1-16-62   56-8546

THE RISE OF THE VICE PRESIDENCY

The Rise of the Vice Presidency

IRVING G. WILLIAMS

*Chairman, Departments of History and
Social Studies, St. John's University*

Introduction by Edward R. Murrow

Public Affairs Press, Washington, D. C.

AS ALWAYS — TO
MURIEL, CAROL ANN, AND GREGORY

Introduction

The American system of government is revered by its people, admired by its foreign friends, respected by most of its opponents, and understood in its entirety by only a few specialists, who, however, do not always agree about it. As an organism it is complex and often obscure. Not unlike the organism of the body, its strengths and its weaknesses are not always easy to account for. The fact that the system has survived so long in a changing world, and seems likely to go on surviving, certainly proves that it is viable, and what has been said about the wisdom shown in devising it is justified. To be sure, part of the wisdom was to allow the system to be adapted to new conditions. The Constitution has been drastically modified, and in many other ways the present form of government departs from the original design of the Constitutional Convention. But modern America differs still more from colonial America which had just won its independence, so the original plan had plenty of merit.

But there are weak spots in the system that still have not been dealt with. One of these is the Vice-Presidency. This office was almost an after-thought at the Constitutional Convention; it was proposed fairly late in the proceedings, was worked out by a committee over a weekend, and then adopted after only brief debate. Because the Vice-President was made presiding officer of the Senate the chief criticism at the time was that the separation of powers between executive and legislature was being blurred, a consideration that in practice has really not mattered. What at the time the convention did not realize was how difficult it might be to decide when a President was incapacitated, how many of his powers the Vice-President should exercise, and what powers he was to have if he took over the presidency by succession. The Constitution was not specific on these points.

The idea of the Founding Fathers was that the Vice-President should be the man next best qualified in the country to be President, surely a notably wise concept. It was implemented by an arrangement under which the Vice-President was to be the man to get the second highest vote for President in the Electoral College. But this could only work if there was no party system; and when that was introduced the Constitution was amended to provide a separate vote for Vice-President. This amendment threw the high office of Vice-President into the dust of party politics, where it has remained for most of our subsequent history.

Seven Vice-Presidents have succeeded to the presidency as a result of death. For more than one year in every five, since Tyler's accession,

17401

we have been governed by men not selected or elected for their fitness to be President. That this should not have produced a Harding is remarkable. But it is due to luck, not to the excellence of our system of government in this one regard.

For much of our history the Vice-President was a fifth wheel. He had no real part in government, and was not informed about national and international policies and events. But as the presidency came to tower higher in world importance, the Vice-President received more notice in Washington. At last he attended Cabinet meetings, became a member of the National Security Council, and was used on foreign missions. But national conventions continued to play politics in choosing vice-presidential nominees, and they are still to be moved first of all by the caliber of the nominee as a possible President. A gap also remains in understanding how a President's incapacity is to be determined, and how, and for how long, the Vice-President is to substitute for him, though it now is law that a Vice-President succeeding to the Presidency by death becomes a full President.

So a considerable element of gamble in the vice-presidency persists. It does so at a time when the President of the United States is virtually the chief officer of the free world, with ever greater burdens weighing upon him. In this situation, the choice of Vice-President no longer can be regarded as an internal affair of a party or a convention. It affects the world.

Fortunately the vice-presidency is now being both studied and discussed. The history of the office is being analyzed with scholarly objectivity, and as a nation we all know the problem as we could not before. We also are bound to be more conscious of the importance of the office because of President Eisenhower's heart attack last year.

Prof. Irving G. Williams, who has devoted his academic career to research on this subject, has established his authority in this field. No scholar could ask that a new work on his favorite subject should appear with greater timeliness. His good fortune in this respect is the good fortune as well of the reading public.

EDWARD R. MURROW

Preface

The purpose of this book is to portray a changing and dynamic institution—the American vice-presidency. It is the result of six years of study and research. It was written to close a serious gap in the literature of American politics and government for, strangely enough, there are only two other volumes which treat the vice-presidency as a whole. One of these books is a scholarly, but out-of-date work; the other is fairly contemporary but reportorial and careless as to facts.

Although the present work does not pretend to be definitive, I have tried to make it reasonably comprehensive, authoritative without being academic, and up-to-date. Particular attention is given to the historic forces that have brought the vice-presidential office to an unprecedented importance in recent years, to the hazards and consequences of succession by death and incapacity, and to the great constitutional issue of presidential inability. These matters are highlighted in the first chapter and followed by a discussion of what the framers of the Constitution had in mind when they created the vice-presidency. The remainder of the book deals with the men who have served as Vice-Presidents, with the problems that arose during their terms and with the ways in which they shaped their high office.

Chapters 3-5 inclusive deal with the vice-presidency from Washington's first term to the assassination of McKinley. This long time-span in the life of the American nation began with high hopes and great promise for the vice-presidency, but they were soon shattered, largely by the deadlock between Burr and Jefferson which resulted in the Twelfth Amendment.

The ensuing century, during which the vice-presidency was practically eclipsed, is treated relatively briefly. Of the 21 men who served out their terms during this period only one—Theodore Roosevelt—reached the presidency by the will of the electors. They were for the most part mediocre men preoccupied with small problems. Their chief formal function was to preside over the Senate. Some of them spent their incumbency seeking to slake their thirst for patronage, conniving against the Chief Executive or else leading an ornamental social life in Washington. The annals of the vice-presidency during this horse-and-buggy period are not particularly interesting nor do they cast any brilliant light on problems of the office in the modern age.

The main emphasis of the present book is on the period stretching from Theodore Roosevelt to Richard M. Nixon, a period roughly coterminous with the first half of the present century. Particular attention is given to the tendency manifest mainly in the last 20 years, to draw the Vice-President from his prior comparative obscurity and involve him in such diverse functions as roving ambassadorships, wartime administration of defense agencies, the role of high policy adviser to the President, attendance at Cabinet meetings and membership in the National Security Council.

*   ❋   *

It should be explained that, due to the insistence of the publisher, I have not used the customary footnotes. However, I have included in the bibliography most of the works I have consulted and/or cited.

I should like to take this opportunity to thank the many people who have helped me in the course of writing this work. Though it would be impossible to list them all, I should like to thank Associate Professor Raph B. Flanders of the History Department, Professor Edward C. Smith of the Government Department, and former Dean Joseph H. Park, all of the Graduate School of Arts and Science, New York University, for their advice and wise counsel. Professor William A. Gillard, Director of Libraries, St. John's University, on many occasions went out of his way to procure needed research materials. Richard C. Snyder, Professor of Politics, Northwestern University, first gave me the opportunity to publish in this field. I am grateful likewise to the Reverend Frederick J. Easterly, C.M., Dean at St. John's, for his unfailing interest, support and understanding. Edward R. Murrow and Fred W. Friendly by their perceptive reporting in the *See It Now* telecast "Report On The Vice-Presidency"—which I had the pleasure to help plan with them—showed me the significance of the lean word and the pertinent illustration. Special thanks go to Mrs. John Collins who typed practically the entire manuscript from crabbed, scratched and all but unintelligible handwritten pages. Nor should I forget the students in my American History and Government classes; many of the evaluations contained in these pages were first tested on them. Their discerning questions and comments were most stimulating. Finally, I wish to acknowledge my deep indebtedness to my wife, Muriel, for her patience and understanding during these long years when I fear I may have neglected my role of parent and husband.

Needless to say, errors of fact or judgment that may be contained in this work are not to be imputed to any of the persons named above, or any others who may have aided me. Such errors as there may be are my sole responsibility.

IRVING G. WILLIAMS

Contents

VICE-PRESIDENTS OF THE UNITED STATES

Name of Vice-President	President Served	Term Served	Party Affiliation	Relevant Chapters
JOHN ADAMS*	George Washington	1789-1797	Federalist	3
THOMAS JEFFERSON*	John Adams	1797-1801	Republican	3
AARON BURR	Thomas Jefferson	1801-1805	Republican	3
GEORGE CLINTON†	Thomas Jefferson and James Madison	1805-1812	Republican	4
ELBRIDGE GERRY†	James Madison	1813	Republican	4
DANIEL D. TOMPKINS	James Monroe	1817-1825	Republican	4
JOHN C. CALHOUN	John Quincy Adams		Natl. Republican	
JOHN C. CALHOUN	and Andrew Jackson	1825-1832	and Democratic	4
MARTIN VAN BUREN*	Andrew Jackson	1833-1837	Democratic	4
RICHARD M. JOHNSON	Martin Van Buren	1837-1841	Democratic	4
JOHN TYLER*	William H. Harrison	1841	Whig	4
GEORGE M. DALLAS	James K. Polk	1845-1849	Democratic	5
MILLARD FILLMORE*	Zachary Taylor	1849-1850	Whig	5
WILLIAM R. KING†	Franklin Pierce	1853	Democratic	5
JOHN C. BRECKINRIDGE	James Buchanan	1857-1861	Democratic	5
HANNIBAL HAMLIN	Abraham Lincoln	1861-1865	Republican	5
ANDREW JOHNSON*	Abraham Lincoln	1865	Republican	5
SCHUYLER COLFAX	Ulysses S. Grant	1869-1873	Republican	5
HENRY WILSON†	Ulysses S. Grant	1873-1875	Republican	5
WILLIAM A. WHEELER	Rutherford B. Hayes	1877-1881	Republican	5
CHESTER A. ARTHUR*	James A. Garfield	1881	Republican	5
THOMAS A. HENDRICKS†	Grover Cleveland	1885	Democratic	5
LEVI P. MORTON	Benjamin Harrison	1889-1893	Republican	5
ADLAI E. STEVENSON	Grover Cleveland	1893-1897	Democratic	5
GARRET A. HOBART†	William A. McKinley	1897-1899	Republican	5
THEODORE ROOSEVELT*	William McKinley	1901	Republican	6
CHARLES W. FAIRBANKS	Theodore Roosevelt	1905-1909	Republican	7
JAMES S. SHERMAN†	William H. Taft	1909-1912	Republican	7
THOMAS R. MARSHALL	Woodrow Wilson	1913-1921	Democratic	7
CALVIN COOLIDGE*	Warren G. Harding	1921-1923	Republican	8
CHARLES G. DAWES	Calvin Coolidge	1925-1929	Republican	9
CHARLES CURTIS	Herbert Hoover	1929-1933	Republican	9
JOHN N. GARNER	Franklin D. Roosevelt	1933-1941	Democratic	10
HENRY A. WALLACE	Franklin D. Roosevelt	1941-1945	Democratic	11
HARRY S. TRUMAN*	Franklin D. Roosevelt	1945	Democratic	12
ALBEN W. BARKLEY	Harry S. Truman	1949-1953	Democratic	12
RICHARD M. NIXON	Dwight D. Eisenhower	1953-	Republican	13

* Subsequently became President.   † Died while in office.

CHAPTER 1

Forgotten Office

During most of the 167 years of the existence of the American nation under the Constitution, the vice-presidential office has been deemed either insignificant or merely honorific and the men chosen for that position have often tended to be too mediocre in caliber to serve as Chief Executives with either wisdom or distinction.

Yet if we consider the full significance of the vice-presidential office, its *raison d'être* is to provide, when necessary, continuity in the presidential succession through a fully qualified successor. It follows, then, that the "President-in-waiting" should be selected, not because of his political ability to "balance the ticket" and least of all to reconcile disgruntled and defeated factions within the party, but rather on the basis of the most lofty considerations. He should be the person who, next to the presidential candidate, is deemed best able to meet the complex and increasingly exacting requirements of the American Chief Executive. This was what the framers of the Constitution envisaged. Such were the very first American Vice-Presidents in that early era of our government under the Constitution. In like manner was that era distinguished by the titanic stature of the men who wielded the executive power.

A promising beginning for the vice-presidency was, however, succeeded by what might well be termed the century of the Throttlebottoms, an age in which the office was a political football, a pawn for factions, a reward for loyal mediocrities, and a pasture for superannuated men.

The twentieth century has seen something of a slow but clearly discernible renaissance of the vice-presidential office. Since this process has reached no fixed resting place, it cannot be gauged with any of the finality of history, but the trend by mid-century has at least been powerful enough to awaken the American people to the realization that their future Vice-Presidents must be men of outstanding ability and character. This realization has in large part been due to the increasing significance of the office during the administrations of Franklin D. Roosevelt, Harry S. Truman, and Dwight D. Eisenhower. The first major step in this direction was the establishment of the

1

principle that the Vice-President is an *ex-officio* member of the Cabinet. The second, which reached its apogee during the incumbency of Henry Wallace, was to make the Vice-President a top policy adviser, diplomatic representative and executive officer. The third step was the institutionalizing of vice-presidential participation on the stratospheric level of American security policy formation—a step taken in the Truman Administration when the Vice-President was made a member of the National Security Council by statute. A corollary of this process in recent years has been a greater tendency on the part of the American people to feel that the vice-presidential nomination must take into major consideration fitness for presidential succession.

Today neither the nation nor the free world can afford the succession to the American presidency of a man who is not fully capable, intellectually and morally, of making the complex decisions that will rush upon him from the first day of his succession. The growth of American power in the world and the rise of the executive branch within that power structure are, of course, the causal decisive factors and they are forces so well known and readily visible as to need little detailing here.

Within the general expansion of the world influence of the American Chief Executive, there is another process which makes the succession even more important—the persistence of international tension, varying from uneasy peace to full-fledged war, a tension which has prevailed with only brief interruptions since 1914, which has taken the form of continuing struggle between free and totalitarian alliances, and which has had as its stake the future ideological shape of the entire earth.

A Vice-President who succeeds to the presidency in the hydrogen age must make decisions which, if erroneous or unsoundly based, could result in radical shifts in the world balance of power and/or plunge the United States into the abyss of total war. Advances in the technology of lethal weapons have eliminated much of the traditional leeway in both space and time. Today total war, once launched, cannot be retracted, compromised or withdrawn from; nor can it be spatially limited. Thus presidential decision, insofar as it impinges on war or peace, is fraught with unprecedented consequences; the margin of permissible error has been greatly reduced, and the potential consequences of having incapable men succeed through death are too dreadful to tolerate.

The cavalier attitude toward the vice-presidency during most of America's national life has not been warranted by the statistics of

succession. Thirty-three men have been President of the United
States and have held the office for a total of 167 years (1789-1956).
Of these 33 men, ten were former Vice-Presidents; three reached the
presidency by election and the remaining seven through the death of
the Chief Executive. These ten men held the presidency for almost
51 years; 28 years of this period represented election or re-election;
23 years represented filling out the balance of presidential terms after
an assassination or illness had killed the elected Chief Executive.
Thus, roughly one-third of the American Vice-Presidents have succeeded to the highest office and have occupied that office for roughly
one-third of the total time span.

The overall picture deserves close inspection. Comparing the twentieth century experience with that of the preceding 111 years, there
appears to be a distinct tendency to nominate vice-presidential candidates on the basis of their putative capacity to fill the presidential
office. Moreover, there is a discernible tendency to choose vice-presidential candidates while bearing in mind the succession potential.
Thus Theodore Roosevelt, although he accepted the vice-presidential
nomination essentially because he was unable to get a second term
as Governor of New York, hoped that it would serve as a stepping
stone to the White House. The nomination of Harry S. Truman was
not the accident it appeared to be at the time; it was the result of
a careful search by Democratic leaders, some of whom anticipated
Roosevelt's death in the fourth term, for the man politically, adminis-
tratively, and ideologically best qualified to succeed. In the case of
Richard M. Nixon, his selection was due to a mixture of considerations disclosed later in this work.

Succession by death has been far more frequent in the twentieth
century than in the previous 111 years. Between 1789 and 1900, the
presidency was occupied by Vice-Presidents who succeeded *via* death
for a total of 14 years—only 13% of the time. In the first 55 years
of the twentieth century, by contrast, the Executive Mansion was
occupied by Vice-Presidents succeeding through death (including
three terms in their own right by election) for 21 years—or 38% of
the time. Moreover, presidential incapacity, leaving the country without any executive leadership in the White House capable of discharging the presidential functions imposed by the Constitution, covered
but 80 days in the nineteenth century (the time-span between Garfield's bullet wound and his death); thus far in the twentieth century
presidential incapacity has existed in varying degrees for about two
years. Woodrow Wilson's stroke and partial paralysis left him—and
the nation—handicapped from September 25, 1919, to March 4, 1921,

when he was succeeded by Harding. In the case of President Eisenhower a period of 143 days lapsed between his heart attack and the announcement as to his recovery.

During the nineteenth century, four Presidents died in office: two by natural causes and two by assassins' bullets. By contrast, of the three transfers of office by death during half of the present century, only the earliest was the result of assassination; the other two were due to natural causes. Although attempts were made to murder Franklin D. Roosevelt and Harry S. Truman, they failed. It is possibly safe to assume that the likelihood of presidential death by violence has decreased significantly because of improved protective measures.

But if the danger of political assassination has decreased, the probability of death or incapacitation because of natural causes seems to have correspondingly increased. The physical and psychological burdens of the presidency have grown inordinately. The sheer volume of work involved, the proliferation of problems which must funnel to the Chief Executive for decision, the psychic burden of the immense and unparalleled responsibility which the office today carries, the denial to the President of personal privacy and the necessity imposed upon him of being on the *qui vive* at all times—these are among the factors which inexorably affect presidential disability and mortality.

Excluding James A. Garfield, who was assassinated, 19 first inaugurals of Presidents, occurred before 1900. Their average age at inauguration was 56; they survived an average of 15½ years after that; their average age at death was 71. But contrast this record with the average for twentieth century Presidents. Excluding McKinley, who was assassinated, and omitting for obvious reasons any Chief Executive still living or who served subsequent to the term of a President still living, five Presidents are considered. Their average age at first inauguration was 51; they lived on the average 12 years after that; their average age at death was 63. Thus, despite the great advances in medical care and in life expectancy, the twentieth century Presidents were on the average eight years younger when they died than their predecessors. This is perhaps as good as any other empirical measure of the increasing strain of the office.

Another factor affecting the picture is the more recent tendency to select older Presidents, particularly during periods of world tension and anxiety. What the cause for this may be is not now germane. The facts are plain, however. During the present century, five presidential elections took place in time of defense preparation, war or cold war (Wilson's second term, Franklin D. Roosevelt's third and fourth terms, Truman's full term and Eisenhower's term). The average age at inauguration of the Presidents chosen during such periods has been 61 years. Three of those five terms of office involved a medical crisis. Wilson suffered stroke and paralysis and, for at least part of the terminal year and a half of his incumbency, was unable to discharge the duties which the Constitution imposed upon his office. The fourth term of Franklin D. Roosevelt featured agreements at Yalta that he might have refused to make had he enjoyed normal health. It terminated after three months in cerebral hemorrhage and death. Finally, the first term of Eisenhower was punctuated by a heart attack which came after he had served less than three years in office. The only President free of this chronicle of crisis or disaster which has followed the induction into office of Chief Executives at ages which are advanced in relation to the burdens of the presidency in time of war or cold war was Harry S. Truman.

This aspect of the problem of vice-presidential succession thus has become considerably more acute. There seems to be a propensity of the parties to nominate and of the people to elect to the presidency men too old to carry the burdens of the office in times of grave crisis. But it is precisely during periods of national peril that the probability of vice-presidential succession by death is greatest.

While the selection of Vice-Presidents capable of assuming the higher office is the most important single step in solving the succession problem, it is also eminently desirable that the vice-presidential office be a training ground for the White House, that the second executive officer in the land be given full information about the problems the President faces and that he be trained in top policy formulation and decision. Vice-presidential attendance at cabinet meetings and membership on the National Security Council constitute at least a *formal* solution of the problem of lack of training in the event of sudden succession through death. We say *formal* because the heart of the issue is cooperation between the President and Vice-President. That must always define its scope and dimensions; and being a personal relationship, it cannot be legislated.

The caliber and experience of the vice-presidential choice may well be more important than the training he will receive in the office. First term Vice-Presidents cannot under the best of circumstances be adequately groomed for the presidency—if the Chief Executive dies early in that term. Yet it has been the American experience that five of the seven successions by death have occurred during a Vice-President's first year of a first term. (Two Vice-Presidents succeeded within the first month, three more between one and six months, with only one of the seven—Coolidge—having as long as 2½ years of "prepa-ration.")   The record emphasizes the need for insisting that national conventions always select as running-mates men who are the best equipped by character and training for any eventuality that may arise in office, whether it come early or late.

The American people must learn to study both halves of the national tickets at election time—and vote accordingly.   Otherwise the lower half could prove to be the Achilles heel of the whole Ameri-can system—both governmental and worldwide.   The political parties must always do a proper job of vice-presidential selection or expect to suffer political defeat.

The Vice-President can succeed to the presidency in other ways than by the death of the Chief Executive.   The latter may be re-moved from office, resign, or be found ineligible to occupy it.   No one of these possible succession modes presents major practical or constitutional problems.   In terms of history, they do not seem very likely to occur.   (However, it should be noted that in his statement of March 6, 1956, President Eisenhower seemed to imply that he might resign if his health deteriorated again.)

Far more significant is the "inability" of the President to discharge the powers and duties of his office.   Article II, Section 1, clause 5 of the Constitution plainly enjoins under such circumstances that "the same shall devolve on the Vice-President."   For reasons already ad-vanced, the danger of new inability situations arising is likely to in-crease with time unless either younger or more vigorous Presidents are chosen or the burdens of the office are somehow lightened.

Obviously there are various kinds of inability, though what kind or kinds the Constitution includes one cannot categorically state.   We do know that in the course of our national existence we have had three probable instances of physical inability.   Their examination will help us understand the magnitude and complexity of this possible way for a Vice-President to reach the White House.

President James A. Garfield was shot on July 2, 1881, receiving a mortal wound that caused his total inability until his death on Sep-tember 19—an eighty-day period.   As to what to do, Vice-President Chester Alan Arthur found little guidance in the Constitution.   Though it unqualifiedly declared that in case of the President's "Inability to discharge the Powers and Duties of the said Office, the same shall devolve on the Vice President," no machinery for its implementation was stated there or in any statute.   Numerous questions presented themselves: Who should declare that inability existed?   What con-stituted inability?   Was temporary or permanent inability (or both) intended? If temporary, what would be the procedure if the inability terminated?

During the inability period, Arthur was sympathetic and self-effacing, doing nothing to precipitate deeper crisis. At first he came to the Capital to stand by for any eventuality. Though he never saw Garfield, he received daily reports from Secretary of State James G. Blaine, who seemed to be regent during the illness. When by late August it seemed that the danger of death had passed, the Vice-President returned to his New York City home where he stayed until the succession by death.

Added to the natural embarrassment any Vice-President suffers during such a period, Arthur was also in the difficult position of being quite generally considered a political puppet. Popular opinion believed him to have been chosen in the 1880 Convention in order to placate Senator Roscoe B. Conkling of New York, the Stalwart boss. Garfield's assassin had proclaimed his loyalty to stalwartism and to Conkling. Wild rumors flew that the whole affair had been planned to advance Conkling's crony to the presidency. The rumors were false, but, given such a climate of speculation, Arthur had little freedom to press for a definitive answer as to his constitutional position. After he had succeeded, he repeatedly asked Congress to formulate answers to the problem, but they never did. As he once pointedly told the national legislature: "Questions which concern the very existence of the Government and the liberties of the people were suggested by the prolonged illness of the late President and his consequent incapacity [*sic*; Arthur could have said 'inability'] to perform the functions of the office."

Of course much discussion took place both in and out of Congress as to what ought to be done in such cases. The chief propositions were these:

1. The Vice-President alone had the duty to decide inability since he was the one affected by the Constitutional sanction;

2. He had the initial responsibility but his affirmative action would have to be approved by Congress. This in effect having been what was done in cases of succession by death, it was argued that the Vice-President would be a "*de facto* acting president" until approved by Congress in his assumption of power; or

3. Congress had the initial responsibility of establishing beforehand a procedure or apparatus to gather evidence, present it, and leave to Congress the duty to decide whether in fact "inability" existed.

No one of these views or any other was acted upon and the whole question ultimately dropped from sight. The country entered on its second and more serious constitutional crisis nearly four decades later just as unprepared as it had been for its first.

While touring the West in a vain effort to save the League of Nations from being rejected in the Senate, President Woodrow Wilson became ill and abandoned his speaking trip (September 26, 1919). In the White House he suffered a cerebral thrombosis which left him partially paralyzed (October 2, 1919). Ike Hoover, chief usher, said "for one month absolutely no business came" to Wilson. For the rest of the fall and winter, selected items were presented but there was "very little even of this sort of business."

A palace regency was established, the Vice-President was never officially informed of the nature of Wilson's illness, Secretary of State Lansing was ultimately fired for seeming to want to turn over the presidency to Vice-President Thomas R. Marshall and for holding Cabinet meetings without Wilson's express permission, and bills passed by Congress became law without his signature. Wilson met his Cabinet on April 13, 1920, for the first time since his illness. Though he continued to do so quite regularly thereafter, he never seemed to have his former vigor. His left arm remained paralyzed and he appeared to be quite out of touch with public affairs for the remainder of his term.

Wilson's retirement from public view evoked congressional action. Four measures were introduced on the question of implementing the disability clause, but none ever got beyond the House Judiciary Committee. One proposal viewed the question as requiring a constitutional amendment and would have empowered the Supreme Court to determine disability when requested by a concurrent resolution of Congress. It also provided that if Congress were not in session, the Vice-President was authorized to call it into special session upon the Cabinet's recommendation. The other measures sought to handle the matter by legislation, one by giving the fact-finding job to the Supreme Court on call by either House, and by its certification either alone or on call again to determine whether or not inability had been removed. This proposal would have established the point that a Vice-President succeeds on a temporary basis, i.e., only for the duration of the disability. The final two measures assumed that the Cabinet was the most competent judge of disability, and one of these even defined inability as illness for thirty days.

Through all this crisis and discussion, Vice-President Thomas R. Marshall tried to thread his way equably. Though he had no political embarrassment, such as Arthur had had to contend with in 1881, that advantage was more than overcome by the fact that 1919 was not a quiet time. The future role of the United States in world affairs was in balance, and with Congress in session all sorts of frenzied advice and plans of action were proposed to Marshall with regard to his "rights" and "duties." But he refused to move, or indeed to make any public statements on the matter.

When President Eisenhower had a "moderate coronary thrombosis" on September 24, 1955, the nation was presented for the second time in thirty-six years with the question of the applicability of the Constitution's inability clause and the position of the Vice-President during such a period. After some twenty weeks of rest, convalescence, part-time activity, and regular checkups, his doctors announced "the President has made a good recovery." This all meant that for a substantial but indeterminate part of the period the United States had at worst no Chief Executive and at best a part-time one. The situation was unparalleled in American history. In no former case was the public so immediately and accurately informed of the exact nature of a President's illness and the details of his day-to-day condition. In the prior instances mass communications media were either non-existent or much less developed; in 1955 more people were hearing more facts in more different ways than had ever been possible heretofore. Moreover, the Eisenhower case had other elements that were unique. Garfield's illness had come during "quiet" times in the world when the United States exerted very little influence on major international affairs. Death came decisively after about 11 weeks. Wilson's illness was both of international importance and of long duration, but in 1919-1920 the attitudes of Congress and the nation could not be properly focussed since they never were given the whole truth of his condition. The Eisenhower illness combined and intensified all the elements previously listed, compounding their domestic and international facets by reason of the post-World War II leadership role of the United States in a shrunken, fearful world.

If under the unparalleled conditions of the past year no solution to the inability clause of the Constitution was forthcoming, it could well be doubted whether any ever would be reached. As on former occasions of serious presidential illness, numerous proposals were advanced in 1955 and 1956. Most of these were recapitulations of the plans brought forth in 1881 and in 1919-1920. But among the new ideas proposed was one which the present author had included in his short monograph, *The American Vice-Presidency*, published more than a year before President Eisenhower's heart attack. The author had written then that the inability question should be given immediate attention: "The usual American habit of avoiding decision until compelled to by *ad hoc* circumstances will no longer serve us in the coming age of continued global involvement. The time to begin to define *inability* is when there is none; the time to establish the mode of procedure involving the Vice-President's succession is when the personalities of the affected President and Vice-President will not fashion the solution."

The main objective of the author's 1954 proposed solution of the disability problem was to secure enactment, by appropriate legislation or constitutional amendment, of the following procedure:

1. Assignment of an official physician to the White House charged with the duty to check the President's health periodically and to notify in writing the Vice-President and the chairman of a special Inability Committee whenever the state of the President's health might deviate from normal to such an extent that the President was seriously ill. Such a report should include a full diagnosis and prognosis, to the best of the doctor's professional ability either with or without other professional opinion.

2. On the basis of said medical report, the Vice-President should, as a ministerial act, request the Inability Committee to meet to consider whether inability within the meaning of the Constitution existed.

3. The said Committee (which might be composed of the Chief Justice of the United States Supreme Court as chairman, the Secretary of State, the Senate majority and minority leaders, the Speaker of the House, and the House majority and minority leaders) could then take such steps as would help them determine whether in fact constitutional inability was present or not. Their majority decision would be final and would determine whether or not succession by the Vice-President should take place.

4. If decided in the affirmative, such succession should be for the duration of the term to which the disabled incumbent was elected, regardless of whether the inability turned out to have been only temporary or not.

Such a proposal has at least the merits of relative certainty and directness. The "court physician" would be a governmental official (presumably a career-service physician) not a personal one. He would be compelled to record his opinion in the medical sense as to whether the illness was totally or permanently disabling or whether it was likely to become so. He would be compelled to publish his findings to the person most constitutionally concerned—the Vice-President of the United States (and as an additional safeguard to the Chief Justice to prevent burying of the issue if such should be contemplated). The

Vice-President thus would be taken off the spot in the matter of what to do. He would have no legal course but to request the immediate convening of the Inability Committee. The inclusion of the minority party leader of both houses would be an additional guarantee that a hush policy would not be followed in a matter so vital to constitutional government. The majority vote as to whether or not succession was required would of course presumably rest with the dominant party's four members (the Cabinet official, the House Speaker, and the majority leaders of both Houses), so that the minority party members could not prevent decision even if they were disposed to, which it may be hoped they would not be. The presence of the Chief Justice would be a balancing factor, injecting a judicial note into what under any circumstances would be already a complex of physical and political factors. Any such succession would have to be permanent, lest the problem arise as to what constitutes removal of the disability. Was Wilson recovered after April, 1920? Is a pale, wan, shawl-covered President with a withered left arm a President restored to what he was before a paralytic stroke? Obviously a medical answer would be different from the constitutional one. No, it would seem that the nation would be best served if all sides knew in advance that a disability succession, taking place on evidence and in good faith, would be final and definite.

Some such law would also have the auxiliary effect of impressing further on the people and parties the abiding necessity of choosing to be Vice-President "the second man felt to be most fit" for the presidency.

The constitutional injunction exists that the Vice-President shall succeed to the presidency on the inability of the incumbent; it is not a matter of the Vice-President's craving for promotion versus his humility to the point of publicly rejecting any desire for the post under any circumstances.

The general nature of this plan received some support after Eisenhower's attack. One political scientist, Professor James M. Burns of Williams College, revised it as follows: "Congress should provide for a permanent committee on Presidential disability, which, with the assistance of a panel of physicians of its own choice, would have power to authorize the Vice-President to take over, and if conditions later permitted, to authorize the President to resume office . . . such a committee should represent all three branches of government . . . the Secretary of State and the Attorney General, the Vice-President . . . Speaker of the House, and the Chief Justice . . . as chairman."

By February, 1956, ex-Vice-Presidents Barkley and Wallace seemed disposed to go along with the essentials of the present writer's plan.

More recently, Professor James Hart of the University of Virginia submitted a somewhat similar plan to the House Judiciary Committee. *New York Times* pundit Arthur Krock felt that this plan was "less vulnerable" than other propositions and was "viable both legally and politically." Hart's proposition called for Congress to create "The Commission on Presidential Inability." The members of the Commission would be appointed by the Supreme Court, serve for life, and make all findings by a majority vote. The core of their power would be "to have authority to investigate on their own motion, whether or not formally asked to do so, and empowered to make simple findings of Presidential inability, of permanent inability, of the removal of inability. These findings not to be subject to question by other authority, and when permanent, not reversible by the Commissioners."

The present author would not be so foolish as to believe his 1954 proposal cannot be improved on and he has no intention of starting a debate in these pages. But he would offer this: both the Burns and the Hart plans, like his own, recognize the need for a special group to decide the inability question. However, the author feels that the Vice-President should not be a part of the fact-finding body (as in the Burns proposal) or totally disregarded (as he appears to be in the Hart plan). He feels that since the Vice-President is the person charged with succeeding he should be in a position to know that the Inability Commission *is* investigating, which would not necessarily be the case under Hart's proposal. He does not feel that in the medical, political, legal, and judicial complex of determining the presence or absence of inability the Vice-President should be a responsible party in the substantive proceedings, lest he be accused of behind-the-scenes skullduggery.

All Vice-Presidents during inability crises have suffered from unwarranted criticism and "inside" stories of grasping for power. Richard M. Nixon was no exception. Wide circulation was given to Drew Pearson's report that on the night of September 24, 1955, Nixon had fled to the home of Acting Attorney General William P. Rogers to get him "to make a legal ruling that he, as Vice-President, could take over the powers of the President." But Assistant Attorney General J. Lee Rankin, in charge of legal opinions, was skeptical and suggested telephoning Attorney General Herbert Brownell, then visiting Spain with Thomas E. Dewey. According to Pearson, Brownell was "extremely loath to give a ruling" and shortly thereafter Assistant President Sherman Adams, "then enjoying a junket in Europe," was rushed back to Washington in the private military plane of General Alfred

Gruenther, NATO Commander. "Next day a meeting was held in the office of Secretary of the Treasury George Humphrey . . . at which Brownell's position was clinched . . . The Vice President politely deferred to the Secretary of the Treasury."

The facts are that Nixon did spend that first night (Saturday-Sunday) in his friend's home to avoid the embarrassment of press phone calls and to be able to have an open phone wire to and from Denver. Sherman Adams did return post-haste from Spain (arriving on Monday), which was the normal thing to do. There was a Tuesday luncheon meeting of Brownell (who arrived on Tuesday) with Humphrey, Adams, Nixon, and Rogers after which the Attorney General announced that there was no urgent need to delegate presidential powers to anyone. Brownell said that despite the request of the summer White House in Denver, "I don't know that it will be necessary to deliver a legal opinion." It was his opinion that there were sufficient legal arrangements to carry on "the day-to-day operations of the government."

Every action of Vice-President Nixon after September 24, 1955, was in conformity with the traditions of American history. He stood by at the Capital, cancelled plans that would have taken him away from Washington, expressed prayerful sympathy for the President, and told reporters on September 25: "I share with all the American people [concern] for the early and complete recovery of the President. In comparison with this, all other questions and problems are not worthy of discussion." Never by word or action did he raise any embarrassing questions or make any effort to precipitate deeper crisis. But Vice-Presidents will undoubtedly continue to be subjects of unfriendly rumors in the future unless their status during inability periods is more precisely defined.

However the inability provision may ultimately be settled, as sooner or later it must be, it is necessary first to make a start. One must walk before he can run and any solution would be better than the existing situation. Regarding the first two disability crises the nation muddled through, Professor Edward Corwin of Princeton University observes that "at least we have never seen the country plunged into civil war by a scheming Vice-President." This opinion offers small comfort. The oldest living government under a written Constitution should be able to point to a greater accomplishment than that it has proved itself superior to a Central American *caudillo*-ridden "constitutional" government. Whatever solution to the disability question is forthcoming, the rights and responsibilities of the Vice-President in the matter must be provided for fully and unequivocally.

CHAPTER 2

The Formative Period

Since, by its very nature, the office of the Vice-President is part of the executive branch of government, its establishment was necessarily contingent on the development of a federal executive branch. This had not been provided for either in the Revolutionary Continental Congresses or in the *de jure* Congress of the Confederation. The dependence on the legislative branch alone for the adequate governance of the nation was indeed one of the glaring weaknesses of the Articles of Confederation. Thus, at the convening of the Constitutional Convention in Philadelphia in May 1787, there was virtual unanimity among the delegates that an executive branch be included in any new arrangements that might be agreed upon. The disagreements that ensued there concerned the form and character of the executive branch, not its existence. The establishment of the vice-presidency was a corollary to the shaping of the office of the presidency.

Having early decided to accept the Randolph Plan rather than the already existing Articles as the basis for discussion, the delegates to the Convention agreed on May 30, 1787, to debate the proposition that there be a National Executive to be selected by the National Legislature for an unspecified term and to be ineligible for a second election. The Virginia proposals had nothing to say about a second-in-command. Randolph, in fact, favored a plural executive and fought most strenuously against "a unity . . . as the foetus of monarchy."

After the submission of Randolph's proposals, three other general schemes of government were placed before the body: Charles Pinckney's draft, William Paterson's plan, and Alexander Hamilton's sketch. For many years, Pinckney was commonly credited with having first proposed the vice-presidential office to the Convention, the occasion being his reading his draft constitution to the entire body immediately following Randolph's speech. Pinckney's plan was then referred to the Committee of the Whole along with Randolph's proposals. However, no copy of this original draft remained with the records of the Convention. In 1818, acting upon a directive of Congress, Secretary of State John Quincy Adams proceeded to prepare the Convention papers for publication. Noting the absence of a draft of Pinckney's proposals, he wrote the latter for a copy. Pinckney replied that, as he had a variety of drafts among his papers, it was impossible to be sure, after thirty-odd years, which was the one he had read to the Convention on May 29, 1787, but he thought it to be the enclosed one. This draft provided for a single executive, eligible for re-election, whose duties in times of necessity were to be exercised by a "President of the Senate" to be chosen by that body. These proposals were a great advance over the generalities or silence of the Randolph plan and seemed to embody at least the germ of the ultimate constitutional provision. However, early in the twentieth century, James F. Jameson and Andrew C. McLaughlin, after a scholarly investigation of all pertinent facts, conclusively demonstrated that the "Pinckney draft" was a third or fourth emendation arrived at toward the close of the Convention, shaped by the deliberations of that body, rather than — as much of the nineteenth century thought—shaping them. Like Randolph, Pinckney was silent on the matter of a second-in-command, and more indefensibly so, since he did desire a single executive.

The Paterson or New Jersey Plan was offered on June 15, 1787, by the small states in opposition to Randolph's concept of a legislative government. The basis of Paterson's proposals was the already existing Articles, but it included in its fourth point: "Resolved, that the U. S. in Congress be authorized to elect a federal Executive to consist of—Persons, to continue in office for the Term of—years." Here, again, the idea of a plural executive was explicitly advanced, thus rendering any provision for a second executive officer superfluous.

The Convention divided into large and small states blocs. As some of the former and virtually all of the latter favored a council as executive, it is all the more remarkable that a Vice-President was ultimately provided for.

Alexander Hamilton's views on government were as well-known as they were unpopular. Nonetheless, he spoke about six hours for the record in the general debate of June 18, "sketching" his concepts of what the contemplated general government should be like. "He was obliged to declare himself unfriendly to both plans" and offered instead a frankly monarchical scheme. His fourth point called for "a *Governor* to serve *during good behaviour*. His election to be made by *Electors* chosen by *Electors* chosen by the people." Hamilton's fifth point provided that, when it became necessary to install a successor, the Governor's "Authorities be exercised by the President of the Senate." Thus, in terms of the gestation of the office of Vice-President, Hamilton's sketch must be acknowledged as the embryo. Of the delegates presenting overall schemes, he alone made a place for a deputy executive who, in addition to his succession potential, should regularly preside over the upper legislative chamber.

Hamilton's plan was to apply nationally the system prevailing in his native New York and nine other states. All had either a Lieutenant-Governor or (as in Pennsylvania) a Vice-President who, in most instances, was also the presiding officer of the upper house.

Acknowledgment by the states of the need for immediate and undisputed succession for continuity in the executive power was the counterpart of colonial experience dating from the beginning of the seventeenth century. A deputy governor for Jamestown was named as early as 1610, three years after the colony was founded. Moreover, due to the Chief Executive's inability to depart for his post, the deputy governor was obliged to assume office and thus launched the first unitary executive authority in the English colonies on the American mainland. For most of the next decade, deputy governors remained as acting chiefs due to the continuing absence of the nominal executive. As further colonies were established, whether by proprietary grants, commercial and religious enterprise, or under crown aegis, the same apparatus of a governor and his "substitute" appeared. And before the colonial period's close, the idea that the deputy when not administering the governorship should be the presiding officer of the deliberative branch of government had been advanced. Thus Hamilton's concepts were wholly conservative and consistent with American governmental development.

Hamilton's sketch of June 18, 1787, though never voted upon, nor even discussed as a basis for constitution-making, was known to the Constitutional Convention and had made enough impression among some of the delegates for him later to fill out his ideas and hand the results to James Madison at the Convention's close. Hamilton's explicit provision for a successor became all the more important when the Convention tentatively decided that the Executive should consist of one man, despite strong pleas for a plural executive expressed by George Mason, Benjamin Franklin, and Edmund Randolph.

Having adjourned after Hamilton's speech, the Convention proceeded next day to discuss whether Randolph's propositions should be adhered to as preferable to those of Paterson. It was decided to retain the Randolph Plan. Almost immediately the great crisis of the Convention was joined — namely, how to apportion seats in the national legislature. Was the principle to be equality of the states or representation proportionate to population? The clash on this issue jeopardized the continued existence of the Convention and no headway could be made on the vice-presidential question until it was solved. When a compromise was finally reached, the Convention, as if worn out by its struggle to avoid shipwreck, appointed a Committee of Detail to prepare a draft on the matters thus far agreed upon, and then took its only recess.

The five-man Committee of Detail made its report to the Convention on August 6. Article V, Section 4, of its draft constitution provided that "the Senate shall chuse its own President and other officers." This clause occasioned no opposition and was agreed to unanimously three days later. Article X, providing for a single person to be called the President, was passed unanimously on August 24. Not so fortunate were the ensuing clauses, whereby the President was to be elected by ballot of the national legislature for a seven-year term without eligibility of re-election. The Convention, unable to agree on these clauses, postponed their consideration. Also postponed was the second section of Article X, which provided for the succession: "In case of his [the President's] removal as aforesaid, death, resignation, or disability to discharge the powers and duties of his office, the President of the Senate shall exercise those powers and duties, until another President of the United States be chosen, or until the disability . . . be removed."

Accordingly, the Committee of Detail had filled in the lacunae and made specific provision for executive continuity should the Chief Executive die or become incapacitated. The caretaker of the interregnum would be the President of the Senate, himself a Senator and chosen by the Senate itself as presiding officer. This official would carry on until Congress named a new President or the disability of the incumbent was removed.

The link between the vice-presidency and the upper chamber had been definitively asserted. Yet opposition and questioning continued. Daniel Carrol's motion to have the President elected by the people having been voted down by nine states to two, the Convention considered whether the President should be chosen by joint or separate ballot of Congress. James Madison felt that the situation required joint balloting for electing the Chief Executive since the President of the Senate "also is to be occasionally President of the United States . . . This is another advantage enjoyed by the Senate." Election of the President by a joint ballot of the two houses was agreed upon by seven states to four.

Other aspects of the great constitutional problem of succession were touched upon. Madison thought the executive powers during vacancy could be handled by a Council. John Dickinson considered the whole succession clause too vague: "What is the extent of the term 'disability' and who is to be the judge of it?" Since no one could provide the answer to this prescient question, it was agreed to postpone consideration of the clause.

On Friday, August 31, the Convention established by ballot the Committee of the States. Over the ensuing weekend, some unknown member or group of members established the vice-presidency of the United States essentially as formulated in the final draft. Unfortunately, there are no notes extant of the work of this committee. Hence, the mystery of authorship as to the choice of name, the mode of election of President and Vice-President, the casting vote, and the supervision by the Vice-President of the electoral count remains impenetrable. In truth, this is the only "lost weekend" of the well-documented Constitutional Convention. In conning the membership of the committee, however, one is tempted to essay a probable *situs* of origin. Given the strong personal and ideological compatability between Rufus King and Gouverneur Morris of the committee on the one hand and the influence of the absent Hamilton on the other, one is led to suspect that the seed of Hamilton's June 18 speech bore fruit through his friends.

In reporting on September 4, the Committee of the States called for a "vice-President, chosen for the same term," elected at the same time and in the same manner as the President. The manner—the electoral college method—provided for each elector's voting in the same ballot two presidential preferences. The person receiving the greatest majority of votes cast would be President, "and in every case after the choice of the President, the Person having the greatest number of votes shall be vice-President." In other words, the runner-up in the presidential vote would be Vice-President, regardless of whether the number of votes was a majority or not. Other points of the committee's report concerning the Vice-President included making him the President of the Senate with the right to vote in case of a tie and making him the successor to the executive in case of emergency.

For three days the Convention debated the proposed change in the method of electing the President. Randolph and Pinckney demanded an explanation for the change. Nathaniel Gorham objected to the automatic election to the vice-presidency of the runner-up for the presidency because he feared that "a very obscure man with very few votes may arrive at that appointment." He felt the Vice-President should also be a majority selection. Gouverneur Morris defended the Committee and offered six reasons for the alteration in the election mode. Among these were: "the danger of intrigue and faction" in election of the President by the legislature; the common principle of having the Senate as the impeachment court with the House as prosecutor would be impossible under legislative election; and the indispensable necessity to make "the Executive independent of the Legislature." To Morris, the great "advantage aimed at was that of taking away the opportunity for cabal" inherent in the former plan.

With acceptance of the electoral system, the way was cleared for discussion on whether to establish the office of Vice-President. To it the Convention turned on September 7. Paradoxically, Elbridge Gerry, who alone among the delegates to the Constitutional Convention would be elected Vice-President, opposed making that official the President of the Senate and, indeed, was "against having any vice-President . . . We might as well put the President himself at the head of the Legislature. The close intimacy that must subsist between the President & vice-president makes it absolutely improper." To which Gouverneur Morris made his oft-quoted rejoinder: "The vice president then will be the first heir apparent that ever loved his father. If there should be no vice president, the President of the Senate would be temporary successor, which would amount to the same thing."

Sherman, also a member of the Committee of the States, remarked that "if the vice-President were not to be President of the Senate, he would be without employment"; moreover, he pointed out, if a Senator occupied this position he would "be deprived of his vote, unless when an equal division . . . might happen." But on this proposition, Gerry was joined by Randolph, Williamson, and Mason. Randolph objected on general principles; Williamson felt that the "officer . . . was not wanted"; Mason contended that the vice-presidency "mixed too much the Legislative and Executive, which, as well as the Judicial departments, ought to be kept as separate as possible." The latter suggested that a Council act as regency on all occasions calling for the succession.

The issue finally came to a vote and the proposal that the Vice-President be the President of the Senate was carried, eight states to two.

The views of the Founding Fathers on the vice-presidency were amazing in view of the subsequent history of the office. Many saw him as a presidential spy in the upper chamber, the *alter ego* of the Chief Executive, and an *eminence grise* of an executive-ridden Congress and country. In the composite, the Vice-President would be a second-rater, pleasant enough, but neither taken seriously nor taking himself seriously, a man sharing the popular belief that election to the office was the surest way to obscurity. In these matters Gerry himself was to be as typical a Vice-President as the nineteenth century would produce. If indeed he looked for "the close intimacy" between Madison and himself in 1813 that he had feared in 1787, his expectation was in vain.

With the basic decisions made as to the method of election of the President and Vice-President, and the duty of the latter to preside over the Senate, the Convention's work was practically at an end. The rough edges of the emerging Constitution were planed down; a Committee on Style re-worked the agreements into a smooth whole; their product was gone over clause by clause. One oblique argument by Elbridge Gerry on the vice-presidency helped to alter a legislative provision. It had always stood that a three-fourths vote of the legislature would be required to override a presidential veto. On September 12th, Williamson moved its alteration to two-thirds, as "the former puts too much in the power of the President." Among his supporters was Gerry who argued, "If three fourths be required, a few Senators having hopes from the nomination of the President to offices, will combine with him and impede proper laws. Making the vice-President Speaker increases the danger." In the vote that followed, the amendment passed by the narrow margin of six to four, with one state divided.

Gerry carried his suspicions against the Constitution as a whole and the vice-presidency in particular to the point of refusing to sign the engrossed parchment. In this he was joined by Mason and Randolph. The Convention having decided that the signing would take place on Monday, September 17, 1787, the preceding Saturday was spent largely in formal declarations by the dissidents of their reasons for refusing to sign. Gerry listed eleven. His eighth objection was making the Vice-President head of the Senate, which to him "destroys the independence of the Legislature." He felt that a second convention should be held — which was unanimously rejected. The completed Constitution was sent to the country for its consideration by state conventions.

The vice-presidency was discussed in only three of the states, and of the hundreds of amendments proposed by the various conventions, not one dealt with the vice-presidential office. It was clear that the office of Vice-President of the United States was the national counterpart of the lieutenant-governor — a familiar, traditional state official.

CHAPTER 3

The First Vice-Presidents

Four elections were held under the original mode establishing the vice-presidency. Geographical and political factors were involved in determining the second electoral choice from the beginning. George Washington seemed to put his stamp of approval on these factors when he wrote in October 1788: "I have never entered into a single discussion . . . respecting the appointment of a Vice-President. From the extent and respectability of Massachusetts, it might reasonably be expected, that he would be chosen from that State. But having taken it for granted that the person selected for that important place would be a true Federalist . . . I was . . . disposed to acquiesce in the prevailing sentiments of the Electors."

Thus, to offset the Virginian Washington, availability narrowed to a person from Massachusetts, a "true Federalist," and a supporter of the new Constitution. Opinion jelled in favor of John Adams, then chief of mission to England, a man with an impeccable Revolutionary record and more latterly a convert to stable, ordered, aristocratically principled government. The anti-Federalists, less well-organized and leaderless, made George Clinton, New York's perennial governor, their second choice for this first national election.

JOHN ADAMS

The electoral result was a unanimous vote for Washington as first choice; Adams was merely a minority winner over a field of eleven. Already staking out his role as *deus ex machina* of the Federalist forces, Alexander Hamilton had sabotaged the pro-Adams movement by having second-choice votes scattered. Publicly he justified his maneuver by declaring it would be unbecoming for anyone to tread too closely on the heels of Washington; a more plausible motive was rivalry with Adams for party leadership. The running battle between Adams and Hamilton was thus joined. Over the years, it would wax and wane; never being resolved, it would permit the anti-Federalists to slip into the vice-presidency in 1796 and the presidency in 1800—to the ultimate complete extinction of the Federalist party.

John Adams, the first Vice-President of the United States, assumed the office in his fifty-third year. A Massachusetts lawyer, his opposition to the Stamp Act had brought him quickly to the forefront as a moderate but determined revolutionist. He was a signer of the Declaration of Independence and helped to draft that document. As a means of ensuring Virginia's support of the patriot cause, Adams urged that Washington be named Commander in Chief.

During most of the Revolutionary War, Adams was abroad on diplomatic missions, where he met rebuffs, had indifferent success, and showed less skill than Franklin or Jefferson. Yet he obtained a loan from the Netherlands and was one of the negotiators of the Treaty of Paris (1783) which brought the revolutionary struggle to its victorious conclusion. His three years as American envoy to England, a thankless task in view of British coldness and unwillingness to negotiate, kept him abroad at the time the Constitution was drafted.

When Adams assumed the vice-presidency, he seemed to be much concerned with etiquette and leaned toward monarchical pomp. He pondered over whether the new Chief Executive should be addressed as "Majesty," "Elective Highness" or perhaps "His Highness the President of the United States and Protector of the Rights of the Same."

John Adams was to serve eight full years as Vice-President and to be the first of a select group of only six who were re-elected during more than a century and a half of the office's existence. (The other five were George Clinton, 1805-13; Daniel D. Tompkins, 1817-25; John C. Calhoun, 1825- resigned as Vice-President in 1832; Thomas R. Marshall, 1913-21; John N. Garner, 1933-41). No future Vice-President was to be more significant as a partner in government. Adams enjoyed the personal esteem of the President and was frequently consulted by him in those social and diplomatic affairs that were considered his specialties. On the occasion of the President's southern tour in 1791, the heads of the Executive Departments were ordered to include him in any consultative meetings they might find it necessary to hold. As a matter of fact, one such was held, which Adams attended; we have Jefferson's testimony that this was the only time the Vice-President sat in at a cabinet meeting.

President Washington established a clear-cut rule of conduct for himself with regard to his heir apparent:

"Whosoever shall be found to enjoy the confidence of the States so far as to be elected Vice-President, cannot be disagreeable to me in that office. And even if I had any predilections, I flatter myself, I possess patriotism enough to sacrifice it [sic] at the shrine of my Country.

". . . supposing myself to be connected in office with any gentleman of character, I would most certainly treat him with perfect sincerity and the greatest candour in every respect. I would give him my full confidence, and use my utmost endeavours to cooperate with him, in promoting and rendering permanent the national prosperity; this should be my great, my only aim."

Washington's formula could well serve as a model for relations between President and Vice-President. There was nothing to indicate from these beginnings that the latter would shrink into the "forgotten man" of American politics.

Since the only regular constitutional duty of the vice-presidency is to preside over the Senate, the tenure of John Adams in this respect is instructive. In that the Senate then had a working membership that averaged twenty-two, the personality of the presiding officer was a major factor in its deliberations. John Adams early stamped the chamber as his plaything; from the first he refused to be the impartial chairman. He conceived the office as a place to exercise the functions of majority leader and thus was for all practical purposes a member of the Senate. He presented the agenda, intervened in debate, apostrophized the Senate for real or fancied derelictions of duty, refused to yield the chair when the Senate turned itself into Committee of the Whole, gave his opinions on any matters before it when he felt like it, and exercised his right of the casting vote more than any other future Vice-President would. Throughout all his legislative activities ran a consistent pattern of shoring up administration policies, strengthening the freedom of action of the national executive, and creating the climate for a "due respect" by the people for a central government controlled by Federalists.

The Vice-President's decisive position was early recognized. The following opinion was expressed at a dinner given by Pennsylvania's congressional delegation to the chief Federal officers: "It was remarked that, as every question of moment was carried only by one majority, or for the most part by the casting vote . . . it might be as well to vest the whole senatorial power in the President of the Senate." Fittingly enough, Adams' faithful party adherence earned him the undivided support of the Federalists in 1792—including even that of Alexander Hamilton.

Although importuned on all sides to stand for re-election, Washington had at first determined to step aside at the end of one term. In a conversation with Madison, who was assigned to write a farewell speech, he implied that their fellow-Virginian, Thomas Jefferson, the Secretary of State, ought to be encouraged to run. Both Madison and Jefferson scotched the idea. Thus, despite the fact that the original electoral procedure may have implied that the Vice-President was the second most fit person to serve as Chief Executive, it is clear that the first American President did not think of him as his successor. A stronger factor than the Vice-President's implicit right to the succession was Washington's loyalty to a compatriot from the Old Dominion. Here then was the essence of the Virginia Dynasty even though its full implementation was to be delayed by the Adams interlude as Chief Executive.

As the organization of the Senate was perfected and its membership increased, the strategic importance of the Vice-President declined. John Adams' latter years were more comparable to those of a modern incumbent. Tie votes fell off and he tended to retreat into silence during debates which he was powerless to affect.

When John Adams became the Federalists' choice to succeed Washington in 1796, it was more because John Jay had eliminated himself by the unpopularity of his treaty with England than because of any general belief that his tenure as Vice-President made him the logical nominee. Again Alexander Hamilton intervened with devious politics, urging Southern Federalist electors to back Thomas Pinckney, the caucus choice for second place, and throw away votes to some Federalist other than John Adams. The success of this plan was predicated on the Northern Federalist electors supporting Pinckney equally with Adams, in which case Pinckney could get the majority vote and be elected President. All this assumed that the Northern Federalists were unaware of the strategem or indifferent to its outcome. As they were neither, there were more defections from Pinckney in the North, where Federalism was strongest, than from Adams in the South.

THOMAS JEFFERSON

The net effect was distinctly beneficial for Thomas Jefferson, the standard bearer of the anti-Federalists. He became the second Vice-President of the United States and by all odds the most illustrious man in the nation's history to occupy that office.

Born in 1743, Jefferson assumed the vice-presidential office in his fifty-third year. His authorship of the Declaration of Independence and of the Bill for Establishing Religious Freedom earned him deserved renown. He had served as Governor of Virginia, carried out his diplomatic mission to France with distinction, fought successfully for the incorporation of the Bill of Rights in the Constitution and as George Washington's Secretary of State, helped thwart Hamilton's pro-British, monarchical and financially centralizing policies.

Both President-elect Adams and Vice-President-elect Jefferson contemplated an *entente* which might have had profound effects on the political development of the United States. Jefferson's projected overture took the form of a draft letter to Adams congratulatory of his electoral success and pledging the Vice-President's support. "Jeemie" Madison, at the seat of government, was asked to judge whether an attempt should be made to incorporate the Adams brand of Federalism into the Jeffersonian party, leaving the Hamiltonian wing in lofty loneliness. The pragmatic Madison vetoed the idea as impactical, buried the letter, and there the matter rested. On his part, Adams on the eve of inauguration visited Jefferson to ask him if he would go to France as a special presidential emissary to bring about better relations with the revolutionary government there. Jefferson declined to do this on the theoretical grounds that it was outside his constitutional domain and on the practical side that it was not his responsibility to lighten his opponent's burden. To Adams' further request that Madison undertake the job, the answer was likewise a definite "no," so that the whole unsatisfactory course of events that characterized Adams' single term—relations with France culminating in undeclared war—was set in motion on the first and perhaps only occasion in which the highest executive offices were filled in accordance with the Founding Fathers' intentions. As Jefferson himself testifies, that was the end of his dealings with the President except on purely formal occasions. In short, the first test of political incompatibles in the two chief national offices resulted in practical mutual non-intercourse and embargo.

The failure of Adams and Jefferson to rise above party and achieve a *modus vivendi* from 1797 to 1801 helped to bring upon the country alarums, tensions, preparations for war, curtailment of civil liberties, and limited war. Correctly figuring that French relations would be the major problem his administration would have to face, President Adams had attempted to use the men most likely to be *persona grata* to Republican France as a demonstration of American good-will. The refusal of Jefferson and Madison to take any responsibility to work out a diplomatic solution to a threatening international situation entailed placing political considerations above the nation's welfare. However, Adams' own case was weak; in 1794, when he had been approached to undertake the mission to England (to which Jay was ultimately appointed), he had deprecated the whole idea and forbade consideration of his name. The very arguments he had expressed then were now used against him.

The whole affair illustrated the virtual independence between the offices of President and Vice-President. The former could not command the latter and the degree of liaison between them would flow more from the desire to cooperate than from the power to control. When in subsequent years the vice-presidency was filled with far less talented men the question of their availability for *ad hoc* foreign missions lapsed and the constitutional question of whether the successor could and/or should be sent abroad dropped from view. The negative answer was not successfully challenged until President Franklin D. Roosevelt sent Vice-President Henry A. Wallace to East Asia in 1944.

Jefferson never left an office he held quite the same as it was before he entered it. His tenure as Vice-President was no exception. He did not disdain the second place; in view of the squalls he saw coming he could think of no other office he would have preferred. "It will give me philosophical evenings in the winter, and rural days in summer" he told a friend. But he did intend to work at his new job. Finding the practices of the Senate rudimentary and contradictory, Jefferson drew up a *Manual of Parliamentary Practice* which, though never formally adopted, became the Bible for Senate procedure, and indeed an authority for the procedure of public and private organizations throughout the United States.

Jefferson's period of "semi-retirement" in the vice-presidency gave him leisure to contemplate political fundamentals and avoid absorption in ephemeral problems and tasks. From this fallow period sprang the Kentucky Resolutions; it is not wholly accidental that the two outstanding theoretical justifications for state supremacy, the Kentucky Resolutions (1798) and The Exposition and Protest (1828) were written by Jefferson and John C. Calhoun while both were serving as Vice-Presidents.

Jefferson's vice-presidency also was unique in the opportunities it offered him as the acknowledged leader of the opposition to provide leads to his political lieutenants on how best to attack Adams' Administration in the forthcoming presidential election. Whether this would have worked if the Federalist party had been united under Adams is problematical, but, given the intra-party split that became unbridgeable when Adams chose peace against the war tendencies of his cabinet, it succeeded.

In the campaign of 1800 the Federalists ran on their record, choosing Adams for a second term and another Pinckney—Charles Cotesworth, elder brother of the defeated Federalist candidate of 1796—as his running mate.

As in 1796, the Republican ticket was Thomas Jefferson and Aaron Burr. The latter insisted on receiving equal support with Jefferson in the electoral college. When the Republicans swept to electoral victory, a tie occurred in the electoral college between Burr and Jefferson which was to prove fateful in the history of American politics.

No one doubted that Jefferson was the first choice of the Republicans and that Burr had been chosen merely for the vice-presidency, but the Constitution did not recognize this distinction. Since Jefferson and Burr were tied with 73 votes each, the issue was thrown into the House of Representatives for decision, where the vote would be by states. However, the "lame-duck" House with its strong Federalist bloc had no interest in easing the tasks or solving the problems of the victorious Republicans. Through 35 ballots, a decision was delayed while the House defied the popular mandate and Jeffersonian stalwarts threatened that "ten thousand republican swords will instantly leap from their scabbards" if their hero were cheated out of the White House. Throughout this crisis, Burr remained in Albany, watchful and waiting, contenting himself with avowing in a letter that, given a tie between Jefferson and himself, he would wish his friends to prefer the former. This attitude paralleled Jefferson's in 1796 when the Monticello statesman had announced that in the event of a tie between himself and Adams he would renounce the presidency rather than precipitate a constitutional crisis.

Hamilton threw what influence he still had against Burr, denouncing him as a conspirator, "as true a Cataline as ever met in midnight conclave," as a man who "thinks everything possible to adventure and perseverance and . . . will attempt usurpation." Burr could well have had the Federalist support necessary for the presidency if he had cared to become a hostage of the conservatives; he declined to do so, disgusting Federalists such as Bayard who thought he played "a miserable, paultry part." On the thirty-sixth ballot, Thomas Jefferson was elected the third President of the United States, inaugurating what he was to call "the second American revolution."

This crisis, which had brought the threat of civil war, illustrated dramatically the weakness of the method of choosing the Chief Executive contemplated by the authors of the Constitution. This weakness was not absolute, however, and it has perhaps been exaggerated by superficial observers. The fact is often overlooked, for example, that on the Federalist side, John Adams and Charles C. Pinckney did not receive equal support simply because one Rhode Island elector threw away his second choice vote. Thus, had the Federalists been returned to power, there would have been no tie and no ambiguity as to who was to be President. Astute politicians as they were, the Republicans inexplicably neglected to make some similar arrangement and thus forestall the possibility of a tie. And this was indicated clearly enough by Jefferson's comment to Burr that "it was badly managed not to have arranged with certainty what seems to have been left to hazard." Such an extra-constitutional device might have made the system workable, but only on the condition that the political parties were subject to a strong, centralized discipline and that the members of the electoral college were similarly bound. Under different conditions, the solution of throwing away votes to prevent ties from occurring would have opened the vista of election of the President by intrigue, bribery and cabal. Given good faith and disciplined parties, the system could have been patched up, but, by its very nature, it invited dishonest conduct above and beyond the norm in politics.

The solution arrived at was the Twelfth Amendment, which provided that the members of the electoral college would have to distinguish between their ballots for the President and the Vice-President. "Slight as this change might appear," wrote Henry Adams in 1889, "it tended toward centralizing powers hitherto jealously guarded. It swept away one of the checks on which the framers had counted to resist majority rule by the great States. Lessening the influence of the small States, and exaggerating the office of President by lowering the dignity of Vice-president, it made the processes of election and government smoother and more efficient—a gain to politicians, but the result most feared by the States-rights school."

With extraordinary prescience, Roger Griswold, Jefferson's virulent critic in the House, declared: "The man voted for as Vice-president will be selected without any decisive view to his qualifications to administer the government. The office will generally be carried into the market to be exchanged for the votes of some large state for President; and the only criterion which will be regarded as a qualification for the office of Vice-president will be the temporary influence of the candidate over the electors of his State . . . The momentary views of party may perhaps be promoted by such arrangements, but the permanent interests of the country are sacrificed."

The Twelfth Amendment was approved on October 17, 1803; the vote in the House was along party lines. The measure became effective on September 25, 1804.

Thus both the structure and the intent of the Constitution were radically altered less than twenty years after its adoption. The Founding Fathers had recognized the twin needs of an undisputed immediate successor to the Chief Executive when the necessity arose and an impartial presiding officer for the Senate. Not foreseeing the rise of political parties (there were none in 1787), they had expected each elector to vote for two men on the theory that after Washington's retirement the first choice would be for a "favorite son" and the second for a leader of national stature. These first votes would thus cancel each other out and the successful candidates would be truly outstanding men.

By 1800 this perspective had become unrealistic because national parties had begun to dominate the scene. Had the Jeffersonians wished to retain the original purpose of the framers of the Constitution—that is, to ensure that the Vice-Presidents be men of sufficient stature to fill the highest office and not merely "favorite sons," mediocrities or selections based on purely electoral considerations — they could have amended the Constitution to provide that the electors have only one vote and that the victor be President and the runner-up Vice-President. Such a procedure would have tended to make the defeated presidential candidate the occupant of the second office. While it might have provided a large inducement to political assassins (since it would have ensured that the death of the President would bring in to office the candidate he had defeated), it would at least have ensured a line of Vice-Presidents fit for the highest office. But the problem was never viewed in this light and the only alternative presented to the actual separate balloting for two offices was the total abolition of the vice-presidential office.

The immediate effect of the Twelfth Amendment was to shrink the caliber of the men chosen to occupy the vice-presidential office. Senator Plumer of New Hampshire prophetically foresaw this possibility. During the debate on the Amendment he warned: "The Electors will not require those qualifications requisite for supreme command. The office . . . will be a sinecure . . . exposed to sale to . . . aspiring candidates for the Presidency. Will his friends . . . promote . . . a man of talents . . . for Vice-President . . . who may become his rival? No! They will seek a man of moderate talents, whose ambition is bounded by that office, and whose influence will aid them in electing the President."

In the first three administrations, Vice-Presidents succeeded the President. In Jefferson's first term, his running mate, Aaron Burr, while certainly not one of the most honorable politicians in the country, was a national figure, a man of outstanding intelligence backed by a powerful political machine. Then came the Twelfth Amendment. Of the 33 men who subsequently became Vice-Presidents, only one, Martin Van Buren, came into the Presidency initially through election rather than through death of the Chief Executive.

AARON BURR

The third Vice-President of the United States was incongruous to the office and an historic enigma. Brilliant, secretive, devoted to underhanded machinations, Burr believed all things to be possible for a man with unbounded ambition in an age of turmoil. His favorite maxim was Napoleon's: "Great spirits are not bothered by small morals."

He was born in 1756 to one of the most distinguished families in American scholarship and theology. At sixteen, he graduated from Princeton, which his father had founded. A few years later, he left a sick bed to join Benedict Arnold in the terrible march to Quebec. Throughout the Revolutionary War, Burr served with outstanding valor and a firm, precocious grasp of strategy. The war over, Burr married a woman ten years his senior; loved her, but had numerous mistresses; suffered from violent headaches and considered suicide. An extraordinarily successful lawyer, he entered politics and took control over the Society of Tammany.

He was forty-four when he became Vice-President. Wielding sufficient power to be wooed by both Federalists and Republicans, Burr had his eye on the succession. Jefferson considered him "a crooked gun, or other perverted instrument, whose aim or shot you could never be sure of." The President was not disposed to have any more dealings with his running-mate than ceremony required. His suspicions of Burr's conduct during the disputed election of 1800 were reinforced by the latter's conduct as Senate presiding officer under conditions where the early techniques of Adams would have saved administration measures. Worse than this, Burr's hatred of Virginia was notorious. In 1801 he attended a Federalist dinner and toasted "the union of all honest men"; this was neither innocuous nor naive. Burr believed he had been betrayed by his party and the implication of his toast was that the Jeffersonians were scoundrels.

The Republicans attempted to wrest control of the federal judiciary from the Federalists and proceeded to impeach justices whose conduct had been flagrantly biased in the days of the Alien and Sedition laws. When the impeached men were tried by the Senate, Vice-President Burr sat as presiding officer, conducting himself with impartiality and good sense.

The Weehawken duel in which Burr shot and killed Alexander Hamilton made the latter a posthumous popular hero (in contrast to his unpopularity while living), but resulted in Burr's being branded as an assassin. The Vice-President of the United States was indicted for murder by New York and New Jersey and his political influence in the Northeast was destroyed.

Yet he continued to follow the *ignis fatuus* of political power. The normal roads to the summit seemed closed to him and he plunged, *faute de mieux*, into a labyrinthine maze of conspiracies. From the English Minister, Anthony Merry, Burr tried to get $500,000 and the aid of an English squadron off New Orleans for the "liberation" of Louisiana Territory from the United States. He proposed a treasonable plot to "General" William Eaton, the alcoholic hero of the Barbary War; the plan was to "turn Congress neck and heels out of doors, assassinate the President, seize the treasury and Navy; and declare himself the protector of an energetic government." At least, so Eaton was to testify when Burr stood charged with treason.

In 1806, Burr proceeded west where he recruited a small band of adventurers, armed them, and moved them by barge down the Ohio and Mississippi. The plan was to seize New Orleans in collaboration with Burr's fellow conspirator, General James Wilkinson, Governor of Upper Louisiana and in command of whatever skeleton forces the United States had in that territory. From New Orleans, Burr planned to march against Mexico and realize grandiose visions of founding a dynasty in the Aztec capital.

General Wilkinson was no tyro at conspiracy. Although he was the senior general of the United States Army, he had secretly sworn allegiance to Spain, become an agent of the Spanish Foreign Office and collected $38,000 from that government during 14 years of duplicity. When it became expedient to do so, he betrayed Burr, had him arrested and denounced the plot to Jefferson.

Thus, in 1807, Aaron Burr, former Vice-President of the United States, stood trial for treason in Richmond, Virginia, before Chief Justice John Marshall. In part, the trial was a continuance of the power struggle between Jefferson and the scattered remnants of Federalism. Marshall, intellectual leader of Federalism and the greatest of Adams' midnight judges, found subtle constitutional reasons for exonerating Burr of technical guilt, but the substantive fact of his treachery can scarcely be doubted — a fact which gives Burr a status among American Vice-Presidents which is happily unique.

At all events, by 1805 the office of Vice-President of the United States had suffered definite diminution from its Constitutional conception and early promise. The main causal agents for this were the rise of national parties and adoption of the Twelfth Amendment.

CHAPTER 4

Politicians in the Saddle

The history of the office of Vice-President in the nineteenth century may be divided into four periods: 1805-25, 1825-45, 1845-69, and 1869-99. Overall the century was one of diminishing significance of the office when compared to the development of the presidency, the legislature, and the judiciary. However, the forces acting on the vice-presidency were sufficiently varied and important to warrant careful examination.

During 1805-1825, the vice-presidency definitely declined. The tendencies apparent with the rise of national political parties, and codified as it were in the Twelfth Amendment, ended even the fiction that the second officer of the national government should be the second best man in the land. That the vice-presidency was now bait to hold out to state favorites was clearly illustrated by the incumbents of the period: George Clinton, Elbridge Gerry and Daniel D. Tompkins. These men helped stamp the office as one suitable for "has beens"—illustrious relics who refused to fade away—or for those whose ambitions were greater than their talents.

GEORGE CLINTON

For Jefferson's second-term running mate, a Republican congressional caucus nominated George Clinton, the Governor of New York, giving him 65 votes to Burr's 41. As Griswold had predicted, the regional consideration had become a major factor in nominations for the vice-presidency. The choice was between Burr and Clinton because, with a Virginia President, the Republicans wanted a strong New York leader who could build the party in the North.

George Clinton was over 65 when he took office as Vice-President. He had been a privateer before the age of 20 and had risen, more because of courage and family than any strategic brilliance, to the rank of brigadier general in the Revolutionary Army. Between 1777 and 1795, he served six successive terms as Governor of New York State. He was a strong believer in states' rights and opposed the Constitution in the Cato letters which Alexander Hamilton answered. Supported by Livingston and Burr, he became Governor of New

32

York for a seventh time in 1800. To all indications he used patronage with ruthless efficiency to eliminate Federalists from all offices.

Essentially a state boss, Clinton was acceptable from a narrow political view as a means of continuing the Virginia dynasty in power, but from the standpoint of the vice-presidency he was a catastrophe. Clinton was out of his surroundings in the national capital; he had no liking for the climate or terrain of the federal district and was quick to say so. He was repeatedly irregular in attendance at the Senate's sessions, lingering as long as possible in his beloved "North," and departing for it again long before the Senate's close. By the time of his second inaugural, he did not even come to Washington to see James Madison installed as President; he delayed his arrival until May of 1809. Not that the Senate missed his presence, for when he was in the chair confusion often reigned. On one occasion procedure got so mixed up that three committees devoted to the same subject were created. "A worse choice than Mr. Clinton could scarcely have been made," observed John Quincy Adams, then a member of the upper chamber.

Vice-President Clinton let it be known that he desired to be fore-warned by Senators whenever they intended making long speeches so "that he might take the opportunity to warm himself at the fire." He would frequently forget points of order and even miscounted votes. Under such conditions it is not surprising that the Senate had scant respect for the man and that the office began to be thought of in terms of the incumbent's characteristics. If, according to Senator William Giles of Virginia, Clinton's friends "had sent him here with a view to push him on to the Presidency, they had been unlucky in the choice of their expedient. It was a dangerous experiment . . . for in such conspicuous stations a man was apt to be seen through."

Since Giles was close to the anti-third term Jefferson, here was clear indication that Clinton was not considered a suitable successor to the President. Nor had he ever been in Jefferson's mind; the mantle would fall on Secretary of State James Madison, despite Jefferson's public protestations of disinterestedness to the contrary. Stephen Bradley of Vermont disclosed the Administration viewpoint when he invited John Quincy Adams to attend the Republican nominating caucus in January 1808. He remarked that he "hoped the old gentleman, Mr. Clinton, would be complimented with a *unanimous* vote for reelection as Vice-President, though he did not expect he would serve. I [Adams] asked whether he was not to be supported for the presidency. He said no; he was too old; and we are all witnesses that his faculties were failing; that Madison was the man for the presidency."

In other words, the "old gentleman" with "failing faculties" was conceivably suitable for another four years as Vice-President (and potential President) but "too old" for the actual presidency.

Giles and Bradley dominated the caucus that brought about renewal of the Virginia-New York axis. Clinton never did reconcile himself to this repeat performance or to the small glory of being the first Vice-President to serve under two different Chief Executives. He let it be widely known that he was angered clear through at Jefferson and once found occasion to vent to the Senate his feelings toward the President. Jefferson had sent a confidential message to the Senate through Clinton, but the latter failed to notice that it was so stamped. When the document was read in public, the newspapers got wind of the situation and commented on it "as evidence of Mr. Clinton's *declining* years." The sixty-eight year old Vice-President thought Jefferson had intentionally set about to "ensnare him and expose him to derision." He let it be known that "he thought the *Executive* would have had more magnanimity than to have treated him thus."

Clinton made no secret of his antipathy toward Madison. Even during the election campaign of 1808 he was in open rivalry with the head of the ticket and used his own political machine to attack Madison. In office, Clinton openly attacked the administration's foreign and domestic policies. He vocally opposed non-intercourse with England and brazenly let the British minister know this. Domestically, about the last important public act of Clinton was to cast the decisive vote against renewal of the charter of the United States Bank in 1811. This measure, strongly urged by Madison's administration, fell on the Vice-President's adverse vote. The bank collapsed and the federal government was left without a credit source to aid in financing the War of 1812. The aging Clinton died shortly after the war began.

ELBRIDGE GERRY

To Madisonians, Clinton's death was badly timed for it threatened the liaison between New York and Virginia just as they were launching a war against Britain which was highly unpopular in the New England states. Clinton's political heir and nephew, De Witt Clinton would have been acceptable, but he had no intention of following his uncle's path up the blind alley of the vice-presidency. The caucus selected John Langdon of New Hampshire over Elbridge Gerry and adjourned, but was forced to reconvene at once when the nominee declined, ostensibly because of poor health. The re-assembled caucus then chose Gerry of Massachusetts with the hope that he would be able to cool his state's molten hatred of Madison's policies.

De Witt Clinton ran for President with Federalist support, but was beaten by the regular Republicans. A curiosity of this first wartime election was that although Gerry failed to carry his own state he polled three more electoral votes than President-elect Madison.

The new Vice-President was neither a newcomer to politics nor a cipher. Born in 1744 to the prosperous merchant, Thomas Gerry, he graduated from Harvard, entered his father's business, and joined the powerful Committee of Correspondence under Samuel Adams which played such a large role in readying the Colonies for armed resistance. A member of the Committee of Safety and the Continental Congress, he signed the Declaration of Independence. He opposed a strong national government, bitterly attacked the Order of Cincinnati as the germ of aristocracy, and publicly opposed the final version of the Constitution. He served in Congress and was appointed in 1797, together with C. C. Pinckney and John Marshall, to go to France and negotiate American grievances with Napoleon. In essence, he was the minority representative of the Jeffersonian faction on that committee. When the XYZ scandal broke and it became known that Talleyrand had asked the American envoys to pay him a £50,000 bribe through intermediaries, Marshall and Pinckney went home, but Gerry, an ardent Francophile, earned public odium by staying on in France, ignoring the insult and attempting to patch matters up. He was elected Governor of Massachusetts in 1810 and again in 1811. In his second term, the Jeffersonians rearranged the election districts in a grotesque manner as a means of ensuring political control; hence the word "gerrymander," a hybrid of Gerry and salamander.

A strong Administration man, pro-war and anti-British, Gerry left no imprint on the vice-presidential office. Although in bad health throughout his term, he persisted in presiding over the Senate until stricken with a fatal hemorrhage in November 1814.

DANIEL D. TOMPKINS

Chastened Republicans, musing over the two successive deaths in the vice-presidency, sought to retrieve the situation by selecting Daniel D. Tompkins, Governor of New York since 1807, as James Monroe's running-mate in 1816. Several purposes were served by this choice: the Virginia-NewYork axis could be safely resumed (De Witt Clinton was never more to be as significant a figure on the national scale as he had been in 1812), Tompkins was young and vigorous with an able record of enthusiastic support of "Mr. Madison's War," and at least the hope could be held out to long-suffering Northern Republicans that perhaps a future ticket might be headed by someone other than a Virginian (a rising young New Yorker named Martin Van Buren was even pushing Tompkins for the presidential nomination itself).

Tompkins seemed indeed to be the most talented vice-presidential choice since pre-Twelfth Amendment days. Only forty-two years old in 1816, he had demonstrated executive ability both in peace and war from Albany; his politics were "always . . . moderate and consistent," as even the Federalist Rufus King admitted, and he had the indispensable political asset of always remembering the name or the face of anyone with whom he had conversed. His prompt and generous financial disbursement of New York funds for prosecution of the War of 1812 was so unlike the frosty, niggardly efforts of other Northern governors that a grateful Madison offered to appoint him Secretary of State in 1814, the position which since 1801 had been reserved for presidential successors. However, Tompkins had turned it down in the belief he could do more useful work in the war from his gubernatorial post.

The prospect that Tompkins might raise the prestige of the office of Vice-President, perhaps even to the point of again being considered as a logical pre-presidential post, never materialized. A characteristically American post-war investigation of war-time governmental activities put Tompkins under a cloud during his vice-presidency and left him broken in spirit and burnt-out in energy. His mistake as Governor was excessive zeal in expenditures without keeping adequate records and affidavits. Thus Tompkins spent more time and effort in trying to clear his name than as a working Vice-President. Nor did it help when, in 1820, he sought vindication at the polls by running for governor of New York against De Witt Clinton, the incumbent and his persecutor. Clinton narrowly defeated the Vice-President, but Tompkins' strong showing warranted his being considered as the party's choice for reelection in the "era of good feeling" vote of 1820.

Tompkins' absences became more pronounced during his second term. A special messenger had to be sent to him by Monroe to inform him of his reelection and he took the oath of office in New York. It began to be rumored that he was taking to drink while persisting in a law suit to establish definitely the facts of his wartime stewardship. The vice-presidency of the United States was of no concern to him now, and it appeared likely he would not be in Washington at all for the 1821-22 session. As Representative John Taylor of New York had it from a friend of Tompkins: "He says there is nothing for him to do here, and any other man may preside in the Senate as well as he."

Tompkins did attempt, from the fall of 1822 to the beginning of

1824, to work at being Vice-President and to test his chances for the wide-open race that was developing for the presidency, but he was unsuccessful. In January 1824, Tompkins confessed to Secretary of State John Quincy Adams that though "he had recovered . . . with the exception of sleepless nights, and . . . was relieved from all his embarrassments . . . he had no intention of being a candidate either for election to the presidency or for reelection as Vice-President. All he wanted was justice . . . had determined to take no part in the approaching election, and wished for nothing hereafter but quiet and retirement." He kept his word, retiring to his Staten Island home to muse over what might have been, receiving General Lafayette on the occasion of that hero's visit in August, and allowing the president *pro tempore* of the Senate, John Gaillard of South Carolina, to handle the electoral crisis of 1825. Tompkins died at fifty-one, only three months after his term of office expired.

*   *   *

From 1825 to 1845, the vice-presidency recovered much of its prestige due to such strong incumbents as Calhoun, Van Buren, and Tyler. The first two men were considered presidential material while they occupied the vice-presidency. Tyler was the first to succeed to the presidency by the death of the chief executive.

JOHN CALDWELL CALHOUN

John Caldwell Calhoun of South Carolina had been a rising luminary ever since his first entrance on the national stage in 1811 as one of the "war hawks" in Congress. As Secretary of War in the Monroe Administration, he had been active and brilliant, and, as the Virginia dynasty appeared to be running out of heirs, he made his bid for the presidency along with most of the other leading members of the second Monroe Administration.

The woods were full of potential presidential candidates for 1824. The one-party system prevailed and unified caucus nomination and support would have been equivalent to election. In this situation the congressional caucus system of nomination fortunately broke down. The delegation which met to pick Secretary of the Treasury William H. Crawford of Georgia for President and the Swiss-born Albert Gallatin for Vice-President was merely a rump assemblage.

Partisans of the other major candidates, John C. Calhoun, Secretary of State John Quincy Adams, Speaker Henry Clay and General Andrew Jackson scoffed at the Crawfordite pleas for party discipline and continued their electioneering. Calhoun sought to keep his boom alive in the manner of the times—by destroying the reputation of others engaged in the pursuit of the office. Gallatin felt he was "a smart fellow . . . but of lax political principles and a disordinate ambition, not over delicate in the means of satisfying them."

By February 1824, Calhoun was out of the presidential picture for that election. However, he was still a young man—only forty—with a bright future ahead of him, and there still remained certain possibilities even for 1824. Calhoun decided to exploit these. There was a distinct possibility that there might be no majority electoral choice for President. With the House having to choose from among the three highest, there might be a deadlock in the body. In that case said ex-Speaker John W. Taylor, "the Executive Government must be administered by the Vice-President," though no one knew "whether for a Presidential term or only until a new election for President could be held." Calhoun accordingly worked to get several major presidential candidates to endorse him for second place on their ticket in return for the Southern votes he could deliver. Behind this scheme lurked the prospect of obtaining the presidency *de facto* for himself through the processes of factional paralysis in the House of Representatives.

Given the unique party conditions that prevailed, intriguing for the vice-presidency was more complex in the campaign of 1824 than it had been before or was to be since. Several of the presidential candidates offered it to each other: Crawford to Adams, Adams to Jackson, Crawford to Clay—among other projected combinations. When Adams broached to friends his idea of having General Jackson as a running-mate, they protested that the latter was a barbarian who liked to hang people. Adams retorted that "the vice-presidency was a station in which the General could hang no one, and in which he would need to quarrel with no one. His name . . . would . . . restore the forgotten dignity of the place, and it would afford an easy and dignified retirement to his old age." Jackson's stormy reaction, had he known of this evaluation, can be imagined. Far from seeking retirement, the General would be in the White House 12 years later.

As it turned out, both Adams' and Jackson's supporters endorsed Calhoun for the vice-presidency—thus ensuring his election. Calhoun's only campaign problem was to convince New Englanders that he was for Adams and Westerners that he favored Jackson.

True to the forecast, the election was thrown into the House. Vice-President-elect Calhoun was in a delicate position. Which one of his running-mates would be chosen? The effective race was between Jackson as front-runner and Adams in second place. Calhoun tried to play it both ways and lost out. When Adams received reports that Calhoun was "neutral" on the question for public purposes but that his "personal wish" was for Adams' election, he ironically replied: "This contrasts singularly with the conduct of all his electioneering partisans."

After the House chose Adams on the first ballot, the Vice-President-elect sought to make Adams recognize his influence and sent an emissary to him to outline the sort of cabinet that would be acceptable to the Southern group. Adams reacted furiously to this as attempted intimidation, as an effort "to bring in General Jackson as the next President, under the auspices of Calhoun."

This was the inauspicious beginning of an Administration in which the President and Vice-President were not merely at loggerheads (for this had been a commonplace), but in active, vehement and continuous quarrels. At the height of the struggle, Adams and Calhoun attacked each other in the press under the thinly disguised pseudonyms of "Patrick Henry" and "Onslow." The occasion was a difference of opinion over the powers of the presiding officer of the Senate. Calhoun sought every opportunity, direct and indirect, to needle the Administration, and it was soon apparent that Senator John Randolph of Virginia was a worthy instrument. A master of invective, Randolph often excoriated John Quincy Adams on the Senate floor while the Vice-President impassively sat in his great chair. Though the castigations sometimes lasted six hours, Calhoun "alone retained his seat, seldom ever changing his position." Adams, fuming, believed Calhoun should have restrained Randolph under his power "to preside." Insisting that only the Senate itself had authority to limit senatorial speech, Calhoun declared: "I trust that it will never be the ambition of him who occupys this chair to enlarge its powers." It was one thing, then, for the Vice-President to call to order when the Senate's rules were violated (as when Senators read newspapers during debate), but with regard to words uttered during debate, the widest latitude was to be given. The traditional unlimited debate of the Senate received its greatest impetus during Calhoun's tenure.

Administration Senators introduced resolutions that they thought would satisfy Adams. But he objected because "additional rules conceded that the power of repressing disorder did not exist." He believed that such power did exist and that Calhoun was evading his duty. The Senate ultimately resolved the dispute to its own satisfaction by granting power to the presiding officer to call to order for words spoken in debate, with the allegedly offending Senator having the right of appeal to the Senate.

Vice-President Calhoun also used another power of his office to irk further the Adams Administration. The rules of the Senate empowered him to appoint the members of all committees, and he failed so noticeably to name Administration men that John Randolph himself pushed through a motion stripping the Vice-President of the power.   One reason the United States failed to participate effectively in the Panama Congress of 1826 was because of a Calhoun-controlled committee's tardy action in handling President Adams' appointment of delegates.

Calhoun's power extended to the Cabinet itself, especially through the Postmaster General, who was, in Adams' own words "devoted to Calhoun."   The result was that patronage distribution in the Post Office department was practically confined to the Vice-President's "tools."

Though all this anti-administration activity on the Vice-President's part could have been interpreted as designed to advance Calhoun's prospects for 1828, Andrew Jackson chose to interpret it otherwise. He selected Calhoun as his running-mate for the "vindication of the people" election in that year. For his part, Adams had decided as early as December 1826 that he needed a new running-mate.   When Clay offered to sacrifice himself, the President put the matter on a health basis.   If Secretary of State Henry Clay was not up to the "oppressive" burdens of the State Department, the President would be glad to have him as Vice-President, "but otherwise I think it more advantageous both for the public and personally for him that he should continue in the far more arduous and important office."   Clay stayed on as Secretary until March 4, 1829.

Calhoun's second vice-presidential term began auspiciously for he seemed to be the heir apparent to the soldier-President. This pleasant state did not last long.   In the maze of bitter personal struggles embracing Jackson, Calhoun, Van Buren, Crawford and various other members both of the official and "kitchen" cabinets, Calhoun lost the inside track to Van Buren and was spewed out ignominiously and publicly on the states' rights issue at the famous Jefferson Day dinner in April 1830.

President Andrew Jackson had already decided who was to be his chief of staff, writing of Van Buren: "I have found him everything that I could desire him to be . . . well qualified to fill the highest office in the gift of the people . . . I wish I could say as much for Mr. Calhoun." Whatever possibilities existed for the Vice-President to retrieve his situation vanished with the disclosures that Calhoun, as Secretary of War in the Monroe Administration, had been critical of Jackson's conduct in 1818. Calhoun's explanations failed; Jackson wrote him: "I . . . never expected to say to you . . . *Et tu Brute.*"   Calhoun unsuccessfully attempted to vindicate himself, at which point Van Buren played the master card that ultimately won him both the vice-presidency and the presidency. His resignation as Secretary of State precipitated Jackson's request for all members of the Cabinet, Calhoun men mostly, to do likewise. With Calhoun isolated now in his vice-presidential chair, Van Buren was rewarded with a recess appointment as Minister to England. He was already at his post when the Senate divided equally on confirmation. Calhoun triumphantly cast the decisive vote of rejection, and descending the rostrum, gleefully announced "It will kill him, sir, kill him dead. He will never kick, sir, never kick." But Senator Thomas Hart Benton, a Jacksonian, saw it differently: "You have broken a Minister, and elected a Vice-President."

Calhoun's action was the signal for Administration Senators to apply to him some of the medicine of castigation that he had allowed Randolph to apply to Adams during the preceding administration. But since the attack was directed at him and not the President, he now sought to answer it. When John Forsyth of Georgia lashed out at the pro-Calhoun press Calhoun said: "Does the Senator allude to me?" Forsyth looked at him. "By what right does the Chair ask that question?" he demanded. As the Chair had no right to speak, Calhoun remained mute.

Even his seat as presiding officer was now becoming uncomfortable. With his state's nullification movement growing more radical, Calhoun was glad to accept Senatorial status when his state offered him Hayne's seat. Now no Forsyth would question his right to speak! Thus occurred the letter, unique in the history of the vice-presidency, addressed to Van Buren's successor in the State Department and dated 28, 1832: "Having concluded to accept of a seat in the United States Senate, I herewith resign the office of Vice-President of the United States."

(Margaret Coit's account of this episode deserves discussion as it illustrates the degree of ignorance of the vice-presidential office that prevails. In a book that won the 1951 Pulitzer Prize for biography, Miss Coit wrote: "Such was the excitement that even Calhoun, the stickler for constitutional legalities, wasted no time seeking a way to submit his resignation to the people of the United States to whom he was, of course, responsible. Instead, he addressed a brief note to Secretary of State Edward Livingston, next in the line of presidential succession . . . To this extraordinary document, neither the Secretary of State nor the United States government paid the least attention . . . The Senate . . . disdained to recognize the withdrawal of their presiding officer. Instead they elected a President *pro tempore* and continued business as usual." Coit, *John C. Calhoun, American Portrait.* Boston, 1950, pp. 239-40 passim.

(Passing over the ambiguous phrase "constitutional legalities," one wonders how a public officer could "submit his resignation to the people of the United States" as Miss Coit imagines Calhoun should have done. To whom would he send it? Calhoun's procedure was not only correct, but legally mandatory under the Act of March 1, 1792 [1 *Statutes At Large,* 239]. Miss Coit is also in error in calling the Secretary of State "next in line of presidential succession" after the Vice-President. This was to be the case 54 years later; in 1832, the 1792 statute governed and provided for the President *pro tempore* and, if none existed, then the Speaker of the House. Finally, the Senate did not wait until Calhoun had resigned before electing a President *pro tem;* it already had one in the person of Hugh L. White of Tennessee, who was elected 25 days before Calhoun resigned and who continued his functions until June 28, 1834, when George Poindexter of Mississippi replaced him.)

Thus ended the vice-presidential career of Calhoun. No other man would be reelected to that office for the next 84 years. He had timed his departure to avoid the unpleasant duty that soon would have confronted him of formally pronouncing Martin Van Buren—whom he had personally barred from a lesser office—his successor as Vice-President.

MARTIN VAN BUREN

Van Buren's term was in some respects pivotal for the office. He had been Secretary of State for most of one term and now was to be Vice-President with the full confidence of Jackson throughout the term and with assurance of selection as the next Democratic standard-bearer. Thus he fused what up to that time had been the two most likely qualifying offices for the presidency. He was to be the last Secretary of State or Vice-President who would ever be directly elected from either office to the chief executiveship of the United States.

As the gossipy Perley Poore saw him, the new Vice-President was "exasperatingly unruffled," smiled easily, took snuff or "read a novel when under attack," and liked to lounge in the presiding chair. Senators could indulge their freedom of speech to the maximum; gallery noises went unheeded, and, when Benton called Senator Calhoun a liar, the Vice-President refused to call his fellow Democrat out of order. In this incident, the Senate, however, overruled him. On one occasion, Van Buren's Olympian aplomb was unsettled and he presided with a brace of pistols to ward off possible attack from "that bloated mass of corruption," President *pro tempore* Poindexter, a Clay Whig. This was the exception and even Adams conceded that Van Buren would succeed Jackson because of his ability to be friends with everybody who counted.

A New York machine politician, a man of great manipulative skill, Van Buren's stand on the large issues of the day—states' rights, internal improvements, slavery—had veered with the winds of expediency. He dominated the Albany Regency and was to that extent in control of the politics of his own state. The most influential of Jackson's advisers, he was further entrenched when he paid his respects to Peggy Eaton. Nominated as Jackson's man at the 1836 Democratic Convention, Van Buren was carried into the White House by his patron's popularity and by the absence of an effective opposition.

RICHARD MENTOR JOHNSON

With considerably greater misgivings, the convention accepted Jackson's second-place choice, Richard Mentor Johnson of Kentucky. There was substantial difference of opinion as to his fitness for the office, but Jackson was determined to prevent the "Richmond Junto" from promoting William C. Rives, thus re-establishing the traditional Virginia-New York axis and getting Rives in as successor to Van Buren in 1840.

Johnson was a lawyer-politician who had an excellent record in the War of 1812 and was chiefly famous as the alleged killer of Tecumseh. His *Report on the Transportation of the Mail on Sunday* was characterized as "probably the ablest state document on record on the noninterference of government with the observance of the Sabbath, and the noblest political plea for the rights of conscience produced in modern times." Though Johnson was incapable of having actually written this Congressional paper, he at least signed his name to it and supported it. In Congress, he had pushed a bill for the abolition of imprisonment for debt and his political strength in the Northern cities was based on his reputation as a Jacksonian radical and friend of the working class. Burly, genial, good-looking, a convivial man who wore flaming scarlet waistcoats, he was, in Schlesinger's judgment, during the 1820s "the one Senator who consistently advocated the rights of the common man, from his attack on the Supreme Court to his defense of the Sunday mails, from his attack on debtors' prisons to his defense of settlers' rights in the public land." The verdict of some of his contemporaries was less flattering. As early as 1821, John Quincy Adams judged that "his weight and influence . . . is at market to the highest bidder." In the vice-presidency, he was a gladhander and to the Senate door keeper "the most vulgar man of all vulgar men in this world."

He did not receive a majority and, in accordance with the Twelfth Amendment, the Senate had to choose between the two top ranking candidates, the quorum being two-thirds of the membership and the vote necessary for election a majority of the whole number. The Senate chose Johnson over his anti-Masonic Whig opponent, Francis Granger, by 33 to 16 votes, thus making him the West's first Vice-President.

Johnson was vehemently criticized because of his personal life. He had a liaison with a Negro girl for a number of years, had educated their children and tried to bring them into society. Another slave mistress ran off with an Indian, for which offense Johnson sold her. While he was Vice-President, there was gossip about his third mistress, young and also Negro, who played the piano and called him "my dear Colonel" when white guests were present. Johnson made no effort to keep his unconventional life *sub rosa*.

In the vice-presidency, Johnson deteriorated into vulgarity and cheap politics. He became absorbed with making money and left Washington one summer to run an inn, personally supervising the purchase and sale of edibles.

The party felt he would be a liability in 1840 and should withdraw since he had failed to carry his state four years earlier. Weakened by the panic of 1837, the Administration felt that the defection of Virginia would be the last straw. Johnson resisted all pressures—even Jackson's—and refused to withdraw. Banking all on his one asset, he felt he could go into the fight, show his scars, and be reelected. The Convention so divided on him, that it chose no vice-presidential candidate at all (a unique event in political party history). Though it was generally accepted that he was Van Buren's running-mate, the ticket was unequally supported. Kentucky again went for Clay's party but Virginia was to prefer Johnson to her own aristocratic John Tyler. The 1840 "Tippecanoe and Tyler Too" campaign of bombast and bosh was a case where *neither* vice-presidential candidate carried his own state, a circumstance which should have given cause for reflection to the exponents of one of the oldest superstitions of "practical" politics.

JOHN TYLER

John Tyler was a college graduate, a gentleman, a former Governor of the Commonwealth and an ardent and uncompromising advocate of states' rights. Since Whig success was to be so portentous for the history of the vice-presidency, the motivations for the 1840 second place choice are of interest. Geography required a Southerner to offset the Ohioan, William Henry Harrison, but which one? John Tyler had a lot to commend him, especially a past history of election to office. For over a quarter of a century he had been in the Virginia House of Delegates, the national House of Representatives, and the Senate. While it was true he had failed in 1836 in his bid for the vice-presidency, he had gotten 47 Southern electoral votes, twice as many as William Smith of Alabama, the other splinter candidate of the Southern Whigs. But Tyler was proving an obstacle to Henry Clay's plans in Virginia. He wanted his old Senatorial seat back for a new term and William C. Rives was not disposed to step aside. Desiring to build up all forms of anti-Democratic feeling into a winning combination for 1840, Clay backed Rives. The Great Compromiser promised to support Tyler for the Whig vice-presidential nomination in 1840 if Rives should be allowed to succeed himself. This deal was closed, but the election of Rives was deferred until Tyler won the vice-presidency. Thus for nearly two years, Virginia had a reduced Senatorial representation, and Rives had to content himself with another attenuated term of office. So angry was the Virginia delegation that it refused to sponsor John Tyler at the Whig Harrisburg Convention, and in the ensuing election, the state preferred Richard M. Johnson to him.

The well-laid plans of Northern and Western Whigs to have a docile Harrison in the White House, so that national affairs could be run from a Clay-dominated Congress and a Webster-dominated Cabinet, went awry with the death one month after inauguration of the soldier President. In the first 52 years of the United States under the Constitution, no vice-presidential succession by reason of death had occurred. Such a long period would prove to be unprecedented. Thus the shock in 1841 was real and widespread. John Quincy Adams was depressed—and voluble: "The influence of this event upon the condition and history of the country can scarcely be foreseen. It makes the Vice-President . . . Acting President of the Union for four years less one month . . . This is the first instance of a Vice-President being called to act as President of the United States, and brings to the test that provision of the Constitution which places in the Executive chair a man never thought of for it by anybody. This day was in every sense gloomy—rain the whole day." Sooner or later, a succession to the presidency through death had been bound to occur and Adams' characterization of the Vice-President as a man "never thought of" for that succession was fantastic.

It will be noted that ex-President Adams was careful to call Tyler the "Acting President" or the person called upon to "act as President." Obviously "to act as" is not the same as "to be." Throughout Tyler's administration, the burning question would be his exact status in the presidency. From the very outset, the Virginian showed that he believed himself to be the Chief Executive of the United States.

Arriving from Williamsburg, where he was found by the emissary from Harrison's Cabinet playing marbles with his two sons, Tyler first met that body at noon on April sixth. Immediately, Secretary of State Webster sought to enlighten him on how business had been done in the Cabinet previously. Decisions, he explained, had been by majority vote with each member *including the President* having one vote. Webster was sure Tyler would wish to abide by that custom. The latter answered with a ringing statement of personal and presidential independence. He would be glad to have all of them continue in office for their "counsel and advice, but I can never consent to being dictated to as to what I shall or shall not do. I, as President, will be responsible for my administration. I hope to have your co-operation . . . So long as you . . . do this, I shall be glad to have you with me— when you think otherwise, your resignations will be accepted."

Having thus declared himself President, he sought Chief Justice Taney to take the presidential oath, but in his absence was sworn in by Justice William Cranch. Being also a lawyer, Tyler requested Cranch to prepare the following certificate: "I . . . certify that the above named John Tyler personally appeared before me this day, and although he deems himself qualified to perform the duties and exercise the powers and office of President . . . without any other oath than that which he has taken as Vice President, yet as doubts may arise, and for greater caution, took and subscribed the foregoing other [oath] before me."

Thus it was apparent that Tyler felt he succeeded to the office by reason of being the legal Vice-President automatically upon his predecessor's death. Just as in hereditary succession where, although the flow of power is automatic, there is still a formal coronation, so in like manner Tyler established the precedent which has never since been departed from that all Vice-Presidents take the President's oath as soon as practicable after hearing of the death of the incumbent.

Was John Tyler correct in his assumption that he was in fact President and not, as John Quincy Adams believed, Acting President? The debate has continued from then till now; the answer hinges on the construction of the pertinent Constitutional clause, which reads: "In case of the Removal of the President from Office, or of his Death, Resignation, or Inability to discharge the Powers and Duties of the said Office, the same shall devolve on the Vice-President, and the Congress may by Law provide for the Case of Removal . . . both of the President and Vice-President, declaring what Officer shall then act as President, and such Officer shall act accordingly, until the Disability be removed, or a President shall be elected." (Article II, Section 1, Clause 5)

Taking the clause as a whole, one thing is immediately clear: succession after the removal of both President and Vice-President would confer the right merely to "act as" and not to be President. The larger question is whether the Founding Fathers intended the Vice-President to succeed to the office of President or merely again to the "acting" status. The answer depends on the construction of what is at best ambiguous grammar. Does "the same shall devolve on the Vice-President" refer to "Powers and Duties" or to "said Office"? Adams insisted it was the former. As he wrote after a visit with Tyler, he "styles himself President of the United States, and not Vice-President acting as President, which would be the correct style. But it is a construction in direct violation both of the grammar and context of the Constitution, which confers upon the Vice-President, on the decease of the President, not the office, but the powers and duties of the said office. . . . a strict constructionist would doubt whether the Vice-President has the right to occupy the President's house, or to claim his salary, without an Act of Congress. He moved into the house two days ago."

Tyler chose to assume the opposite construction, namely, that "the same" referred to the noun closest to it which is "office." He made this interpretation stick by usage and eventually wore down even the stubborn Adams. Thus, on May 21, 1841, Adams wrote: "I feel an utter distrust of the principles of John Tyler, now acting as President of the United States"; but by June 26 he gave up the ghost and entered in his diary: "President Tyler . . . was present."

What was in the mind of the 1787 Convention in this respect? Though a categorical answer is impossible, the trend of argument on the vice-presidency, as outlined above, indicates that the founders never conceived of the Vice-President as more than an acting Chief Executive. Any ambiguity that exists springs from the fact that the Committee on Style of the Convention altered the clearer language of the Committee of Detail and the States. As altered, the language dealing with the vice-presidency was accepted in the closing days of the Convention without any recorded debate and hence without any elaboration of the framers' intent.

In the first session of the Senate, a discussion occurred which sheds some light on this matter. John Adams, as first Vice-President, asked the Senate whether he should sign a communication of that body as "Vice-President" or "President of the Senate." The irascible Senator

Maclay of Pennsylvania replied that he should sign only as President of the Senate, for Adams could only be Vice-President and use the title after he had succeeded to the presidency. He held that "every act done by the Vice-President as such implied that when so acting he held the place of the President." Needless to say, the elder Adams did not think much of Maclay's solution and soon he began to use the title "Vice-President and President of the Senate."

A body of opinion existed from the early days of the Republic that the Framers of the Constitution intended the Vice-President to be at most an acting President. Also germane to a solution is the word "devolve" in the pertinent clause, "the same shall devolve on the Vice-President." Modernly, it is axiomatic to political scientists that an office passes but that powers and duties devolve. If one accepts the distinction between "succession" and "devolution," and if the Founding Fathers accepted it (which is more important and not known), then the Vice-President on "devolution" became "acting President" as John Quincy Adams maintained.

Finally one may ask whether the Twelfth Amendment sheds any light? The pertinent sentence reads: "And if the House of Representatives shall not choose a President whenever the right of choice shall devolve upon them, before the fourth day of March next following, then *the Vice-President shall act as President as in the case of the death or other constitutional disability of the President.*" (Italics added.) The italicized portion above seems to settle the argument in favor of John Quincy Adams, though he never used it.

So, most probably, John Tyler had no *right* to the office and title of President in 1841, but only to its "powers and duties." The practice commenced by him and continued down through seven successions —even with the same words of the Twelfth Amendment carried into the Twentieth Amendment (ratified January 23, 1933) — meant in effect that usage had prevailed over the plain meaning of the Constitution and that the Vice-President on succeeding would become President of the United States in every sense of the word.

Tyler's ultimate triumph came exactly a century later when, in 1951, the Twenty-second Amendment was ratified. This Amendment incorporated unambiguous phraseology to distinguish a vice-presidential succession from other kinds of succession, and in so doing completely vindicated Tyler's belief and the practice of six other vice-presidential successors. The text of the current governing Amendment is as follows, with the applicable words italicized:

"No person shall be elected to the office of the President more than twice, and *no person who has held the office of President, or acted as*

President, for more than two years of a term to which some other person was elected President shall be elected to the office of President more than once.

"*But this Article shall not apply to any person holding the office of President when this Article was proposed by the Congress*, and shall not prevent any person who may be holding the office of President, or acting as President, during the term within which this Article becomes operative from holding the office of President or acting as President during the remainder of such term."

"Holding the office of President" is distinguished three times in the short text above from "or acting as President." It should be noted that the italicized part of the second paragraph could apply to but one person, Harry S. Truman. Since the Amendment "shall not apply to any person holding the office of President when this Article was proposed by the Congress", and since the Eightieth Congress proposed "this Article" on March 26, 1947 and had it sent out then to the States for action, it unequivocally meant that Vice-President-Successor Harry S. Truman was in 1947 "holding" the office of President and not "acting as President."

Whatever the Founding Fathers had in mind in 1787, and regardless of the clear language of the Twelfth and Twentieth Amendments, the fact is that by now practice and the Constitution have at last been synchronized and are henceforth indistinguishable in this matter. John Tyler's presumption has become Constitutional law.

Tyler's experience was significant in another respect. It illustrated that choosing a Vice-President whose views differed radically from those of the President might be a shrewd way to collect votes, but was bound to bring chaos to the Executive Branch and disunity to the Government should the Chief Executive die in office. In the Tyler administration, party liaison between the Executive and Legislature completely broke down. His two vetoes of the Bank bills—being sustained—illustrated the power of the President in the face of his party's wishes. His punishment was immediate and was expected to prove overwhelming: the entire Cabinet, except Daniel Webster, resigned in September 1841. However, as we have seen, Tyler had envisaged this possibility at the very outset of his succession. He formed a new cabinet from friendly elements and it carried on in as competent a manner as the regency bequeathed by Harrison. Nevertheless, before his administration was over, Tyler ran through five Secretaries of War, three Attorneys-General, four Secretaries of the Treasury, four Secretaries of State, two Postmasters General, and five Secretaries of the Navy. Needless to say, this is a record.

In 1842, Tyler was read out of the Whig Party by Clay's Congress-men. The curious spectacle was thus present of a Chief Executive in a bipartisan system self-exiled from the one party and formally cashiered from the other. Stalemate was the inevitable result. The President was refused appointment; Congress was refused the Presi-dent's signature to bills. Democrats, hugely enjoying the situation, saw to it that Tyler's vetoes were not overridden by the angry Whig Congress. Clay Whigs were forced to make the supreme effort to get rid of Tyler by invoking the impeachment clauses of the Constitution.

On January 11, 1843 a resolution was introduced in the House to establish a committee of inquiry looking toward the impeachment of "John Tyler, Vice-President, acting as President." Nine charges were specified which, in the view of the sponsoring Whigs, constituted "the high crimes and misdemeanors" specified in the Constitution; to a modern observer they merely illustrate a basic difference of political judgment between Executive and Legislature, with no demonstrable evidence that the President was using ungranted powers or using granted powers unconstitutionally. Fortunately, the resolution failed of adoption, 83 to 127. Democrats, Tylerites and a scattering of neutral Whigs beat down the first attempt to impeach a President of the United States for what was essentially a failure of the Whig Party in convention assembled to take into account the fact that only a heartbeat separates the Vice-President from the presidency. The first successful attempt at impeachment was deferred until another Vice-President should succeed to the presidency by death (Andrew John-son), and should be unable also to control the party which had selected him as potential President.

CHAPTER 5

Accession by Assassination

The third nineteenth century period for the vice-presidency, 1845 to 1869, may be termed its critical period. Though two successions by death occurred which should theoretically have strengthened the office's significance, neither one was very successful from a party viewpoint and the real lesson of Tyler's accession was not learned. In general, the period was one that saw the forces tending to strengthen the office in shifting contention with those that used the vice-presidency to repair temporary sectional or political intraparty divisions. On balance the disruptive forces triumphed, and hence for the rest of the century the Vice-President became fixed in the popular and political mind as an inferior officer to be selected as an afterthought at convention time and to be forgotten during the administration. The idea that it was a place for actual presidential timber died out and, despite the succession of Arthur, its potentiality was not a controlling factor in selection.

* * *

The Whigs in 1844 had learned nothing from the debacle of the Tyler Administration. They chose for the vice-presidency Theodore W. Frelinghuysen of New Jersey, a prominent sponsor of a Bible society engaged in changing Catholics to Protestants, as a means of appealing to nativist elements in the North. The strategy failed; the Whigs lost New York by a margin of 5,026 votes. This cost them the election due, in Millard Fillmore's opinion, to "the Native Americans and Mr. Frelinghuysen" who "drove the foreign Catholics from us."

The Democrats for their part selected running-mates not thought of in pre-convention plans. Ex-Vice-President Calhoun and ex-President Van Buren cancelled each other out, Tyler was given no consideration, and Lewis W. Cass of Michigan (a confirmed expansionist with or without war) began to be strongly favored by the southern elements. The New York delegation, controlled by Van Buren, therefore swung the convention to the comparatively unknown James K. Polk of Tennessee. A minor contender before, with his backers more interested in keeping his name in view for the vice-presidency, Polk became the presidential choice as a compromise between the pro- and anti-slavery wings.

GEORGE MIFFLIN DALLAS

To appease the still disgruntled Van Buren, the Democrats chose Silas Wright of New York for the second place on the ticket. Senator Wright, Van Buren's personal friend as well as political ally, was an able man. The aristocratic Clay Whig, Philip Hone, agreed with the reaction to the Polk-Wright ticket; it was "like a kangaroo—it goes upon its hind legs." The man in second place was felt to be much superior to Polk, possessing qualities "little short of superb," "honest and courageous, a man of high personal honor." Momentary consternation thus swept the convention when Wright refused the already-voted selection. Back to work it went, ultimately choosing George Mifflin Dallas of Pennsylvania.

A Princeton graduate and a lawyer, Dallas had had a fairly distinguished record as secretary to Albert Gallatin, solicitor of the Bank of the United States and Mayor of Philadelphia. He had been a Senator, Attorney-General of Pennsylvania, and Minister to Russia. Throughout, he remained active in the Democratic Party and the inveterate political enemy of the pro-slavery expansionist, James Buchanan. With his wide variety of experience in all levels of government, his diplomatic manner and financial independence of government salary, he was in contrast to most of his political contemporaries to whom office-holding was their life's blood. A gentleman with a view of public office as public service, he and President Polk found each other congenial and their official relationship was comparable to the *ententes* between Washington and Adams and between Jackson and Van Buren.

Polk made it clear in the party that he had a definite job to perform and, accomplishing it on schedule, resisted all pressure to take more from a prostrate Mexico, and paid no attention to a "fifty-four forty or fight" solution for Oregon. Having no desire for a second term, he refused to consider it—an unusual stand for an American President.

George M. Dallas fortified Polk in his approach to his conception of the presidential office. Polk in turn made an effort, the first since 1833, to keep the second officer *au courant* with affairs of state, both foreign and domestic. Dallas presided efficiently over the Senate and was a loyal supporter there of the Administration. Indeed it was his loyalty that blasted his chances for the future. When he used his casting vote in support of Polk's low tariff bill of 1846, he became anathema to his protectionist home state supporters. As one Pennsylvania newspaper put it: "Farewell to all Vice-Presidents from Pennsylvania for the future. We have had enough of one to last us while all who live now shall continue to breathe." (The "curse" has held to date; no party has since selected a vice-presidential candidate from Pennsylvania). By his one act, Dallas destroyed all his long-maintained home state support and prestige.

MILLARD FILLMORE

In 1848 the election again hinged on New York and when Democrats chose Cass over Van Buren, adherents of the latter "took a walk," choosing him for the presidency on a "Free Soil" party ticket. In this situation the Whigs turned to a soldier-hero of the Mexican War—Zachary Taylor. Henry Clay, who had again been passed over, was given the consolation prize of a Clay Whig, Millard Fillmore of New York, in the second place.

The new vice-presidential candidate was an upstate politician in his late forties. Despite an erratic and irregular education, interrupted by his need to work at odd jobs to support himself, Fillmore was admitted to the New York bar. After a few years of practice, he gravitated to politics, joining the Anti-Masonic Party, an organization brought into being by lurid charges that Freemasonry was a species of Murder Incorporated. By the 1830s, Fillmore graduated from state politics to the House and, after the 1840 election, held the powerful patronage-plum of chairman of the Ways and Means Committee. In 1844, he was considered, but not chosen, for the vice-presidency; in the same year, he ran for Governor of New York, but was beaten.

To Hone, Fillmore's selection was "judicious . . . it will serve to reconcile the party in good measure." He was much too optimistic. Fillmore's selection was a great defeat for Boss Thurlow Weed of New York who had expected to name both Convention candidates and had succeeded in choosing neither. Seward and Weed now worried about the distribution of federal patronage in New York with the dissident Fillmore close by "Old Rough and Ready" Zachary Taylor. The Vice-President might well furnish a rallying point for all those discontented with Weed's leadership. To checkmate Fillmore, Seward decided to run for the Senate. Senatorial courtesy could then be urged to control New York appointments. When Seward defeated a Fillmore man, the Vice-President expressed "the fervent wish that he could exchange places with the Senator-elect." Even that early, Fillmore had assessed the relative powers of Vice-President and Senator in terms of patronage. The Seward-Weed coalition proved unbeatable;

President Taylor came to place more and more reliance on Seward's judgment, "and the great bulk of the New York patronage passed under the latter's control." If Fillmore, as Seward wrote, was "too dull of comprehension really to understand what had happened," the Vice-President was made painfully aware that his early intimacy with the President was lost when the latter travelled through Fillmore's own state without even consulting him on the itinerary, constantly shepherded by Weed men.

The Vice-President subsided into his constitutional chore of presiding over the violent debates that ensued in the Senate after California's request to be admitted as a free state. Again the whole searing question of slavery, Union, and potential civil warfare was re-opened. Passion so ruled both Houses that it prevented "the despatch of public business of any kind." The great debaters, Clay, Webster, Calhoun, all spoke their views—conciliatory or fiery. The New York Senator, William H. Seward, was uncompromisingly anti-slavery and spoke of a "higher law" than the Constitution of the United States. Lesser lights more vituperative than eloquent also had their day, turning the Senate topsy-turvy. Senators Foote and Benton created "a most disgraceful scene . . . in which epithets were applied to each other."

The Vice-President's patience was overborne by the plethora of base talk during the great debate of 1850, and he decided to use his oft-neglected power of calling the Senate to order. On April 3, in a masterpiece of understatement, Fillmore lectured the Senate: "Many little irregularities may be tolerated in a small body that would cause much disorder in a large one. . . . A practice seems to have grown up of interrupting a Senator when speaking, by addressing him directly, instead of . . . the Chair, as required by the rule." Nevins concludes that as a result of this intervention "members mended their ways, and reverted to a due formality," but the fact is that the Senate was not chastened at all by Fillmore's censure. Within a fortnight "personal conflict" occurred on the floor of the Senate between Foote and Benton in which the latter went after his tormentor only to be met by Foote's drawing a pistol. Quick action by "the gentlemen near by" probably saved the deliberative body from the infamy of gunplay.

The Vice-President could do nothing in such tempestuous times and by mid-year no business had yet been transacted. It was well-known that one reason why Clay's package compromise was being held up was because the President, fortified by Seward's viewpoint, wanted the California question to be settled apart from any other considerations. To Daniel Webster, this policy was "flatly impossible." Fillmore favored Clay's compromise solutions and early in July called on President Taylor to outline his views: "I said to him in substance . . . that from present appearances, I might be called upon to give a casting vote . . . and if I should feel it my duty to vote for it, as I might, I wished him to understand that it was not out of any hostility to him or his Administration, but . . . because I deemed it for the best interests of the country."

A week later, Taylor was dead and Fillmore was President. Though again there was shock and foreboding, these were only momentary. There was no disposition to contest Fillmore's right to the office, and it was soon apparent that the new President was more conciliatory in the Texas-California crisis than the old had been. Before Taylor was even buried, Webster wrote optimistically: "I believe Mr. Fillmore favors the Compromise, and . . . recent events have increased the probability of the passage of that measure."

The jam had indeed been broken by the removal of Taylor from the scene. Paradoxically, the extreme slavery wing and the "higher law" Sewardites were aligned against the majority coalition of moderates who quailed before the full implications of an "irrepressible" question. The measures comprising the Omnibus Bill were successively passed by Congress in August and September and duly signed into law by President Fillmore. The Union was saved for a decade, and as Nevins puts it, Americans "may well rejoice that death [had] intervened; that the clash of two civilizations was postponed until the North was relatively much stronger, and a far wiser leader sat in the White House."

Four men are generally considered principally responsible for the enactment of the Great Compromise: Clay, Webster, Fillmore, and Stephen A. Douglas. Fillmore's contribution was in reorganizing the Cabinet and with it "energetically" applying "the influence . . . which brought over enough Northern Whigs to make victory certain."

He was to close out his Administration not without drama. Though no genius — to Weed and Seward he was even obtuse — Fillmore enforced the Compromise equitably, earning public odium in the North which heartily hated the Fugitive Slave Law. Before 1851 was out, despite overall acquiescence in the Compromise, it was clear that Fillmore could not be nominated for a term in his own right. It was not merely a case of New York Weed-Seward opposition; even conservative Whigs were of the same opinion. As one wrote: "We can rally on a man pledged to *let the Compromise alone*, but not for one who figured in the enactment of the Fugitive Law."

WILLIAM RUFUS DEVANE KING

The vacancy in the vice-presidency that had begun with Fillmore's accession on July 9, 1850, was to last with a trivial exception until March 4, 1857—the longest period in the history of the office. The Democratic winners in 1852 were Franklin Pierce and William Rufus Devane King, a North Carolina born politician who had migrated to Alabama in time to become one of that state's first Senators. In 1844, he left the Senate to serve as Minister to France and dissuade the government of Louis Philippe from joining England's protest against the annexation of Texas. He was back in the Senate in 1848 and won the election to the vice-presidency in 1852. King, who was 66, lived just long enough to take the oath of office in Cuba, but died on April 18, 1853 without ever presiding in the Senate *qua* Vice-President. This was ironical for he had been president *pro tempore* under five former Vice-Presidents, was a recognized expert on parliamentary law, and had in fact taken Fillmore's place in the Senate chair.

JOHN CABELL BRECKINRIDGE

It was partly due to King's untimely death that the Democratic Party accented youth in 1856 by choosing John C. Breckinridge of Kentucky to serve as running mate for the aging bachelor, James Buchanan. Breckinridge at 35 was the youngest man ever to hold the vice-presidential office at inauguration, Nixon not excepted, whereas James Buchanan at 65 was the second oldest in the presidency, the record being held by the 68-year-old William Henry Harrison who died a month after inauguration.

Breckinridge was a Southern lawyer-politician. He had been politically weaned, having served two terms in the House and, remarkably enough, won office in Henry Clay's home district. Stephen A. Douglas, the disappointed presidential aspirant, was instrumental in having the Convention pick Breckinridge because of his appeal to "young America." Breckinridge carried Kentucky for the Democrats and retained its confidence throughout his tenure, so much so that his native state voted him into the United States Senate in 1859 "if and when he is no longer Vice-President." He was a dignified and popular presiding officer.

With the vacillating Buchanan failing entirely to stop the drift toward disunion and war, the 1860 Democratic Convention could find no standard bearer to agree upon. Breckinridge was named as presidential choice of the extremist pro-slavery wing. The disruption of the party made Lincoln's election possible and in time sent Breckinridge into the Confederate States Army and the Richmond War Office.

While the powerful Democratic Party was nominating Buchanan and Breckinridge in 1856, the newly organized Republican Party held its first national convention in Philadelphia, deciding on John C. Fremont for President and William L. Dayton as his running mate. That summer, the Urbana, Illinois, newspapers brought the news that the runner-up for the second place on the ticket had been a man named Lincoln who had polled 110 votes to Dayton's 259. Abraham Lincoln, the circuit lawyer, joked about it with his Urbana friends. "I reckon that ain't me," he said; "there's another great man in Massachusetts named Lincoln and I reckon it's him."

HANNIBAL HAMLIN

In 1860, "Lincoln's friends started him only for the second place" on the ticket, but the Republican Convention decided otherwise and William H. Seward, the leading contestant, went down to bitter defeat. As usual, the defeated elements were offered the vice-presidential place. New York rejected it for one of her own sons, but acquiesced in Hannibal Hamlin of Maine who was duly nominated and elected.

Successively farmer, schoolmaster, newspaperman and attorney, Hamlin had entered politics in his early thirties as an anti-slavery Democrat and had advanced methodically. At 34, he was elected to Congress where he served two terms. Taking his place in the Senate in 1848, he also served two terms there and earned a reputation for his vigorous opposition to the Kansas-Nebraska Bill and other measures designed to strengthen slavery. In 1856, he resigned from the Democratic Party because of its position on slavery and, as a candidate of the newly organized Republicans, won the governorship of Maine by an overwhelming majority. The next year he resigned to again take a seat in the Senate where he served until January 1861.

Having been a Senator off and on since 1848, Vice-President Hamlin was completely at home in that body and a successful presiding officer. Presidential relations were more complex. Seeking to establish close rapport with Hamlin, Lincoln wrote him "a sort of introduction" in July 1860. Hamlin replied by expressing the hope that they would "become intimately acquainted in the coming four years." He desired to be Lincoln's confidant, writing "I have enough prudence not to injure the cause or any one, by what may be communicated to me." Lincoln took him at his word; after election he conferred with Hamlin in Chicago. Each pledged trust and friendship, and Lincoln offered him the choice of a New England cabinet member from a panel of three names. Hamlin picked Gideon Welles of Connecticut, who became Secretary of the Navy. He was later to regret this choice, for the two came to dislike each other; nevertheless Welles remained throughout both the Lincoln and Johnson regimes.

On his way to Chicago, Hamlin had been intercepted by New York boss Thurlow Weed who urged him to prevail upon Lincoln to offer Seward the secretaryship of State. Seward intended to retire and was certain to turn it down, Weed insinuated, but the offer should nonetheless be made in the interests of party harmony. Lincoln made it plain that he did not want Seward in the State Department, but gave Hamlin "a letter tendering the appointment to Seward" which he could, in his own judgment, deliver or withhold. Accordingly, Hamlin had a private talk with Seward, heard the latter repeat several times "that he would not go into the Cabinet," then fell into the prepared trap and handed over the letter. To both Lincoln's and Hamlin's chagrin, Seward accepted. The foundation had been laid for Lincoln's questioning his judgment in matters requiring delicate negotiation.

Lincoln's relationship to Hamlin cooled further when it became apparent that the Vice-President questioned his Fabian policy on slavery. When in 1863, Mrs. Fremont, wife of the first Republican candidate for President, wrote Hamlin asking for a field command for her husband, the Vice-President replied: "What can I do? The slow and unsatisfactory movements of the government do not meet my approbation, and that is known, and of course I am not consulted at all, nor do I think there is much disposition . . . to regard any counsel I may give."

Hamlin considered himself due a mead of patronage. He asked Lincoln "as a *personal* favor that prizes may be sent to Portland for adjudication, says *he* has not had many favors." When the President turned the matter over to the Navy Department, Welles refused to extend courts to Maine.

On at least two major matters, the promulgation of the Emancipation Proclamation and the arming of Negro troops, Lincoln had taken Hamlin's advice. Nevertheless, as 1864 approached, the President became increasingly dubious about his running-mate. The basic political consideration was that peace loomed on the horizon. Lincoln's great aim, accordingly, was to "bind up the wounds of war" and reunite the nation. For this purpose, he believed a border state man as his running-mate would be far better than an irreconcilable Maine anti-slavery spokesman.

Unaware of all that was in Lincoln's mind, the Cabinet was unanimous for Hamlin, Welles naturally excepted, as the 1864 convention opened. Lincoln indicated that "personally his choice was Johnson" and wrote that it was his "wish not to interfere about Vice-President . . . Convention must judge for itself." The Convention correctly interpreted his inaction as a kiss of death for Hamlin and on the second ballot nominated Andrew Johnson of Tennessee.

ANDREW JOHNSON

The man who took Hamlin's place had lost his father at three and went to work as a tailor's apprentice at 14. He was self-educated and still something of a rough diamond, a man of dogged strength and perseverance, who was helped in his career by a wife who taught him to read after their marriage. A spokesman for the laborers and small farmers, Johnson opposed the slave-holding aristocracy. From the age of 24, he was almost continuously in one local political office or another; he was elected to Congress when he was 35, state governor ten years later, and Senator in 1857.

Johnson's major political interest was free land in the West for laborers. On the slavery issue he, like the mountaineers of east Tennessee where he came from, was Unionist in sentiment. When Civil War broke out, Johnson was the only Southerner in the Senate not to resign his seat. In 1862, Lincoln named him military governor of Tennessee with the rank of brigadier-general, a difficult office which he filled with consummate ability.

The Convention was enthusiastic for vigorous Andy Johnson and apparently oblivious to the possibilities of tragedy ahead. The leading Republican politicians were more far-sighted. Writing to Hamlin's compatriot from Maine, Senator William Fessenden, Simon Cameron said: "Johnson will be a strong candidate . . . but in the contingency of death, I should greatly prefer a man reared and educated in the North." Less articulate but more colorful was Thaddeus Stevens' reaction: "Can't you find a candidate for Vice-President in the United States without going down to one of those damned rebel provinces to pick one up?"

Practically the last official act of Hamlin as Vice-President was to announce the electoral result of the election of 1864. If it was gall and wormwood to have to count in Andrew Johnson, there was at least satisfaction that Johnson could not receive the electoral votes of his own state. The storm clouds that were to burst during the years of Johnson's succession had already been gathering since 1863, and the division between Executive and Legislature over post-war

Southern policy was growing more acute as the military struggle drew to a close. Both Tennessee and Louisiana, rebel conquered states, had been presidentially reconstructed enough to participate in the 1864 election. On February 6, 1865, however, Congress resolved that no electoral votes from states that had rebelled were to be counted. Accordingly, on the day of the count, Hamlin announced that the returns from Louisiana and Tennessee were in his possession but "he held it to be his duty" not to present them.

This decision created constitutional ambiguities and foreshadowed greater ones to come. The February 6th resolution meant that Tennessee had ceased to be a state in the Union ever since it took up arms and, if this were the case, how could Andrew Johnson of the non-existent state be the Vice-President of the United States.

Johnson served as Vice-President for only six weeks. To Lincoln's sorrow he was inaugurated into that office while "under the influence" and gave a rambling, strange harangue which passed for an inaugural speech. Johnson was no drunkard, but not feeling well, had sought the typical American cure-all. His mistake seems to have been over-estimation of his capacity in a weakened condition. Hamlin's role in the incident was to send out for the whiskey Johnson had requested prior to the swearing-in ceremonies.

Catapulted into the presidency only a little more than a month later, Johnson moved toward the fiasco foreshadowed by his ridiculous inauguration. With the best will in the world, he labored in vain to carry out Lincoln's presidential plan for reconstruction. The inevitable legislative revolt that Lincoln would conceivably have been able to stem crushed Johnson and subjected him to the depths of personal humiliation. Whatever chance Johnson had to limit and channel Congressional Radical opinion vanished after his indiscreet harangue in February 1866 "crowing" over the failure of his enemies to override his veto of the Extended Freedmen's Bureau Bill. He was never to be so successful again, and, whereas no veto of Tyler's was overridden except his last, no veto of Johnson's was sustained except his first. Johnson's efforts to take his case (which was Lincoln's, too) to the people was a dismal failure. Here again his distemper and the goadings of planted hecklers made him and his office a laughing stock. After the mid-term elections, Congress was to be even more comfortably Radical than before. As a Seward-Weed conservative Republican put it, after surveying the political wreckage in New York: "Everything has gone wrong since last spring . . . If Andy had staid at home and left the dead to bury their dead there would have been less dead people now."

It was little wonder that Stevens, Sumner, Wade, Butler and their like were emboldened to disregard not only the man in the presidency, but the office itself. Supporters of the President were branded Copperheads and rumors even circulated that Johnson had been a conspirator in Lincoln's assassination (despite the known fact that he himself had been marked for death at the time). As early as January 1867, Representative James Ashley called for his impeachment in terms reminiscent of the 1843 Whig effort to "get" Tyler: "I do impeach Andrew Johnson, Vice-President and acting President of the United States, of high crimes and misdemeanors."

Though referred, 108 to 38, this early movement died in committee. Instead Congress enacted the military reconstruction policy destroying the work built up by Lincoln and Johnson over a period of three years. The President was hamstrung in the application of his executive powers. When Johnson chose to meet the challenge by removing Edwin M. Stanton, Radical Secretary of War, articles of impeachment were duly drawn, passed, and presented to the Senate as the high court of impeachment.

The threat first used in the first succession had thus finally become a reality in the third! Of the trial, it need only be noted that the defense was masterly, the charges were much more political than legal, and by the fortunate failure of the Radicals to make voting a matter of party discipline, the President of the United States was acquitted by one vote short of the necessary two-thirds.

Had Johnson been convicted the President *pro tempore* of the Senate would have succeeded to the presidency, so that that body had an obvious vested interest in the outcome. In 1868, the President *pro tempore* was the Radical Republican Benjamin F. Wade, who allowed no considerations of propriety to keep him from voting "Guilty" on all three ballots that were taken!

The Republican National Convention was meeting at the time the trial was in its decisive stage. By a semantic twist, it made white seem black when it said in its platform that Johnson had been "justly impeached for high crimes and misdemeanors, and properly pronounced guilty thereof by the vote of thirty-five Senators." Perhaps Welles had the right of it when, after Johnson's calamitous administration had ended, he mused: Johnson "has been faithful to the Constitution . . . Of measures he was a good judge, but not always of men."

*   *   *

The Vice-Presidents during the period 1869-1899 are little remembered by even better-informed Americans. Colfax, Henry Wilson,

Wheeler, Arthur, Hendricks, Levi Morton, Stevenson and Hobart have been largely and justly forgotten. On balance they were inferior men in an age that offered a plenitude of inferior men in high positions. Three of them (Wilson, Hendricks, and Hobart) died in office. Chester A. Arthur succeeded to the presidency in September of 1881, but could not overcome the jinx of vice-presidential-successors —namely, ability to win his party's nomination for a presidential term in his own right. The remaining four were dropped from consideration for a second vice-presidential term, thus confirming the trend inaugurated in 1864 in the case of Hamlin. Need it be added that no one of these Vice-Presidents was considered as presidential material on completion of his vice-presidential term. The vice-presidency was no longer the office for the second-best man of the party; it was the office for the second-rate man.

SCHUYLER COLFAX

Schuyler Colfax, who served as Vice-President during Grant's first term, was perhaps typical of the group. He was the victor in a field of at least six aspirants for the office, the death of Lincoln having given it an unusual roseate glow. Welles' estimate of the lot, including Hamlin who was seeking vindication, was "very common men, with no decent pretensions to the second position in the Government."

A product of the New York City public schools who had moved to Indiana with his mother when he was ten, Colfax had begun as a clerk, an auditor and a newspaper reporter. He entered politics and was active in organizing the Republican Party in his adopted state. Entering Congress in 1855, when he was 32 years old, Colfax served there for 14 years, the last six as Speaker of the House. By the end of the War, he was a Radical Republican and a characteristically partisan presiding officer. Thus when Congressman Loan of Missouri implied on the floor of the House on January 14, 1867 that Vice-President Johnson had conspired to murder Lincoln and when a member demanded that the words be taken down, Colfax smiled and ruled that the language was unexceptional.

"Smiler" Colfax had promised that he would disprove the rule of inevitable friction between President and Vice-President, but his ambitions triumphed over this laudable objective. Horace Greeley intimated that Colfax was presidential timber for 1872 and, as an opening gambit in what he hoped would be a "draft Colfax" movement, the Vice-President announced he would retire from public life at the end of his term. Grant countered by offering him the secretaryship of

State immediately, but Colfax feared being under the President's direct control and decided to stay where he was.

Grant disliked office-hungry pretenders and dropped Colfax as his 1872 running-mate. This action was providential, for the Crédit Mobilier scandal broke in the midst of the election campaign. The essential facts were that Oakes Ames and other key stockholders in the Union Pacific Railway had organized this dummy construction company to make contracts with themselves. Crédit Mobilier profits of from $7,000,000 to $23,000,000 gutted the Union Pacific of the money Congress had granted it and by 1869 the insiders were fore-stalling a congressional probe by handing out Crédit Mobilier stock to key members of the House. It turned out that the somewhat sanc-timonious Colfax had received twenty shares of this stock on which he had already received dividends of $3,000.

The Vice-President first denied the whole affair, then recollected that he had bought the stock with a thousand dollar bill which he found in his mail one morning at the breakfast table. On January 25, 1873, the *New York World* demanded Schuyler Colfax's impeach-ment, but he was allowed to fill out the remaining month and a half of his vice-presidential term and then sink from disrepute into oblivion.

HENRY WILSON

The next man to serve as Vice-President was born Jeremiah J. Colbaith. Son of a Farmington, New Hampshire, day laborer, he went to work as a farmhand at the age of ten, began to educate himself and, during his apprenticeship read over a thousand books. He walked to Massachusetts to learn the trade of cobbler, continued his reading and studying and at the same time moved from manual work to the position of successful shoe manufacturer. For some un-specified reason, Colbaith legally changed his name to Henry Wilson.

Oratorical ability brought Wilson into local politics. In 1848, he left the Whigs to become one of the national leaders of the Free Soil Party and four years later presided over its national convention. Defeated for the governorship of Massachusetts, he was briefly active in the American (Know Nothing) Party, which vigorously opposed free immigration and the Catholic Church. His uncompromising an-tagonism to slavery brought him into the Republican Party. Between 1855 and 1873, he served in the United States Senate as one of the most energetic of the Radical Republicans. For the four years of the Civil War, he served as chairman of the Senate's Military Committee.

After the war Senator Wilson and "Pig Iron" Kelley stumped

North Carolina as leaders of the carpetbaggers. They enrolled Negroes in an organization called "Heroes of America" and, with a program of confiscation of rebel property and death to traitors, set up a state Republican Party that was largely dark in complexion and radical to the core. During 1872, while campaigning for the vice-presidency, Wilson returned to North Carolina to see that three thousand of its inhabitants were indicted on Ku Klux Klan charges just before election and to help align the state behind Grant rather than Greeley.

Wilson served two years in the oubliette of the vice-presidency, was tarred and scarred by the Crédit Mobilier scandal, and died in office in 1875.

WILLIAM ALMON WHEELER

A graduate of the University of Vermont and an upper New York State attorney, Wheeler combined politics with the more lucrative fields of banking and railroad financing. First a Whig and then a Republican, he was a congressman during two years of the Civil War and eight years of Reconstruction. He was known for a compromise formula to resolve a disputed Louisiana election — the so-called Wheeler Adjustment. A man of strict principle, he opposed the "salary grab" act of 1873 and, when it went through despite him, bought bonds with the increment to his own salary and then had them cancelled so they could not be redeemed.

Though Rutherford B. Hayes asked "Who is Wheeler?" when President-maker John Sherman informed him in January 1876 that he intended to have the Republican Convention pick the New Yorker as Hayes' running-mate, the two got along famously on a social level throughout their single term. Like Polk, Hayes had had his fill of practical politics in one term, did not desire a second, and groomed no one as his successor, pleasant evenings with Wheeler notwithstanding. Moreover, as an upstate man, Wheeler was outside the control of the new state boss, Roscoe Conkling. For this reason, he was passed over in 1880.

CHESTER ALAN ARTHUR

The Republican National Convention was to be a test of political power between James G. Blaine and Roscoe Conkling, the boss of New York State. Conkling attended personally with his principal lieutenants and had General Grant placed in nomination for a third time in a decisive move to checkmate Blaine's presidential aspirations. With 378 votes needed for choice, the Conkling Stalwarts held Grant in the lead through 35 ballots with totals ranging between 302 and

313, but always ahead of "the Plumed Knight." On the 34th ballot, the dark horse, James A. Garfield of Ohio, first appeared and two ballots later was chosen with 399 votes to Grant's 306.

Resorting to the customary gesture of mollification, the Convention sought a New York Stalwart for Vice-President. General Woodford was approached and asked Conkling's opinion. "I hope no sincere friend of mine will accept it" was the Boss' irate reply. Woodford declined. Levi P. Morton, a banker, who was to be Vice-President eight years later, was next approached. He seemed to want the office, but also refused when Conkling told him: "If you think the ticket will be elected, if you think you will be happy in the association, accept."

The third man to be approached was Chester A. Arthur, a 50-year-old New York lawyer and professional politician, a dyed-in-the-wool Grant-Conkling Stalwart, who had never held an elective office in his life, but had advanced in politics by inner circle maneuvers usually abetted by his crony, Conkling. In 1871, Grant had appointed Arthur Customs Collector for the port of New York. "Chet" Arthur and his Naval officer, Alonzo B. Cornell, administered the office honestly, but stacked it with machine politicians and, in 1878, President Hayes, who was bent on Civil Service reform, investigated the mess and had both men fired.

In a rare moment of independent decision and with the disgusted Conkling absent from the Convention, Arthur accepted the vice-presidential bid, and was duly nominated by the elements of the Republican Party that had kicked him out of office in New York as incompetent three years before. Soon the vice-presidency—and in a little longer while the presidency—would be graced with "a Phi Beta Kappa from Union College, a lawyer and teacher, large, amiable, dandified . . . ; [who] spoke always in a low, pleasant voice . . . eschewed publicity . . . enjoyed nocturnal conferences during which decanters were frequently . . . emptied . . . liked life, and everybody liked him."

If Conkling was displeased with Arthur, he did not show it. They continued to be bosom friends and went fishing after the Convention's close. During the campaign the Boss spoke much more about Arthur than about Garfield and they shared the same house in Washington while Arthur awaited inauguration day. To such an extent did Conkling still dominate Arthur that once in late February when word arrived that Levi P. Morton had been offered the Navy Department post, the Vice-President-elect was sent like an errand boy to fetch the unruly Morton to "the Morgue" (as the house was called) to have his mind changed. Deciding it was high time to have an understanding with the President-elect, Conkling called on Garfield the next day, taking Arthur with him, and probably expatiated on the protocol of senatorial courtesy.

On March 22, 1881, the Garfield-Conkling patronage quarrel erupted. On that day, Vice-President Arthur received a White House notice that a certain Robertson was named as collector at the port of New York. However, Robertson was *persona non grata* to Conkling, as Garfield well knew. The scholar in politics and friend of reform had decided to declare war on the Conkling organization. A petition from both New York Senators, the New York Postmaster-General, and the New York Vice-President was pigeon-holed by Garfield without comment. Arthur personally pleaded with Garfield for withdrawal of the appointment (April 14, 1881), but to no avail. In a passionate statement to the editor of the *New York Herald*, the Vice-President poured forth his resentment. "Garfield has not been square, nor honorable, nor truthful with Conkling. It's a hard thing to say of a President of the United States, but it's only the truth."

Unable to prevent confirmation of Garfield's appointee, Conkling on May 16, 1881 resigned from the United States Senate, followed by Tom "Me Too" Platt. The Vice-President led a group of Conklingites, mostly New Yorkers, who in a meeting at Arthur's New York City home, convinced Conkling to go to Albany and have the state legislature re-elect him. The move failed, and this for all practical purposes ended Conkling's political career. As for Vice-President Chester A. Arthur, he was saved from a similar fate by the assassin's bullet which, fired on July 2, 1881, caused Garfield's death on September 19, 1881. Unfortunately for the Vice-President, the murderer, Charles J. Guiteau, loudly if incoherently espoused Stalwartism, Conkling, and Arthur. On his person was a recent issue of the *New York Herald*, folded to a marked editorial criticizing the President for his treatment of Conkling. Undoubtedly deranged and unknown to Stalwart politicians, Guiteau nevertheless compromised Arthur's situation during the long fatal illness by his insistence that he had been motivated by a desire to make him President "to unite the Republican party." As if this were not humiliating enough, no one disagreed with the opinion of George William Curtis, the great exponent of the merit system in Civil Service, that if Arthur did succeed "in his ignorance and inexperience he would be compelled to rely on some one more capable than himself. Obviously . . . Mr. Conkling . . . would be the controlling influence of the Administration."

During that summer of 1881, for the first time in nearly a century of operation, Americans were driven back to a reading of pertinent clauses of the Constitution to see what it contained in such a situation. The President was critically ill. Of that there was no doubt, but —as has been already shown in Chapter 1—the Constitution offered small guidance. Though it flatly stated that in case of the President's "Inability to discharge the Powers and Duties of the said Office, the same shall devolve on the Vice-President," the clause was too vague to act upon. John Dickinson's query on the floor of the 1787 Convention: "What is the extent of the term 'disability' and who is to be the judge of it?" had been left unanswered for the following ninety-odd years.

Upon receipt of the news about Garfield, Arthur left Albany where he had been lobbying for Conkling and Platt (as if he was a ward-heeler) and returned to Washington. He never saw the sick President but received daily progress reports from Secretary of State James G. Blaine.

The constitutional issues were unresolved when Garfield died. The new Chief Executive, Chester A. Arthur, repeatedly tried to get Congress to formulate answers to the whole problem of succession, but not till five years later did they respond, and then they merely changed the *situs* of succession after the Vice-President and never touched the inability question at all.

Arthur surprised those observers who believed that his accession to the White House meant that the nadir of the American presidency had at last been reached. Edwin L. Godkin had reacted to Arthur's nomination by looking at the bright side, writing that at least New York was rid of his hand in state machine politics and that he could do small "mischief" as Vice-President. Since Garfield was only forty-nine, his death "was too unlikely a contingency to be worth making extraordinary provision for." The "too unlikely a contingency" had now become a fact and few expected anything better than boss rule and unabashed plunder. Strangely enough, Arthur upheld the Civil Service, was not ruled by Conkling and finished his term without any threat of impeachment. While he was acceptable neither to true Half-Breeds nor Stalwarts for a term in his own right, he at least ended the atmosphere of crisis endemic to all previous administrations by vice-presidential successors.

THOMAS ANDREWS HENDRICKS

At the Republican Convention of 1884, Arthur and Conkling joined forces only to the extent necessary to prevent Governor Cornell of New York, Arthur's old associate in the 1878 New York customs scandal, from getting the presidential nomination. James G. Blaine was finally given his chance, but in the election itself was soundly trounced by a relatively obscure mayor of Buffalo, Grover Cleveland.

The second man on the ticket in this first presidential victory of the Democratic Party since the Civil War was Thomas Andrews Hendricks, a 65-year-old Ohio lawyer and politician. A lifelong Democrat and opponent of the resumption of specie payments, Hendricks had been put in nomination for the presidency of the United States at every Democratic National Convention, with one exception, from 1868 until his death in 1885. In these four unsuccessful attempts, he was twice given the consolation prize of second place on the ticket. In 1876, Hendricks had been Tilden's running-mate and, as such, had been part of a ticket which had a majority of the popular votes and probably a majority in the electoral college as well. Now, in 1884, after a generation of defeats and disappointments, he at last won the lesser of the two national offices.

After only eight months in office and with rumors already circulating that he and the President were on the outs because the old guard Democrats had him in mind for 1888 in preference to the reformer Cleveland, Hendricks died.

LEVI PARSONS MORTON

In 1888 the Republicans came back into office with the uninspiring team of Benjamin Harrison and Levi Parsons Morton. The latter was a Vermont-born businessman and financier. During the Civil War he had organized one of the chief financial organizations in the United States. His interest in politics had developed late in life and he entered Congress for the first time at the age of 55. His one term in the House plus four years as American Minister to France were the sum total of his strictly political qualifications for the vice-presidential office. It might have been argued, however, that his business career involved more political responsibility than could have come with twenty years on Capitol Hill. The Morton firm had at least played a significant role in funding the national debt upon the resumption of specie payments and its London branch had served as fiscal agents of the United States from 1873 to 1884.

Morton considered the vice-presidency a prestige office, one in fact that he had wanted for many years. He was rejected for renomination when Boss Thomas Collier Platt withdrew his name from the Convention, ostensibly to save him the embarrassment of being on a losing ticket, but really, it was rumored, to weaken the ticket in New York to ensure its defeat.

ADLAI EWING STEVENSON

A relatively obscure Illinois lawyer and politician, Adlai Ewing Stevenson, was Vice-President during Cleveland's second term (1893-97). Kentucky-born, he rose from master of chancery to an Illinois district attorneyship. In 1875, when 40 years old, he was elected to the House of Representatives, where he served two non-successive terms. A mild, gracious man, he entered the first Cleveland administration as an assistant postmaster general and was assigned the unpleasant job of purging some 40,000 fourth-class postmasters—all Republicans and strongly entrenched after twenty-four years of G.O.P. rule. Subsequently when Cleveland appointed him to a federal judgeship the Senate Republican majority refused to confirm him.

A "soft-money" man, Stevenson was put on the 1892 ticket to offset Cleveland's monetary conservatism. As Vice-President he gave "hard-money" Democrats a bad case of the jitters during the gold crisis of 1894-95, when the President suffered a spell of ill-health. The thought that an inflationist from the home of Populism might succeed Cleveland distinctly frightened businessmen. However, no questions of presidential inability were raised and the crisis passed.

GARRET AUGUSTUS HOBART

The last of the nineteenth century Vice-Presidents, Garret Augustus Hobart, was selected as McKinley's running-mate by Mark Hanna. A New Jersey lawyer, he had been prominent for over a decade in state Republican politics and in the state legislature. He had also found time to build up a successful business and accumulate a considerable fortune. His views and income were consonant with the dominant wing of his party and he was a distinct improvement over most of his predecessors. Genial, tactful and rich, he was qualified to adorn the office in approved public style and his views also harmonized with those of the administration.

From the outset, Hobart proved amenable to McKinley's direction. He turned over his proposed acceptance speech for the latter's perusal. Kohlsaat recalled: "McKinley ripped it to pieces, so that when Hobart returned to New York, it bore little resemblance to the letter he brought to Canton."

Hobart became closely attached to the President during his tenure. He was a frequent caller at the White House, acted as liaison man between the President and the Senate, and was often referred to as "Assistant President." After an initial effort to speed up the Senate's work, Hobart gave up the task and soon became rather well-liked as a presiding officer. Nicholas Murray Butler thought him "the best presiding officer . . . the Senate has ever had in my lifetime." In Hatch's opinion, Hobart ultimately gained "an influence" with Senators "probably greater than any other Vice-President has enjoyed."

With Hobart's death, the period of disintegration of the vice-presidential office came to an end and, as the century closed, the prospect assumed shape that the Vice-Presidents would grow in stature and begin to share the burdens of executive leadership.

In summing up the impact of the 1869-99 period on public opinion, it is not surprising that contemporary commentators found little to commend in the office of Vice-President. As early as 1868, Gideon Welles thought "the office of Vice-President is without responsibility, patronage, or any duty worthy of honorable aspiration." A professor of government at Princeton, one Woodrow Wilson, in a popular analysis of American government, wrote in the middle Eighties:

"It would, doubtless, be considered quite improper to omit . . . all mention of the Senate's President; and yet there is very little to be said about the Vice-President . . . His position is one of anomalous insignificance and curious uncertainty . . . It is hard to find in sketching the government any proper place to discuss him . . . He is simply a judicial officer [of the Senate] . . . whose rules he has had no voice in framing and can have no voice in changing . . .His importance consists in the fact that he may cease to be Vice-President . . . He is awaiting the death or disability of the President. And the chief embarrassment in discussing his office is, that in explaining how little there is to be said about it one has evidently said all there is to say."

Nor did the great British analyst, James Bryce, view the office any differently:

"The Vice-President's office is ill conceived. His only ordinary function is to act as Chairman of the Senate . . . [which] is of little moment. If, however, the President dies, or becomes incapable of acting . . . the Vice-President succeeds. What is the result? The place being in itself unimportant, the choice of a candidate for it excites little interest, and is chiefly used by the party managers as a means of conciliating a section of their party. It becomes what is called a 'complimentary nomination.' The man elected Vice-President is therefore never a man in the front rank. But when the President dies . . . this second-class man steps into a great place for which he was never intended. Sometimes, as in the case of Mr. Arthur, he fills the place respectably. Sometimes, as in that of Andrew Johnson, he throws the country into confusion.

"He is *aut nullus aut Caesar.*"

These judgments indicate the general contempt in which the second office had come to be held.

CHAPTER 6

Rough Riding

At the dawn of the twentieth century there was no Vice-President of the United States. This fact did not seem to bother anyone. Alone of all the major offices in the Federal Government, the vice-presidency could be left vacant until the next presidential election provided a new incumbent. When Vice-President Garret Augustus Hobart died in November 1899, the only problem presented was that the McKinley administration would have to find a new running-mate for the 1900 campaign. Even had he lived, that might have been done anyway, for the practice was to deny a Vice-President renomination for a second term. However, as Hobart was particularly close to the President and enjoyed great popularity with the Senate and important sections of his party, an effort might have been made to defy this tradition.

The year was 1900. It was not merely the beginning of a new century, but of a new and more virile conception of the vice-presidential office. Few of the new century's Vice-Presidents would be second-rate, non-entities or little thought of in party and public circles. Of the five most significant Presidents, three were vice-presidential successors who obtained re-election for a term in their own right (something, as we have seen, no nineteenth century successor ever accomplished). As the century advanced, the tendency would seem to be to install a better type of man. Thomas R. Marshall (1913-21), Charles G. Dawes (1925-29), John N. Garner (1933-41), Henry A. Wallace (1941-45), Alben W. Barkley (1949-53), and Richard M. Nixon (1953-) were not lightweights either with respect to their times or judged in perspective. Thus we are left with a small group who graced the office in approved post-Civil War style: Charles W. Fairbanks (1905-09), James S. Sherman (1909-13) and Charles Curtis (1929-33). These twelve Vice-Presidents of the twentieth century will engage our attention in the chapters that follow.

THEODORE ROOSEVELT

Theodore Roosevelt, Governor of New York since 1898, was first suggested for the vice-presidency by Senator Henry Cabot Lodge of Massachusetts. At the time of T.R.'s gubernatorial nomination, Lodge had told a mutual friend that he "wanted" Roosevelt "to be Vice-President." The idea lay dormant until June 1899, when he was wildly received by fellow Rough Riders and others while en route to and from a soldier's reunion at Las Vegas. It was about this time that Lodge urged him to "accept the popular wish, whatever it is, follow your star, and let the future care for itself." If the presidency was at the moment out of reach, there was always the vice-presidency: "It is the tradition of our politics, and a very poor tradition, that the vice-presidency is a shelf. It ought to be, and there is no reason why it should not be, a stepping-stone. Put there by the popular desire, it would be so to you."

Senator Lodge was willing to pit Roosevelt's national fame, gained in the recent war with Spain, against Vice President Hobart's popularity with President McKinley and the dominant Old Guard of the Republican party. Convinced that Roosevelt could win such a contest, especially in view of the long practice of rotating the vice-presidential nomination, Lodge saw Roosevelt strategically situated for the presidential nomination in 1904.

Roosevelt's reaction was that he was "for Hobart's renomination, if he will take it," but if not "I am inclined to be for it . . . I regard my position as utterly unstable . . . I appreciate how entirely ephemeral is the hold I have for a moment on the voters . . . I have never yet known a hurrah to endure five years; so I should be inclined to accept any honorable position; that the vice-presidency is." However, he felt there were surer paths to continued prominence. The most satisfactory future he could think of was to be re-elected Governor and "then be offered the secretaryship of war for four years." As a matter of fact, the war office did fall vacant in the summer of 1899 but McKinley chose another New Yorker, Elihu Root. Root immediately demonstrated his organizational abilities and Roosevelt concluded that that particular avenue for his own political advancement was now closed.

Others now began to promote Roosevelt as likely material for the vice-presidency: Senator William E. Chandler of New Hampshire (inspired by Lodge), friends from the West (wholly on their own volition), and General Nelson A. Miles (who wanted the Governor as his own running-mate in 1900). Roosevelt held his counsel, concentrated on trying to keep the support of Senator Thomas C. Platt, boss of the New York state machine, and privately told Lodge: "I should like to be reelected Governor, but I do not expect it . . . As for the vice-presidency, I do not think there is anything in that. But in any event, I shall do just as you advise—that is, let it take care of itself."

Such was the situation when in November, 1899, Hobart died. Mc-

Kinley's spokesmen began casting about for a new running-mate. Roosevelt was not one of those sounded out by the White House. McKinley had no love for Roosevelt. To him the Governor was a maverick, politically unpredictable and discomforting. Indeed, for McKinley one of the bright spots of the late war had been Roosevelt's retirement from the administration, and he had no desire to help him return. In New York, Roosevelt was Platt's headache and McKinley was well-satisfied that that situation be not disturbed. No offer to run with McKinley in 1900 was ever to come from the President or his friends.

Meanwhile, Boss Platt was becoming convinced that the Governor was a liability to his own domination in the state. Platt had not promoted the Colonel's 1898 nomination, but had been forced to give it his approval. He had then feared that if Roosevelt "becomes Governor of New York, sooner or later, with his personality, he will have to be President of the United States . . . and, aside from the question of whether he will be fair to me and to our organization, I am afraid to start that thing going." For most of Roosevelt's first year as Governor, Platt had somehow managed to get along with him, even periodically telling him that he would be endorsed for a second term. He had even opposed the growing talk of Roosevelt for the vice-presidency. This was undoubtedly due to the fear that it might prove to be a stepping-stone to the presidency, rather than to any feeling that the Governor was indispensable to him and New York. By the end of the year, Platt reversed his judgment and determined to remove Roosevelt from the state.

Even without definite knowledge of Platt's decision Roosevelt sensed the change. Appreciating Boss Platt's influence, he realized that he could not be renominated without it. This placed the vice-presidency in a new light—it was better than political oblivion—and he now felt: "were my renomination out of the question I should accept the vice-presidency were I offered it." This view is the key to his later complicated backing and filling with respect to that office. As long as he felt that any possibility existed for his renomination, he would oppose the vice-presidential boom, but when he became convinced that Platt was immovable he would not unequivocally take himself out of consideration for the national office, and would permit himself to be "drafted."

T.R. vowed to battle for a second term while keeping open a line of retreat. There was talk of creating a governor-general for the lately acquired Philippine Islands. Roosevelt felt that this would be a post he could ably fill, that it would be a stepping-stone to 1904, but that if he were Vice-President that office "would cut me off definitely from all

chance of doing it." When friends explained that he could resign from
the vice-presidency, Roosevelt thought there would be "a strong . . .
feeling against" it, even though such a feeling would be "unreasonable"
because "the succession is arranged in the Secretaryship of State."

Shortly thereafter, several members of the Republican National
Committee visited T.R. to persuade him to accept the nomination. He
told them he was reluctant because he feared that the forces of political
reaction would return to New York if he left Albany, that the vice-
presidency did not lead to the presidency, and that he did not have the
means to entertain lavishly as recent incumbents had been doing.
Roosevelt was annoyed when these views were published in the *New
York Sun* on February 1, 1900. A few days after, he made a public
statement spurning the vice-presidency. His words seemed quite clear,
his intent unmistakable. "It is proper for me to state definitely that
under no circumstances could I or would I accept the nomination for
the vice-presidency . . . My duty is here in the State . . . I am happy
to state that Senator Platt cordially acquiesces in my views in the
matter." This last was pure fiction, as Roosevelt well knew, but it
was an integral part of his scheme to get renomination as Governor.
As he put it to a friend, "Now if the machine is going to beat me, it
must do so openly and on the ground that it is antagonistic to me."

T.R.'s announcement temporarily quieted matters. Boss Platt made
no overt moves against him. However, in April Admiral George
Dewey announced himself available for nomination as President and
his wife stated Roosevelt would be a suitable running-mate. T.R. replied: "I have been having enough work trying to escape . . . the Republican ticket." But regarding his own chances for a second term as
Governor, Roosevelt was about resigned to defeat. He felt "I have
had a first-class run for my money." Just two days after this gloomy
appraisal he declined a suggestion that he again publicly turn down the
vice-presidency: "I may make myself ridiculous if I announce too
often that I won't take it," he declared in a letter to Joseph B. Bishop.
"Then I have a horror of saying what I may not be able to do . . . If
I were actually nominated; and if I were unable to stem the convention's desire to nominate me, it might be impossible to refuse." [The
caution required in using official authorized biographies is well illustrated by the handling of this letter in Bishop's *Theodore Roosevelt
And His Time Shown In His Own Letters* (New York, 1920). At
T.R.'s request, Bishop began his study "five or more years before"
Roosevelt's death in 1919. The matter "down to . . . 1905 . . . received
his approval . . . I went over with him what I had written and had the
. . . advantage of his suggestions." The letter is partly quoted, but the

above cited portion is omitted. The result is that Bishop and T.R. convey a consistent anti-vice-presidential attitude on the Governor's part which in fact never existed.]

When Lodge heard that Roosevelt planned to attend the approaching convention, he thought he ought not to go if he was adamantly against being nominated; conventions were funny affairs, and the Roosevelt presence was nothing if not galvanic. But Roosevelt felt he "would be looked upon as rather a coward" if he stayed away. When Lodge replied, "If you stay away with your absolute declination which you have already put out, I do not think you will be nominated", Roosevelt tartly retorted, "I did *not* say I would not under any circumstances accept the vice-presidency." Poor Lodge! Not only had Roosevelt said just what Lodge thought he had said in his public statement of February 6, but in a private letter written *on the same day* as his retort to Lodge he again stated: "I shall . . . try to make the National leaders understand . . . *that I will not under any circumstances accept the vice-presidential nomination,* and so we might just as well go on with the consideration of somebody else."

April was the month of decision. To selected correspondents he expostulated more and more, "if it were vital for me to help the ticket by going on, I would feel that the situation was changed." In May, he visited Washington to sound out the administration on the nomination question. He already knew that White House circles were hostile to him. Secretaries Root and Hay were sardonic about the whole business. When he protested against the effort being made to "force" him into the vice-presidency, Root remarked: "Of course not, Theodore, you're not fit for it." Hay added: "I think you are unduly alarmed, there is no instance of an election of a Vice-President by violence." Their sarcasm angered T.R. considerably; he now realized that the vice-presidency was at least preferable to political extinction.

In the meantime, larger movements had gotten under way to ensure his nomination in June. Senator Matthew S. Quay of Pennsylvania, in control there since 1885, had already served two Senate terms when a rebellious legislature refused him a third. An obedient governor appointed him anyway to the resulting vacancy. Hanna, though not renowned for his contributions to open debate on the Senate floor, questioned Quay's right to be seated, and after a year's lapse, secured the passage of a resolution of non-entitlement (April 24, 1900). Though Quay was to be vindicated eventually by being elected, the fact remains that from 1899 to January, 1901, Hanna had him in escrow. Matt Quay, burning for revenge and seeing in Hanna's animus against Roosevelt a chance to retaliate, joined with Platt as early as January,

1900, to help put Roosevelt over as the vice-presidential nominee. In view, then, of the disparate and incongruous Platt-Quay motives, together with the support of Lodge, and *bona fide* Western pro-Roosevelt sentiment, it was little wonder that Platt was to say to an aide: "Why Roosevelt might as well stand under Niagara Falls and try to spit the water back as to stop his nomination by this convention."

As conventions go, the Republican one in 1900 was a dull affair. McKinley was unopposed and the only real interest centered on the vice-presidential selection. When Roosevelt arrived at Philadelphia on the afternoon of June 16th, as a delegate-at-large from New York, he immediately became the center of attraction, delegation after delegation visiting him that first evening. Nicholas Murray Butler, in the Roosevelt entourage, was convinced by the next morning "that only the most drastic steps would prevent T.R.'s nomination." The Pennsylvania delegation came to say that "the entire body of delegates from Pennsylvania intended to vote for Roosevelt's nomination." Quay was ready to push forward his anti-Hanna plans. A young McKinleyite, Charles G. Dawes, felt on that day that "the sentiment is clearly for Roosevelt." The only one who yet refused to give up was Mark Hanna. He still felt as he had in March when "he banged on the table and said that he proposed to control the Philadelphia convention absolutely and that under no circumstances would or could T.R. be nominated for the vice-presidency. He . . . would not have it."

On Monday, the day before the convention was to open, Nicholas Murray Butler, who still believed Roosevelt really did not want to be Vice-President, pressed him to issue a declaration of "definite refusal." Roosevelt "walked up and down for some little time, muttering and protesting, and then said with much impatience: 'What is it you want me to say? I am willing to say it.' " When Butler composed a clear-cut refusal, Roosevelt "improved" its phrasing and then handed it back, saying: "There that is what you want." Butler read it and expostulated: "Theodore, if that is all you will say, you will certainly be nominated. You have taken out of the statement all of the finality and definiteness that was in mine." Though the two argued over the wording for a half-hour more, Roosevelt was adamant. Butler admitted that the incident opened his eyes, "I then began to suspect for the first time that he was really willing to be nominated."

At a press conference that same day, Roosevelt, standing on his hotel bed, read the watered down "refusal" to an overflow crowd including Senator Platt's son, Frank, and Lem Quigg, who were right by the bed. Butler noted than when Roosevelt had finished reading "their faces were wreathed in smiles and they darted for the door to report to Senator Platt that all was well and that he had won his fight. And so he had." "Sunny Jim" Sherman, to be Vice-President under William Howard Taft, chuckled as he read the press statement: "It's a cinch . . . All we have to do is go ahead and nominate him."

When Hanna rapped the gavel opening the Republican National Convention of 1900 a few minutes after 12:30 P.M. Tuesday, the test of strength between him and the Platt-Quay forces began. Roosevelt, arriving late, walked down the main aisle in a broad-brimmed black hat conspicuously like the Rough Rider campaign headgear. An ovation commenced at the sight of the New York Governor and continued while he strode to his seat in the body of the Hall, hat still on until the band struck up the "Star Spangled Banner."

On June 20, Quay moved to the attack. He proposed that the rules be amended to have state representation henceforth proportionate to the size of the Republican vote. The plan was extremely dangerous to Mark Hanna for it meant eliminating the Southern delegations that he controlled and hence destroying his power in the 1904 Convention when, in the normal course of events, a successor to McKinley would have to be chosen. In the midst of the ensuing furor, Quay airily suggested that its discussion might be delayed for a day or so. Plainly he was giving Hanna the choice between possible loss of power in 1904 and accepting T.R. as vice-presidential candidate.

Hanna was disposed to give battle. He exploded to friends: "Don't any of you realize that there is only one life between that mad man and the presidency? Platt and Quay are no better than idiots! What harm can he do as Governor of New York compared to the damage he will do as President if McKinley should die?" He threatened to resign as chairman of the party if Platt or Quay nominated Roosevelt. "Hanna and I almost had an altercation," Dawes confessed. Alarmed at Hanna's stand, Dawes telephoned the White House. After hearing his report, McKinley ordered him to deliver "an ultimatum" to Hanna: "The Administration . . . has no candidate. The convention must make the nomination . . . The President's friends must not dictate to the convention."

That night a conference originally called to unite on a candidate to oppose Roosevelt agreed on Roosevelt. At next day's session (June 21), Quay withdrew his resolution and in "a great burst of enthusiasm," Roosevelt was acclaimed the vice-presidential nominee. T.R. interpreted these proceedings quite differently in his *Autobiography*. There he said: "A meeting of the New York delegation was called. Most . . . were under the control of Senator Platt. The Senator notified me that if I refused to accept the nomination for Vice-President I would be beaten for the nomination for Governor. I answered that I would accept the challenge, that we would have a straight-out fight on the proposition, and that I would begin it at once by telling . . . of the threat . . . This brought Senator Platt to terms. The effort to instruct the New York delegation for me was abandoned . . . I supposed that closed the incident . . . [However] the upset of the New York machine increased the feeling of the delegates from the other States that it was necessary to draft me for the nomination. By the next day Senator Hanna himself concluded that this was a necessity . . . No other candidate was placed in the field." About all one can agree with in this statement is that Platt definitely told Roosevelt it was the vice-presidency or political oblivion.

Shortly after the Convention, Lodge, the real victor in the battle to make Roosevelt "follow his star," wrote him: "We must not permit the President, or any of his friends, who are, of course, in control of the campaign, to imagine that we want to absorb the leadership and the glory . . . Secure by every righteous means the confidence and support for you of the President and of all his large following . . . This is going to be of immense importance to us four years hence, and . . . I desire that you should appear . . . as the President's next friend, as Hobart was." If Roosevelt made no mistakes, Lodge felt, the "nomination for the presidency" was "within our grasp four years hence."

The candidacy of T.R. in 1900 for the vice-presidential office illustrates the divergent judgments of it made by professionals in the art of politics. Roosevelt derided it as being merely an "inactive" post, a "shelf," a consignment to limbo. Platt at first feared putting him into an office that might lead to the highest in the land, then decided he preferred having him in Washington than in Albany. Lodge consistently wanted Roosevelt in the office because it had once been and could again be a stepping-stone to the presidency. Hanna did not want him for exactly the same reasons. Quay just did not think about Roosevelt as Vice-President in any way than as an instrument of vengeance on Hanna.

Two weeks after the Republican Convention, the Democrats assembled in Kansas City to again choose William Jennings Bryan unanimously. After a test ballot for the second place, which saw "Uncle Adlai" Stevenson of Illinois, Cleveland's second term Vice-President, leading Charles A. Towne of Minnesota (darling of the Populist wing) and David Hill (anti-Croker ex-Governor of New York), the delegates unanimously chose Stevenson. To the *Nation,* he was "one of those colorless men who . . . would stand on any platform."

McKinley had no desire to use Bryan's methods; he preferred a quiet, dignified, "front porch" campaign. Hanna, now interested only in victory, put aside his animosity and decided to use Roosevelt in a widespread tour. The Governor agreed, but "I most emphatically do not wish to appear like a second-class Bryan"; and again, "I am strong as a bull moose and you can use me up to the limit, taking heed of ... my throat ... I do not want my throat to give out."

On August 20, T.R. stayed overnight at the White House. He wanted a promotion for his friend Leonard Wood, and to get Root to run for governor of New York. Wood, then military governor of Cuba, desired promotion to the rank of Brigadier-General. Roosevelt told McKinley: "I believed it was customary for the Vice-President to be allowed to ask one favor in the way of appointments, and that I wanted to ask ... now; ... if I was not elected Vice-President I was doing everything ... I could for the ticket and ... the office meant nothing to me, indeed meant only a sacrifice." McKinley offered "no definite promise," replying only: "Governor Roosevelt, you may be certain that I shall take care of General Wood exactly as you would." There is no clear evidence that any custom regarding vice-presidential appointments has ever existed. Some Vice-Presidents had been asked for recommendations and others had not been. Roosevelt may have been thinking of Lincoln, who had permitted Hamlin to pick the New England cabinet member.

The vice-presidential candidate was equally unsuccessful in the Root matter. That he really believed Root had to run as governor in order to strengthen the McKinley-Roosevelt ticket in New York, seems unlikely. Probably he was returning to his old idea of the War Department as a future possibility for himself. McKinley firmly over-ruled the suggestion about Root.

When the campaign formally opened on Labor Day, Roosevelt forgot all his disappointments. From September 5 to October 21, he vigorously stumped in the West. Thereafter he toured New York. In all, he covered 21,209 miles, 567 towns and cities in 24 states, and had delivered 673 speeches to three million listeners. It was a record of stumping unequalled in vice-presidential annals, and except for the vigorous Bryan, equally unmatched by presidential candidates.

The substance of Roosevelt's talks was pretty much the same, and as Pringle says, "all very similar to the ones he made in campaigning for the governorship in 1898. Honor and decency, the preservation of prosperity, the nation's good faith, an unstained Flag; all these depended on a Republican victory." Justifiably proud of his part in the electoral victory, Roosevelt felt "more than content," but "there is nothing in the world for me to do" as Vice-President.

In some ways, the Republican vice-presidential nomination of 1900 was the most remarkable in the history of the office. While it is true that the forces of populism, muckraking and progressivism were running deep and strong as the twentieth century dawned so that they would have found political expression sooner or later, the devious and varied motives that induced the politicians to settle on Theodore Roosevelt for the vice-presidency brought into the presidency a little more than a year later a man of action, color and popular appeal. By propounding reform at home and vigorous internationalism, he took the play away from the theoretical reformers and ideologues and kept within governable channels the movement of protest. Since it is most doubtful whether McKinley would have been able to do this, the 1900 nomination of Roosevelt probably gave the Republicans a lease on the presidency for eight years longer than they had a right to expect when they ratified McKinleyism in the Convention.

CHAPTER 7

Transition Years

The story is told that when Senator Tom Platt was asked if he was going to McKinley's second inaugural, he replied "I am going to Washington to see Theodore Roosevelt take the veil."

Roosevelt himself might not have seriously disagreed with this verdict. Even before taking office, he wrote "I do not see my way very clearly," and again "a Vice-President has mighty little power." He felt frustrated in contemplating his "shelf": "The Vice-President . . . is really a fifth wheel to the coach . . . it is not a stepping stone to anything except oblivion. I fear my bolt is shot." Because of these convictions the forty-two year old Vice-President toyed with a variety of plans to fill up the void of his vice-presidential years, plans which at the same time would be a preparation for the years thereafter, half-expected to be spent in private life. Thus he contemplated studying law, or becoming a graduate school history professor and doing "serious scholarly work."

Roosevelt had had no experience in presiding over a legislative body and seems not to have tried to prepare himself for his one certain duty beyond poring over "back files of the *Congressional Record*" for a few days. As a matter of fact, he was to preside only for five days, (March 5 to 9, 1901), but to Senator Foraker the period was "long enough to show that his peculiar qualifications for the public service fitted him better for wider, broader and more useful fields." Roosevelt himself admitted he "was the poorest presiding officer the Senate ever had." He evinced little interest in this aspect of the vice-presidency —which attitude contrasted with Jefferson's, who worked hard in preparation for his occupancy of the Chair of the Senate.

Most of Roosevelt's vice-presidential activity was devoted to setting political bonfires for himself. He vigorously tried to prevent Platt's hopes (and his own fears) from being fulfilled. Even before March 1901 was ended, he had been virtually endorsed by the Governor of California for the succession and had agreed with that official's suggestion to make a country-wide tour in 1902. McKinley himself was early forced to repudiate third term talk, so the Vice-President had, momentarily, a clear field to "follow his star."

By the end of June, Roosevelt was "receiving . . . conditional offers of friendship . . . from men of tact" in Michigan and Illinois. Of these, the most important was McKinley's Comptroller of the Currency, Charles G. Dawes of Illinois, a masterly manipulator of Republican delegates and campaign chests. At Roosevelt's invitation, Dawes conferred for two hours with him, telling the Vice-President "I was for him."

Roosevelt, scouting the political terrain of the West in August, was "greatly astonished . . .at the feeling displayed for me, not only in Colorado and Kansas, but in Missouri and even in Illinois." Evidently the leaven of Dawes' support was already at work and enthusiasm for Roosevelt was rising even in McKinley territory. In Minnesota, at a dinner given in his honor, the Vice-President could report that Senator Knute Nelson "proceeded to nominate me for President." Swinging East, Roosevelt was in Vermont by September, testing his not inconsiderable strength there. He was especially pleased that other 1904 prospects had no comparable support.

Not since Calhoun's time had there been so much activity so early by a Vice-President in pursuit of a presidential nomination. In race track parlance, Roosevelt had broken fast from the barrier, and was well out in front of the field as the first quarter turn was approaching. Whether he would have been able to maintain his pace and position throughout the entire race if McKinley had lived is a matter of speculation. The obstacles in his path were still formidable. They included the silent disapprobation of McKinley, Hanna, and Platt, the lack of Roosevelt men in the South, and what Lodge had called "the unknown quantity of the next three years."

Roosevelt worked hard to get along with President McKinley. Remembering Lodge's admonition to become a second Hobart, he tried consistently, if in vain, to be a counsellor. Without patronage himself, T.R. answered an appeal for political favor in words that delineate the limitations of his office: "I will try to get it for you, but you must not build high hopes upon my succeeding . . . The Vice-President has no office whatever in his gift. If someone else makes an appointment for him, he has no way of repaying the favor. I want you to understand . . . the extremely narrow limitations of my power."

Even when it was a General desiring only an appointment to Annapolis for his grandson, Roosevelt could not be sure he could get it. As a matter of fact, the General had to wait until T.R. was in the White House himself. (In 1928, Congress permitted Vice-Presidents to make service academy appointments for the first time.) When Roosevelt once suggested a specific person for the Civil Service

Commission, McKinley chose a known enemy. The Vice-President felt his letters were not "even looked at by the President" despite the "courteous acknowledgments" from his secretary. As for McKinley's attitude toward him: "He is perfectly cordial and friendly with me . . . but he does not intend that I shall have any influence of any kind, sort or description in the administration from the top to the bottom. This he has made evident again and again." It was little wonder that T.R. felt "the vice-presidency is an utterly anomalous office (one which I think ought to be abolished)."

A Pan-American Exposition had been in progress at Buffalo, New York, since May 1901. Roosevelt had gone to its opening and in late summer McKinley took the trip. While attending a public reception on September 6th, he was shot by an anarchist. The Vice-President, still in Vermont on his good-will tour, hurried to Buffalo to stand by. On September 8th, the doctors pronounced the President to be "out of danger." At this point, Roosevelt sought out Dawes who had likewise come post-haste to Buffalo with some of the Cabinet and Senator Fairbanks. Roosevelt took Dawes aside, the latter related, "to discuss 1904 presidential politics for an hour. I told him that his prospects seemed good in Illinois."

Vice-President Roosevelt decided it would be more calming to public opinion for him to leave Buffalo. Therefore he joined his family, who were vacationing in the Adirondack Mountains of upper New York. He was in a relatively inaccessible wilderness when he received word that he should return in view of the serious worsening of the President's condition (September 13). With much dramatic difficulty, including a ten-mile hike to a horse and wagon and a forty-mile night ride over bad terrain to a waiting railroad train, he arrived on the afternoon of the 14th. In the meantime, McKinley had died and Secretary of War Elihu Root advised Roosevelt to take the presidential oath of office without further delay.

The fifth succession was thus formally accomplished at the house of Ansley Wilcox, an independent Republican friend. In his first statement as President, Roosevelt followed precedent and sought to allay business fears by accepting Root's rhetoric: "I wish to state that it shall be my aim to continue absolutely unbroken the policy of President McKinley for the peace, prosperity and honor of our beloved country." He also indicated that he wished to have the McKinley Cabinet continue in office. His own reaction to the accidental fulfillment of his most cherished goal was: "It is a dreadful thing to come into the presidency this way; but it would be a far worse thing to be morbid about it. Here is the task, and I have got

to do it to the best of my ability; and that is all there is about it."
That he had the "ability" he did not for an instant doubt. Supremely
confident, he could not see why he should not end the "jinx" of vice-
presidential successions, namely, inability to command the party
throughout the term and gain nomination for one in his own right.
He was well aware of the problem he faced, for he had written on just
this subject in 1896:

"When [William Henry] Harrison died the presidency fell into the
hands of a man who had but a corporal's guard of supporters in the
nation, who proceeded to oppose all the measures of the immense
majority of those who elected him.

"Johnson was put on the ticket largely for geographic reasons, and
on the death of Lincoln tried to reverse the policy of the party which
had put him in office. . . . The death of Garfield meant complete
overturn in the *personnel*. . . . The bitterness caused by his succession
to power nearly tore the party in twain. . . . The Vice-President should
. . . represent the same views and principles . . . [as] the President
. . . standing well in the councils of the party, trusted . . . and able
. . . to take up the work of the latter [President] just where it was
left. . . . It is an unhealthy thing to have the Vice-President and
President represented by principles so far apart that the succession
of one to the place of the other means a change as radical as any
party overturn."

Though one can disagree with details in Roosevelt's interpretation
of the previous successions, the sense of his argument and the remedy
he proposed were correct. He was well aware that his own nomination in 1900 had not been in accordance with these views and he had
no desire to go down in history as another of those who "tore the
party in twain."

As early as June, 1902, state Republican organizations began to
endorse T.R. for 1904. As Edward Stanwood said: "We should probably have to go as far back as the time of General Jackson to cite
similar action, so early in an administration, in favor even of an
elected President." The mid-term elections of 1902, so often the
weather vane for party hopes and fears two years hence, reaffirmed
Republican control throughout the nation and in 1904 the Roosevelt
tide swept all before it

One last facet of Roosevelt's 1901 accession should be noted: his
attitude toward the office he held. With typical directness, he declared
to reporters on his first day in the White House: "I want you to
understand at the start—I feel myself just as much a constitutionally
elected President . . . as McKinley was. I was voted for as Vice-

President, it is true, but the Constitution provides that in the case of the death or inability of the President, the Vice-President shall serve as President, and, therefore, due to the act of a madman, I am President and shall act in every word and deed precisely as if I and not McKinley had been the candidate for whom the electors cast the vote for President. I have no superstitions and no misgivings on that score. That should be understood."

No one was disposed to dispute Roosevelt's executive prerogatives, even when he interpreted them in novel ways (as in Panama, the coal strike, or the Venezuelan debt controversy). Dawes aptly characterized the Roosevelt of this period: "He seeks to wield power—not to avoid wielding it. He apparently loves everybody and nobody—both at once."

Nevertheless, T.R. was grimly aware of his actual position and thus was all the more elated at his 1904 triumph. Meeting Senator Foraker a few days later, the President greeted him with: "You are shaking hands with His Excellency, not his Accidency." At that same meeting, Roosevelt warned the Old Guard Ohioan that in his forthcoming administration "he would feel at liberty to have his own policies" rather than continue McKinley's "which he had until that time been pursuing." A host of McKinleyites felt like the wit who said that Roosevelt carried out McKinley's policies—and buried them.

CHARLES WARREN FAIRBANKS

Reference has already been made to an article on the vice-presidency written by Theodore Roosevelt in 1896 as campaign literature. This serves as an unusually good guide to chart his relations with Charles Warren Fairbanks, Vice-President during his second term. Here, as in the case of George Washington, a rule of action had been laid down for the second office of the land by the man who was to occupy the first.

Roosevelt had said the Vice-President should be of the same "views and principles" as the President; that it was "unhealthy" to have the two ends of the ticket "so far apart" in principles that a succession would cause "change as radical as any party overturn." Were those rules followed in the case of Fairbanks' selection in 1904? They were not.

Senator Charles W. Fairbanks of Indiana had a close inner circle relationship with the hitherto dominant McKinley-Hanna wing of the Republican party. Though an Ohioan by birth, he was a Hoosier by adoption, choosing Indianapolis as the place to hang out his law shingle in 1874. Born of poor farmer parents, he was a shrewd lawyer who became well-to-do early. His specialty was bankrupt railroads, of which there was a plethora after the Panic of 1873. Soon "no railroad enterprise . . . [was] undertaken in Indiana . . . without his having a share in it." In politics more interested in manipulating than in office-holding, Fairbanks had been temporary chairman and keynoter of the 1896 Convention, in which he had eloquently defended the gold standard. In 1897, he accepted his first political office as Senator. Fairbanks, at forty-five, became, together with another freshman, Mark Hanna, the spokesman for McKinley in the Senate. He was the dispenser of the Federal patronage for his state and was American chairman of the Joint High Commission of 1898 which unsuccessfully sought to adjust all outstanding difficulties with Canada. Together with Hanna, Platt and other spokesmen for big business, he had opposed such foreign adventures as the Spanish-Cuban struggle, and had acted as a restraining influence on the tormented McKinley. He was one of Hanna's choices for running-mate in 1900 but turned the offer down. Henry L. Stoddard, a commentator of this period, thought "Fairbanks had dreams of the White House. He preferred to remain in the Senate until the real call came." He helped carry his state in 1900 and accepted senatorial re-election in 1902.

By 1903 a new Indiana luminary arose to contest Fairbanks' grip— the pro-reform Albert J. Beveridge. Roosevelt "originally wanted Beveridge as his teammate" for 1904, but the latter himself planned to become President and found "Fairbanks . . . fighting him in every possible way." The Beveridge boom never got anywhere; by 1904 the President had a new choice, Congressman Robert Roberts Hitt of Illinois, a member of the House since 1882. Again, Roosevelt had no intention of rocking the boat and would only privately indicate his preference for Hitt.

Roosevelt, accordingly, *was* desirous of having a personally or politically compatible person in the vice-presidency, but he was not prepared to fight for it. He acted no differently than had McKinley in 1900 who, in T.R.'s opinion, had "no more backbone than a chocolate eclair." The Convention of 1904 was allowed a free hand. It picked Fairbanks, and Roosevelt meekly acquiesced in the choice.

The Old Guard had early fixed on Fairbanks as the offset to the maverick President. Fairbanks himself was disposed to re-enact Roosevelt's wavering pre-Convention attitude to the vice-presidency. In January, 1904, he discussed with Dawes "the question of whether or not he should be a candidate." He felt the nomination was his "for the asking" and Dawes agreed. Dawes received "the impression that he expected to become a candidate." In May, Fairbanks called on Lodge to authorize him to tell the President that he was at T.R.'s service in any way he might indicate. Lodge correctly interpreted the cryptic words to mean the vice-presidency only and advised Roosevelt to sit tight and let events take care of themselves—the exact public policy McKinley had followed with respect to Roosevelt's candidacy in 1900. As late as June 18, five days before his nomination, Fairbanks (who evidently had not informed his close friend of his talk with Lodge) still was playing cat-and-mouse with the office, Dawes noting: "He has not yet decided as to whether or not to announce his candidacy for the vice-presidency."

And so the deed was done again. The usual compromise between principle and expediency resulted in the victory of expediency. "Practical politics" succeeded, as the euphemism has it, in "balancing the ticket." Thus the essential dichotomy of the Republican party, apparent even by 1904, was submerged in order to ensure that degree of organizational harmony necessary to give Roosevelt a term in his own right. His arguments of 1896 were a mere academic effusion, not a mainspring of action to a man in power.

Fairbanks, duly nominated without any spirited opposition, received fulsome congratulations from Roosevelt: "It is a position of high honor and dignity, and its tremendous importance is shown by the fact that five times . . . the Vice-President has had to assume the duties of President. No man should take it who is not fit to be President, and it is not always easy to induce those who are fit to accept it. I feel that you . . . have rendered a real service by accepting . . . though . . . I do not see how you could refuse in view of the unanimous feeling . . .that you were the man above all others needed for the place."

When the Democrats, on July 9, 1904, nominated a frankly conservative ticket of Alton B. Parker of New York and Henry Gassaway Davis of West Virginia, they wrote finis to the Old Guard's stranglehold on their party. The drubbing this ticket was to take in November would convince Democrats that their only future hope was in a frank espousal of liberal principles and men of the Bryan stamp. Never again would they choose two conservatives.

It was laughable to think of the eighty-one-year-old Davis as a potential President, able to step into the breach that might be caused by death or incapacity. Reports were rife that he had been chosen primarily because of his wealth and heavy contributions to the Democratic campaign chest. But as Foraker said, "Like most men who made their money, he knew how to keep it," and Davis made only a

"nominal" contribution. The Gridiron Club of Washington correspondents were to have a lot of fun that year at their annual dinner
satirizing the Democratic National Committee for receiving $7.39 from
Henry "Gazzaway" Davis. Elihu Root, as chairman of the Republican
vice-presidential notification committee, dwelt long on the contrasting
ages and qualifications of the opponents. His letter of notification to
Fairbanks pointed out that Davis had been born in Monroe's administration.

Fairbanks campaigned vigorously and there was a close liaison between him and T.R. through election. Thereafter, Fairbanks' practical use to Roosevelt was short-lived. Since he was still Senator from
Indiana until March 4, the Vice-President-elect participated in the
lame duck session before becoming politically impotent. In White
House conferences on December 2 and 4, 1904, Fairbanks helped
shape the legislative program. The Vice-President-elect next had an
opportunity to demonstrate loyalty to the administration in the
matter of the proposed ratification of a series of arbitration treaties
with their "special agreement" clauses. The Senate was suspicious
that here was an executive device to thwart its ratification prerogative
in the future. Debate was long and acrid; even Lodge split with the
President on the matter and led the fight against the inclusion of the
clause. Among the handful of Roosevelt supporters during January
and February was Fairbanks. The matter was ultimately tabled.

After March 4, the Roosevelt-Fairbanks *rapport* was short-lived.
Though Fairbanks continued to call on the President in the early
months of his vice-presidency, he was soon made to realize that his
Old Guard advice was neither asked for nor welcome. It was the
McKinley-Roosevelt relationship of 1901 all over again, and given the
basic political incompatability it could hardly have been otherwise.

The President's feelings and actions with respect to his Vice-President were sharply contradictory to his *dicta* of 1896. Then he had
offered specific suggestions to cement relations and to heighten the
prestige of the second officer: "He should always be . . . consulted
by the President on every great party question. It would be very
well if he were given a seat in the Cabinet. It might be well if, in
addition to his vote in the Senate in . . . a tie, he should be given a
vote, on ordinary occasions, and perchance on occasion a voice in the
debates." Of these concrete proposals, the first was very clearly
abandoned by Roosevelt; he appears never to have thought of the
second; the last two would have required legislation and constitutional
amendment, neither of which he ever recommended.

As a matter of fact, Fairbanks was the victim of Roosevelt's real contempt both for the office of the vice-presidency and the man in it. Once when the President was told that he was more powerful than any constitutional king, he had quickly replied: "A constitutional king! Why, a constitutional king is nothing but a combination of the Vice-President and the leader of the Four Hundred." Roosevelt had laughed heartily and often repeated the response F. P. Dunne had made when he told him he was thinking of going down in a submarine: "Well, you really shouldn't do it—unless you take Fairbanks with you." The letters of Archie Butt, his (and later, Taft's) military aide, are filled with T.R.'s "humorous" comments about Fairbanks and are evidence of strong personal dislike.

Though Fairbanks felt his office might be a logical stepping-stone for 1908, he naturally received no support from Roosevelt. The President even found occasion to discuss his personal choices for the nomination in Fairbanks' presence. Needless to say, the Vice-President was not among the prospects.

Isolated though he was, and without any effective role in the administration, Fairbanks sought to promote himself. As well as he could, he manipulated bosses and situations with an eye to 1908. However, having no patronage at his disposal, the Vice-President could do no more than make promises to those who controlled delegates, while the President, aware of those promises, checkmated him at will by shifting the incidence of patronage to the extent required by the situation. Fairbanks was to meet many such frustrating incidents throughout his pre-convention campaign.

As Foraker said, the Old Guard strategy for 1908 was "that by the combination of different elements we might be able to nominate . . . Fairbanks or some other Republican with whom we would be better satisfied" than a hand-picked Rooseveltian. (The Ohio Senator had hopes he might be that "some other Republican.") In the final analysis, Roosevelt's selection of Taft would carry in the 1908 Convention, but the Fairbanks threat was a worry to the end. Shortly before the Convention met, in a conference with Stoddard whose paper, the *New York Evening Mail*, was booming Governor Charles Evans Hughes, Roosevelt sought to persuade him to shift to Taft. Stoddard refused, saying both Taft and Hughes were liberals and "if your hand was not on the convention Hughes would land the prize." To which Roosevelt replied: "You're wrong. . . . Do you know whom we have the most trouble in beating! Not Hughes—but Fairbanks! Think of it— Charley Fairbanks! I was never more surprised in my life. I never dreamt of such a thing. He's got a hold in Kentucky, Indiana and some other States that is hard to break. How and why is beyond me.

It is easier to win delegates away from Hughes right in New York than to win them away from Fairbanks in those States."

The Roosevelt hand was never to relax and Taft was an easy winner though the "bitter-enders" stayed with Fairbanks through the balloting. He peremptorily refused all overtures for the consolation prize of the second place again.

Fairbanks as Vice-President had hit back at Roosevelt as well as he could for the humiliations and ostracisms he met. His only weapon, admittedly insufficient, was his presidency of the Senate. In that capacity, especially after 1906, he used whatever pretense he could find to block the Square Deal program. In combination with Senator Nelson W. Aldrich of Rhode Island and House Speaker Cannon, Fairbanks agreed to a "definite program . . . of burying all progressive measures in committee so that they could never come to a vote." His particular role was to be "on the alert to rule any dangerous speakers 'out of order' on the slightest pretext." The result was that "few were the measures able to run the gauntlet." Fairbanks' most famous ruling came early in 1907 when he declared Beveridge out of order during a renewed fight to put the cost of meat inspection upon the packers. The measure was effectively killed.

The net result of this running-battle between President Roosevelt and Vice-President Fairbanks for political control of the Republican Party was that the welfare of the country suffered. Fairbanks' incumbency was further proof of the "unhealthy" situation Roosevelt had once spoken of, even when there was no succession. After his term of office expired, Fairbanks retired to private life, but retained his hold on the councils of the Republican Party, supported Taft against the Roosevelt bolt in 1912, accepted the chairmanship of the platform committee, and in 1916 again entered the presidential lists as Indiana's favorite son. Though the presidential nomination went to Hughes, Fairbanks was persuaded to accept second place on the ticket again, thus repeating the example of Adlai E. Stevenson in 1900.

THE CAMPAIGN OF 1908

Though in 1908 the forces of reform were too strong to allow the Old Guard of either party to control the presidential nominations, they were more fortunate as concerned the second place. Both conventions chose organization men, stand-patters, symbols of regularity and party discipline. John Worth Kern, of Indiana, was selected by a few leaders meeting in the room of Charles Wayland Bryan on the tenth of June, the last day of the Democratic Convention. Kern was available because New York was uninterested and because he was a deserving Democrat from a pivotal state that might be weaned away from the Republicans. Kern's name was presented to the convention by Thomas Riley Marshall, Democrat of Indiana, who would himself be the incumbent in the Wilson administrations. Kern and Fairbanks had long known each other and when William Jennings Bryan in a pre-convention visit to Indianapolis had referred to Kern as a possible running-mate, the latter pleaded poverty. It was rumored that the office cost Fairbanks $50,000 a year. "I am too poor to think of running. . . . At that rate I could only afford to stop in Washington a day." Bryan thereupon laughingly offered to share the White House with him rent-free and followed up this idea with a later announcement that, if elected, he would invite his Vice-President to sit with the Cabinet. This leaf out of Roosevelt's 1896 campaign article was not echoed by the Republicans.

The Republican vice-presidential selection in 1908 was James Schoolcraft Sherman. Roosevelt, "practical" enough to realize that he should not expect the convention to ratify his choices on both ends of the ticket, again offered no administration favorite. He did, however, believe that Sherman's selection would be embarrassing to Taft, for as a long-time powerful member of the House of Representatives from New York, Sherman was identified with the failure of that body to push through postal savings bank and anti-injunction legislation, items long demanded by reformers and unequivocally embraced by Taft. Nevertheless, the President did not interfere. When Sherman was duly nominated, Roosevelt felt, he "helps us in New York by interesting the organization, but in the upper Mississippi Valley he is considerably identified with Cannon and I have been disturbed by the extent of the hostility to and the revolt against Cannon." Taft too had his doubts about Sherman and would have preferred a Westerner like Fairbanks or Beveridge. However, the former had taken himself out of contention and the latter had insisted that Taft publicly endorse him prior to his agreement to accept the nomination, something that Taft refused to do.

Senator Depew of New York recalled "the Republican congressmen who were at the convention were practically unanimous for Sherman and their leader was Uncle Joe Cannon." With the downfall of every other candidacy and Depew's off-the-floor orations for "Sunny Jim" Sherman, a night conference of the leaders settled on the New York congressman. Speaker Cannon seconded Sherman's nomination, and the business was speedily accomplished. To William Allen White the handwriting on the wall was clear: "I saw how little enthusiasm those delegates had for Mr. Taft. They cheered their reactionary leaders.

Joe Cannon was their idol—not Taft. . . . Alice Roosevelt [daughter of the President] . . . knew what a hollow victory was Taft's. . . . She gave me the tip that . . . James Sherman, the most reactionary of the Republican Congressmen, would be nominated. . . . It was the revolt of the conservative Republican party against . . . liberal leadership. . . . All of the world of change that was abroad in the land . . . the Republican party . . . rejected in scorn with the Sherman nomination."

The reformist *Nation* saw in both vice-presidential selections renewed "proof of the flippant way in which Americans . . . fill . . . the highest offices. . . . It is not personality but geography that has been the decisive factor." While agreeing in part with this interpretation, one must dissent that geography was the decisive factor in 1908. The necessity of "balancing the ticket," ideologically speaking, was the more significant motivating factor in both conventions, just as it had been for the Republicans in 1904.

JAMES SCHOOLCRAFT SHERMAN

James S. Sherman was a native New Yorker, born in Utica, Oneida County, and identified all his life with county and city. A classmate and fraternity brother of Elihu Root at Hamilton College, he had had a successful business and legal career before turning to politics. Though of Democratic origins, Sherman was elected mayor of Utica in 1884 on the Republican ticket and progressed into national politics with his election as Republican Congressman in 1886. Thereafter, except for one term (1891-1893) when he was defeated, he was in the House until he began his vice-presidential duties in 1909. Such long service meant a natural growth in importance in Congress. A loyal organization man, Sherman was the confidant of Speakers Reed and Cannon. No espouser of "causes", he preferred to work behind the scenes and was commonly supposed to have "evolved most of the measures proposed by the committee on rules," the most important of the House standing committees. A master of parliamentary tactics, he alone was trusted to relieve Reed in the Chair during the debates on the Dingley Tariff and the Spanish war revenue bills. Firm and dignified, he was, "next to Reed," the House's "best presiding officer," and Sherman had tried to succeed him in the speakership.

Though he had been regularly returned to the House after his one defeat, these biennial victories were not always easy. In 1902, due to a census reapportionment, he had been in grave danger of being eliminated by having no district to run in. Again, in 1906, he just squeaked through to victory, being then the beneficiary of the rhetori-

cal prowess of his fraternity brother, Elihu Root, who came on to
Utica to save him and the state for the Republican Party.

These narrow escapes influenced him to aspire to a post that carried
with it dignity and prestige and did not react so violently on the nervous system. Sherman, in other words, was a reversion to the latter
nineteenth century vice-presidential candidates, the stately, dignified,
yet genial, aspirants. He was neither well enough nor able enough to
conduct the strenuous campaign that Roosevelt and Fairbanks had
waged in 1900 and 1904. Taft, however, was both able and willing
and, since the ticket would stand or fall on him alone, the silent
geniality of Sherman was good enough.

At his first visit to the White House for a victory luncheon Sherman
looked "unusually well and . . . not . . . the invalid which it was
feared he would be after his attack in the summer." The President-
elect seemed at first to have intended to act independently of Uncle
Joe Cannon, and to have sought to enlist his running-mate in the
effort. Sherman conferred with Taft in December, and was told that
the latter "did not intend to have anything to do with Joe Cannon.
. . . I am going to rely on you, Jim . . . to take care of Cannon for
me. Whatever I have to do there [in the House] will be done through
you." But the Old Guard was nothing if not loyal and Sherman's
answer was direct and unequivocal: "Not through me. . . . You will
have to act on your own account. I am to be Vice-President and
acting as a messenger boy is not part of the duties of a Vice-President."

If Taft was shocked by the directness of Sherman's refusal, he gave
no indication of it. He accepted the Vice-President as a companion in
his famous golf games which, duly publicized, were indeed tame pur-
suits after the strenuous activities of Roosevelt. Unfortunately, Sherman was a bit of a duffer and Taft soon came to think of his dates
as duty games. He felt himself "committed to the Vice-President for
golf and fears to hurt his feelings by not asking him to join him
when he plays."

Sherman sought to atone for his lack of skill on the golf course
by counselling Taft on legislative matters. Tariff reform had long
been in the air and the Republican 1908 platform had promised revision. The President had made tariff reduction the first order of
business in his administration and had Congress sitting in special
session to effect it. The bill was lagging in the House with Republican
agents of local industries seeking to protect their interests. Motoring
with Sherman in April, Taft expressed his disappointment at the way
things were going. Sherman told the President to use his power of
appointment to get results: "You can't cajole [members of Congress]

. . . you have to hit them with a club. . . . Begin to hit. I would . . . shut off the appointments . . . until the bill is passed . . . Shut them all off so that the innocent can get to work on the guilty and it can all be done without any personal threat. . . . The appointing power is your only club."

Sherman's advice was not followed and the resulting Payne-Aldrich Tariff was the opposite of downward revision. When Taft signed it, he was well on his way to the almost complete loss of public support that was to characterize his administration. Captain Archie Butt, his military aide, became worried about his health when the storm of protest broke about him, but Taft recovered and assured Butt he would live "to preserve the country from the sage of Utica."

Both Taft and Butt had begun to suspect Sherman's motives during a legislative battle over the tariff schedule for gloves. They believed the Vice-President was using his influence in favor of a high rate to help a New York colleague in the House of Representatives. In this matter, at least, the President was victorious, the Congress agreeing to his lower figure.

Sherman was held in low esteem by the President until the Ballinger-Pinchot controversy broke wide open. The Vice-President supported the administration and Secretary of the Interior Ballinger. His weapon was use (or abuse) of his power to appoint senators to a special investigating committee.

To assuage the cries of Gifford Pinchot and others that the Interior Department was sabotaging Roosevelt's conservation movement, Congress established a joint twelve-man committee composed of eight Republicans and four Democrats. The House Republican insurgent, George W. Norris of Nebraska, managed to get named to the committee. This meant that the Democrats could expect to muster an additional vote and it became necessary to ensure that there be no defections among the other Republican members. The Senate Old Guard managed to keep the power of naming the Senate's committee delegation in Sherman's hands. Thus everything depended on the Vice-President. Conservationists felt they had a friend when Sherman named Senator Elihu Root, but, as Pinchot later admitted, Root "acted like the counsel for the Administration during the hearings." Many of the committee's significant votes were carried for the Taft Administration by the narrow vote of 7 to 5, thus attesting to the unerring choices Sherman had made. Though the committee's verdict was a victory for the administration, it was joyless and an unappeased public compelled Ballinger's resignation in March 1911.

Meanwhile, ex-President Roosevelt had returned from his African safari and his European triumphs. Dissatisfied with developments in his own state, he re-entered the political arena. In New York, the machine was still safely in control. In its top echelon was Tim Woodruff of the State Central Committee, soon up for reelection. When word began to get around that "the Administration" desired Woodruff eliminated, the latter went directly to Taft to find out. Butt admits Taft wanted Woodruff purged, but alas, here was Woodruff in the flesh, wanting a direct answer. Taft was in a quandary because "Woodruff is one of the closest friends of the Vice-President, and the Vice-President is urging the President to take no part in the fight against Woodruff." "Torn asunder in his desire to please everybody, [Taft] permitted Woodruff to leave thinking that the Administration would not oppose him." The weaknesses of Taft as President were never more cleary evidenced than in this incident, though Butt laid all the blame on the Vice-President. He summed up the situation: "Heavens, why did they ever put such a man as Sherman on the same ticket with Taft?"

Roosevelt decided to contest the Old Guard's control in New York. As he later wrote Root: "I went into the fight . . . because Sherman . . . and Woodruff, from their interview with Taft, gave the impression that he was with them, was pleased to have them continue in control, and would at least indirectly support them." Initially the fight centered around the State Central Committee which would soon name a temporary chairman for the forthcoming state convention. The position was strategically significant for the New York gubernatorial candidate and the composition of the national convention delegation two years hence. Roosevelt was surprised at Taft's apparent backing of Woodruff and more shocked that he seemed to prefer Vice-President Sherman over himself for the temporary chairmanship. Sherman was busy "telephoning every day to the President, giving the plans to defeat Mr. Roosevelt."

The Vice-President drew first blood when the State Central Committee chose him over Roosevelt. Butt felt the whole affair was unfortunate; it involved Taft in anti-Rooseveltism: "As long as the Vice-President is at the bottom of the fight . . . and . . . is running back and forth to Beverly, it will be hard to convince others of the disinterestedness of the President."

Tension mounted at Beverly when a report arrived that Roosevelt was going to issue a statement that his defeat "was the result of a conspiracy on the part of Woodruff, Sherman, Barnes, and the President." Taft's private secretary at this time, Charles D. Norton, who had encouraged Sherman, now began to say "that the President knew nothing of Sherman's acts or intentions . . ." In this Norton was partially successful. Roosevelt did not issue his public statement forthwith, but had an intermediary get Norton to urge Taft to "deny all connection with . . . the old guard of New York and repudiating the Vice-President." Taft yielded, and in a public letter, denied that he had favored the Vice-President over Roosevelt for the position. Taft furthermore stated that "he first learned of the Sherman movement from the newspapers; and that he had done all he could to prevent a contest." The effects of this lying letter assuaged temporarily the feeling against Taft, but left Sherman the arch-villain of the piece —the embodiment of all that was anti-liberal, anti-Roosevelt. It was little wonder that Taft-Sherman relations were strained to the breaking point. Sherman, "very indignant" at the statements and implications of Taft's letter, agreed to "say nothing in contradiction," but to "accept the odium rather than involve the President by a further denial of the facts."

The Taft letter went a long way to retrieve Roosevelt's fortunes. He continued to do battle "to win the Republican party to the cause of reform" and was so successful that "the Vice-President was even defeated for delegate in his own precinct of his own district."

The state convention opened at Saratoga and, as Henry L. Stimson recalled it, immediately "T.R. was triumphantly elected as temporary chairman" over "a personally estimable stand-pat conservative." The actual vote was 568 to 443, hardly a landslide; one tends to agree with Mark Sullivan that it was an "unappetizing triumph for an ex-President." Root—torn between Sherman and Roosevelt—felt like "a sore-headed bear" in voting "against Jim Sherman, but there was absolutely nothing else to be done." In the driver's seat, Roosevelt steered Stimson through to nomination for governor. The professionals were unenthusiastic throughout the campaign, and as Stimson said: "Many Republicans in the Washington administration felt that a Stimson victory would be of no value to Mr. Taft." The Democrats won New York by 60,000 votes. With their capture of 26 governorships and the House of Representatives by a 66 majority, it was a bad year all around for the Republicans.

The Sherman-Taft breach, wide enough by midterm, was widened still further by Stimson's appointment as Secretary of War. Taft wanted to ally himself more to the "decent element" in New York— meaning T.R. He admitted that the move would further alienate Sherman, but from "the way he smiled," Butt was sure the President "seemed to welcome this." Needless to say, the Vice-President reacted as Taft had expected, having "the bitterest feeling" thereafter toward the new appointee and the President.

But Sherman could swallow his pride to help a friend. Senator William Lorimer had been elected Senator from Illinois in May, 1909. Reformers deemed his election invalid and the President decided to support a proposed senatorial investigation. Sherman pleaded with him to desist lest he "lose the Catholic vote." The President was adamant: "If the entire Catholic Church stood before me I should not be moved." The Vice-President persuaded Root to try his luck on Taft, but the President was determined, knew "Sherman has had hold of him" (Root), and brushed aside his arguments. (Lorimer was ultimately unseated in 1912.)

Sherman, now convinced of his complete lack of influence with Taft, concentrated on rebuilding his influence in New York. To Taft men, he was "knifing the Administration . . . in search for delegates" for 1912. They felt he wanted to be the presidential "nominee of the conservative wing" as Fairbanks had aspired. Taft himself was unperturbed: "He knew full well that Sherman would sacrifice him if by doing so he could secure the re-nomination for the vice-presidency. He does not think that Sherman wants to be nominated for President, but . . . wants to be able to be in a position to trade the New York delegation off for the vice-presidency."

Sherman and Taft were pleasant enough to each other when their paths crossed, but there were no more personal relations, no more chatty golf games, motor rides, and private conferences. Also, by the middle of 1911, the only subject Taft and Roosevelt could safely discuss together was the Vice-President. At a ceremony honoring the golden jubilee of Cardinal Gibbons' ordination, while Sherman was quoting the Bible to point up his remarks, the ex-President whispered to Taft: "When Jim Sherman quotes scripture the devil must shake all hell with his laughter . . . I should think it would make the cardinal feel like going out of business." Yet both men had known in 1908 what Sherman was like. He had not changed; indeed he was uncomfortably consistent through the years. His two critics of 1911 were more than any others responsible for his being Vice-President of the United States.

Taft had moments of despondency, especially after the election debacle of 1910 put Administration recommendations at the mercy of a Democratic House and a Senate where insurgents held the balance of power. Taft had taken up the reciprocity idea to soften criticism of his high tariff stand. Congress had authorized the administration to approach Canada on the issue. Taft mused to his secretary: "I wonder, should anything happen to me . . . if Jim Sherman would sign the bill. I am inclined to think that public opinion would force him to do it." Taft added: "Yet again, he and Uncle Joe might think my death a direct visitation of Providence brought about for the sole purpose of upholding the protective doctrine. I think it safer to live." Again, when later in the year he was forced to call off a projected tour because of illness, causing the stock market to sag, he mused: "That is strange. I should think when Wall Street thinks of Jim Sherman and his intimates, stocks would go up."

Sherman gloried in his nickname of "Sunny Jim." Less flattering was the soubriquet of "Short-weight Jim" which Dr. Harvey W. Wiley had once applied to him. Wiley, an outstanding figure in the pure food crusade, had met determined opposition from Congressman Sherman, who was also president of his family's New Hartford Canning Company.

Taft's attitude was almost wholly negative. According to Butt, Sherman by the fall of 1911 was in the same category as Uncle Joe Cannon "and the latter's presence is enough to ruin an evening for him." Mulling over his estrangement from Sherman, Taft professed not to know the reason why, "but as a rule the President and the Vice-President seem to drift apart, no matter how close they are together at the start."

For a time Taft toyed with the possibility of a new running-mate for 1912. He was favorably impressed by Governor Herbert S. Hadley of Missouri, an ardent friend of Roosevelt whose reputation was based on his successful prosecutions of the Standard Oil and Harvester Companies. Taft felt Hadley "could carry Missouri and help me possibly carry some of the Southern states." But it was not to be. Hadley became a "Bull Moose" adherent in 1912; indeed, was Roosevelt's floor manager at the regular Republican Convention. His bolting action was typical of most of the extremely liberal Republicans, so that as a matter of fact, the Old Guard and the Taft Republicans had little choice but to stand on the old ticket of 1908. With fights over credentials of delegates, chairmanship, ideology, presidential nomination, the pro-Roosevelt walk-out and the split in Republican ranks, the 1912 Convention was emotionally exhausting and there was little interest in such an anti-climactic event as the vice-presidential choice. The speech putting Sherman's name before the half-empty hall took only a minute! No others were formally placed in nomination but on the balloting a few scattered protest votes were registered.

The renomination of James S. Sherman in 1912 was noteworthy for two reasons. In the first place, he was the first Vice-President in the Republican Party's history to be given the chance to succeed himself. The precedent, started by Lincoln dropping Hamlin in 1864, was departed from for the first time in half a century of the party's existence. In the second place, 1912 represented the first Republican twentieth century Convention when the vice-presidential nomination was not the major business of interest before it. There had been no real presidential contests over McKinley, Roosevelt, or Taft on the three previous occasions. This apparent 1912 harmony was fictitious. The rump Republican precedent-smashers must have known in their hearts that their ticket of Taft and Sherman was doomed to defeat in November.

Sherman, whom Taft had so often feared might succeed him by death, was not to live to face the ignominy of defeat in 1912. He died on October 30, 1912, deeply mourned by his friends. To Depew was ended "one of the most delightful associations of a lifetime, personally and politically." For the history of the vice-presidency, Sherman's death created a unique situation. Though several incumbents had died in office before, none had done so so shortly before election. It was impossible to get a substitute for him in the popular vote, and so over three million people voted for a dead man for Vice-President in 1912. As far as the electoral votes were concerned, the eight electors from Vermont and Utah were the first in several decades to choose otherwise than as directed by a national convention. The recipient of these Republican electoral votes, Nicholas Murray Butler, recalled: "It rather amused me to find myself . . . receiving the Republican electoral vote for Vice-President. . . . When the Electoral College was about to meet, Senator Reed Smoot of Utah called me by telephone from Washington and asked whether I had any objection. . . . I had . . . [none] provided there was no chance of electing a Republican Vice-President . . . We chaffed each other . . . for a few minutes and that ended the matter. The . . . votes had to be cast for somebody, and under the circumstances it was a matter of complete indifference whether they were cast for me or not."

THE CAMPAIGN OF 1912

The breakup of Republican unity in 1912 led to the first Democratic presidential triumph in twenty years. The "rebel" Republicans, meeting in their separate Bull Moose Convention, chose a strong running mate for Roosevelt. The selection of Governor Hiram Johnson of California marked the first time any party selected a Pacific Coast candidate and, beyond attesting to that section's rising importance, was a tribute to his personal fame. Johnson's effective reform activities were widely known and conformed to the "New Nationalism" the standard bearer espoused. Roosevelt praised the Convention's choice, even admitting that the vice-presidential nomination was more important than the one to the New York governorship.

The Democrats jubilantly met at Baltimore after the regular Republican convention had split wide open. Bryan, refusing overtures for the second place, told Democrats: "there is but one thing left to do, and that is to give us a candidate for Vice-President in harmony with our candidate for President, so there may be no joint debate between our candidates." In the popular view, Thomas R. Marshall was to meet this standard of liberalism and political kinship with Woodrow Wilson. As a matter of fact, his selection for the vice-presidency was due to a combination of factors, not the least of which was the bloc of thirty votes pledged to him as Indiana's favorite son presidential candidate. The organization choice for President was Champ Clark, Speaker of the House after 1911, and though he had a plurality of delegates pledged to him at the opening of the Convention, under the two-thirds rule it was not enough. Thus, in the lengthy balloting that ensued, a solid bloc of thirty votes that solemnly went to Marshall throughout 27 ballots was of significance. On the 28th ballot, the Indiana bloc (controlled by Thomas T. Taggart) switched to Wilson. The latter's son-in-law-to-be, William Gibbs McAdoo, wrote: "This accession of strength . . . produced a magnificent effect upon the crowded galleries. . . . Tom Taggart had done a grand thing for Wilson. It was the first break to him of the delegates from any of the large states. It disheartened the Clark forces and, from that time on, Clark's strength disintegrated with every ballot."

The situation led to no frenzied bandwagon shifts, but it clearly indicated a trend that, confirmed in ballot after ballot, resulted in Wilson's nomination next day on the 46th ballot. This long struggle had left the delegates "completely exhausted" and Wilson's managers were "almost physical wrecks." Everyone was impatient to leave but the Democrats had reversed the usual procedure and selected the nominee before adopting a platform. Thus there was still the vice-president to pick and the platform to be adopted. Immediately after receiving news of his own selection, Wilson, in New Jersey, phoned Albert S. Burleson, one of his managers at Baltimore: "I want you to go to Washington," he said, "and see Underwood, and ask if he will not be Vice-President. He is my candidate."

Senator Oscar W. Underwood of Alabama, who had been the official presidential candidate of the South and had held the bulk of his sectional strength right to the end, rejected the offer. When asked how the convention tended in the matter, Burleson stated it seemed to be "leaning toward Thomas R. Marshall." Wilson protested, "But . . . he is a very small calibre man" to which Burleson agreed, but argued that since he was from the Midwest and a doubtful state, he would be a perfect supplement to Wilson. Wilson accepted Burleson's arguments. However, it was still necessary to get at least 726 delegates dutifully lined up. The perennially smiling McAdoo gives an oversimplified version of what then occurred: "I had got in touch with Governor Wilson and told him that the convention would nominate anyone he desired. . . . He said he did not care to offer a suggestion . . . the convention [could] exercise complete freedom of action . . . I told the Governor that his friends . . . would want . . . his preference. . . . He then asked me to suggest. . . . I suggested . . . Marshall . . . whom I did not know personally, but only by reputation. . . . [which], was that of a liberal, and because he seemed to be generally well regarded . . . Governor Wilson authorized me to say that Marshall would be acceptable to him. I conveyed this . . . to Taggart. He was immensely pleased. A listless convention. . . . voted [for] Marshall."

With so many politicians getting in touch with Wilson at one time or the other, during those seven hours, the lines from Baltimore to Sea Girt, New Jersey, must have been busy indeed! The third manager, titular head of the Wilson effort, has left his account of the proceedings, one which certainly rings more true, since it is more in line with American political practice. William F. McCombs, crippled, dynamic, taut and tense, did not immediately phone Wilson that Tuesday afternoon of July 2. Instead, he wrote: "I went to my hotel and slept for a while. Refreshed, I called up the Governor and asked him what he thought about the vice presidency. I told him the candidates would probably be Governor [John] Burke, of North Dakota, Mayor Preston of Baltimore, and Governor Marshall, of Indiana. I told him that he could have his choice . . . and asked him to make a suggestion. His suggestion was that I do what I was willing as representing him."

McCombs "mulled over" the potential candidates and by a process of elimination "concluded that Marshall was the man." Arriving at the Convention hall that evening, McCombs was shunted into a "private room" where eleven of the Wilson backers had gathered, including Burleson, McAdoo, and A. Mitchell Palmer. McCombs related: "We must decide who should be the Vice President. A vote was proposed. Somebody mentioned Palmer. Then I knew what the vote would be. I also knew that Palmer could not help the ticket at all, because...[he was] from...Pennsylvania. I said that eleven men could not decide who was to be the Vice-President of the United States. I proceeded to the floor. I spoke to the leaders of the large delegations. Marshall was nominated by a tremendous majority." McCombs' cryptic account is cleared up by his editor's explanation which says "Mr. McCombs fulfilled his pledge to Thomas T. Taggart to throw the Wilson vote to Thomas R. Marshall, of Indiana, for Vice President."

Thus, in all probability a trade of the Marshall delegates to Wilson for Wilson's delegates to Marshall took place at the 1912 convention. Therefore the vice-presidential nomination was fixed even before Wilson himself had been nominated, much less "consulted," on his second-place choice. There is little doubt that McCombs' editor is correct when he says in effect that McCombs had no other alternative but to advance Marshall's name.

What then is the influence of a presidential nominee in selecting his running-mate? Probably the best answer is that if the political situation at the convention will allow, his opinion will be decisive, otherwise merely influential.

THOMAS RILEY MARSHALL

The recipient of all this activity, Thomas Riley Marshall, the man of "very small calibre," was a native of Indiana, a lawyer and state governor. He had never engaged in the pursuit of public office prior to his nomination as governor in 1908. He confessed that he was then a compromise selection due to "the inability of the leading candidates to obtain a majority . . . in the Convention." Tirelessly stumping the state, he made 169 speeches, admitting also that his wife's view was more probably correct that it was one speech given 169 times. He accomplished the unusual feat of narrowly winning despite Taft's carrying the state for himself. Marshall gave the state an honest, efficient administration. He gained fame for the so-called "Tom Marshall Constitution," a liberal document which the state Supreme Court declared unconstitutional. Marshall felt that the court's decision was a "clear usurpation of authority," but did nothing. Re-nominated in 1910 he was comfortably returned for a second gubernatorial term and wrote a brother Democrat, Woodrow Wilson, essaying his first political job: "I welcome you into the company of governors who think that principles are worth maintaining." On account of his felicity for phrase-making, and his undoubted strength and popularity, a movement began early in 1911 to make Marshall Indiana's favorite son for the 1912 Democratic nomination.

Governor Marshall was serious in his pursuit of the presidential nomination. He once outlined his hopes and strategy to a friend: "I believe my chance lies in other persons being active and prominent candidates, and when they have exhausted their efforts in the convention, that it will turn to a conservative progressive such as I am known to be. I believe it to be better to not have any alliances with any faction of the party." In other words, he hoped that political lightning would strike him again, as it had first struck in the Indiana convention of 1908. When it did not, and Taggart did the next best thing to prevent a knock-out struggle, Marshall was momentarily irate. He "at first refused" to consider second place, "the salary was too small" ($12,000), but his wife's "tears . . . swayed" him to accept.

Marshall, like Hiram Johnson for the Bull Moose adherents, was considered by the press to be a good choice and was deemed "quite fitted" for the presidency. All in all the 1912 Democratic and Bull Moose tickets were straight-out liberal ones vying with the straight-out reactionary Taft-Sherman one of the Republican Party.

Although 1912 issues had been mainly of a domestic nature, the question of the revolution in Mexico left an unsolved problem that Wilson would have to face. Marshall received a letter from Taft's Ambassador to Mexico, Henry Lane Wilson (a fellow alumnus of Wabash College), proposing that the provisional government of Victoriana Huerta should be recognized. Marshall and Wilson discussed the matter and agreed on a non-intervention policy. The first public hint of this was made by Marshall in late February when he said "he personally did not believe that intervention was advisable at this time." This was shortly followed by the statement of "a close friend" of Wilson's in Congress that the President-elect "thought that intervention would mean war, a horror which must be avoided."

However, Marshall would not continue to operate in the heady atmosphere of international affairs after March 4. As he put it in his quaint book of *Recollections*, "Responsible for nothing and influential nowhere, I only stood on the sidelines and watched the Mexican situation develop." Between the lines it is clear that he was unsympathetic to Wilson's later shift of policy, that meant non-recognition and moral condemnation of the Huerta government. To Marshall the Monroe Doctrine meant that the United States as well as Europe was not to interfere with Latin-American governments. Since he also admitted that he "sought every occasion" to express his views to diplomats when he met them socially, it was little to be wondered Wilson had no use for him in foreign affairs thereafter.

In rare instances, Marshall resented that he was not consulted more by the President. Secretary of the Navy Josephus Daniels recalled that once when he went to the Vice-President's office to relay some request of Wilson, Marshall answered sharply, "I will perform the order, sir." Daniels was surprised at the tone from the usually affable Marshall and remembered later how he had emphasized the word "order."

The Vice-President's role in the Wilson administration was the normal one of smoothing the path for the White House in the upper chamber and of defending Wilson's policies before the country. As he put it: "I soon ascertained that I was of no importance to the administration beyond the duty of being loyal to it and ready, at any time, to act as a sort of pinch hitter . . . I reached the conclusion that I was too small to look dignified in a Prince Albert coat . . . I, therefore, chose . . . to acknowledge the insignificant influence of the office; to take it in a good-natured way; to be friendly and well-disposed to . . . friend and . . . foe alike; to be loyal to my chief and . . . not to be offensive to my associates; and . . . to deal justly with those over whom I was merely nominally presiding."

Marshall largely succeeded in his role, and ultimately became the most popular vice-president up to his time. He humanized the office and advertised it. Contemporaries felt he "was not a great man, but he was an excellent average man. . . . Men . . . repelled by genius would listen to Marshall, and he told them many a homely truth that they needed to hear."

However, some of his remarks were ill-received. The *Indianapolis Star* thought his public complaint of his poverty in bad taste: "He knew in the beginning what the emoluments of the position would be and, incidentally, that they would be greater than any income he had ever known . . . Mr. Marshall should talk less on the subject of his personal finances." He also was long hooted at for his radical suggestion that incomes should be taxed away above a level of $100,000 or so.

Yet, on the whole, Marshall's conservatism came to outweigh his progressivism. In this he bore a strong resemblance to a later Vice-President, John N. Garner (1933-41), although unlike the latter he avoided precipitating any crises. Marshall favored all the 1913-14 reform legislation except the Federal Trade Commission Act, which he felt "approached too close to regimentation." In a public statement at the end of 1913 he said that all needed legislation had been passed and that a breathing spell should now ensue: "There was no need for any anti-trust legislation at present." At the time, Wilson was announcing the necessity for pressing on to that field.

After 1913, Marshall chose silence as the better part of political

valor when party legislation he did not approve was pending. "Even
the Adamson Railway Labor Act (1916) brought no expression of his
deeply felt objection both to the provisions . . . and to the methods"
of its passage. His biographer, Charles M. Thomas, admits that
Marshall's later writings "show the full development of those conservative tendencies which McAdoo had observed in his association
with the Vice-President."

Marshall's manner of presiding in the Senate was also subjected
to liberal criticism in the beginning. McAdoo, speaking for confirmed
Wilsonians, felt he was too impartial and that he "should have
favored . . . his own party" wherever possible, as Sherman had so
recently done. Marshall's defense was that he was bound by oath to
administer the rules as they were and, if the rules were bad, they
should be changed by the Senate and not by the Vice-President. The
fact that Marshall stood on morally firm ground did not endear him
to the more conscienceless of the Democrats.

These varied dissatisfactions with the first-term Marshall were to
account largely for the unsuccessful movement to replace him in 1916.
Marshall sought to overcome this end by keeping open an epistolary
line to Wilson himself, avowing his loyalty. For example, at the close
of the 1914 session he wrote: "I am going . . . to Indiana, Missouri and
Colorado to tell in my own way the story and to help, if I can, heal
any dissensions in our ranks." The President replied that "The
pleasure of being associated with you grows as the months pass."
Marshall was at least spared the belated formal answers Vice-President
Roosevelt had received from McKinley.

Like Roosevelt, Marshall had come from a gubernatorial post and
he, too, was to be irked by the lack of patronage. Though he "gave
more than the ordinary amount of attention to getting jobs for friends
. . . Marshall could not get what he thought he was entitled to as
vice-president." McAdoo in the Treasury said: "He was a great job-
hunter for his friends. . . . I did the best I could . . . but he was
never satisfied."

Not all Wilsonians felt that Marshall should be renominated.
Added to those groups already mentioned was Henry Morgenthau
who, speaking for the banking interests allied with Jacob Schiff, felt
the Vice-President lacked "force." A movement began to build up
the Secretary of War for the post. McCombs' tart reaction to this
pre-convention boom was "the Wilson-McAdoo coterie . . . wanted
Baker because . . . [he] never made a move without Wilson's direction.
Furthermore Baker used classical English." As a professional politician, McCombs led the movement to retain some organizational con-

trol in the 1916 selections. The professionals (Tom Taggart, Charles F. Murphy, the boss of Tammany, Roger Sullivan of Illinois, and Governor James M. Cox of Ohio) opposed Baker and were "offended by . . . Wilson's idea of getting a candidate more to his liking as Vice President" and so combined to smash "the anti-Marshall plot."

McCombs was so anti-Wilson by 1916 that he admitted he would have liked to prevent his nomination if that had been possible but, failing that, the next best thing was to retain Marshall, for: "In my mind, at that very time, Marshall was superior to Wilson. If there were to be any succession by fate, we could not go very far wrong with Marshall."

Marshall superior to Wilson! This absurd judgment merely showed the extent to which passion had blinded the bosses of the Northern machines who resented their lack of influence in the White House.

It was quite clear, however, that Wilson would have a real fight on his hands in the St. Louis Convention if he attempted to drop Marshall. Accordingly, he disavowed any connection with the anti-Marshall movement. In a hastily penned note attached to a letter dated June 2, 1916 from Governor H. R. Fielder of New Jersey, who asked for a statement of preference, Wilson wrote: "I do not feel that I have any right to suggest anything on this head. The attitude of Mr. Marshall towards the administration has been loyal and generous in the extreme. He has given me every reason to admire and trust him." Since, as Ray Stannard Baker says, this was "as good as an order," Marshall was renominated by acclamation.

As for the Roosevelt Progressives and regular Republicans, they had both met at the same time in Chicago, but in different halls. The more militant Progressives wanted to nominate Roosevelt quickly and then leave the Republicans with the dilemma of choosing him too or facing 1912 again if they should refuse. George Perkins, Wall Street "angel" of the Bull Moosers and long-suspected by the more ardent among them, stalled off the Progressive nomination until after the Republican convention had picked Charles E. Hughes. Roosevelt then refused the Progressive nomination and by this and his subsequent backing of Hughes "killed the Progressive party." Vice-President Marshall quipped Roosevelt was "not leading his followers to Armageddon, but deserting them at Bull Moose Run." For better or for worse, the Republican Party had been re-united.

Like a breath from the past, former Vice-President Charles W. Fairbanks was nominated on the first ballot by what amounted to acclamation at the Republican Convention. He disclaimed that he had wanted the post but felt that since it was a true draft he could not refuse. He represented the same conservative elements that had dominated the Republican Party under McKinley and Taft and his selection indicated anew that, if circumstances required a liberal to head the ticket, the Old Guard would have its way in the vice-presidency.

The election of 1916 is notable in the history of the vice-presidency as being the only time that both nominees came from the same state. Indiana was particularly important that year for both senatorial seats were at stake and Republicans hoped to win them and gain a fighting chance to control the Senate.

By the middle of October Colonel Edward M. House, Wilson's "assistant president," began to worry about the outcome. He felt that if both New York and Indiana were lost, "the danger of defeat was real." Supposing defeat came, House felt it would be a calamity to have a repudiated administration remain in power for sixteen weeks pending the formal inauguration. He accordingly wrote the President: "If Hughes is elected—which God forbid—what do you think of asking both Lansing and Marshall to resign, appoint Hughes Secretary of State, and then resign yourself? This would be a patriotic thing to do. . . . [and] would save the situation from danger and embarrassment." To this startling suggestion both Secretary of State Robert Lansing (who had succeeded Bryan in 1915) and President Wilson agreed. Nothing is directly stated as to Marshall's views, but one infers that he would have acquiesced, for Marshall often stated that it was "my custom" to take "orders from my chief." House's project never had to be tested for, though both Indiana and New York were lost, the administration was re-elected. When the results were in, Marshall wired Wilson: "'Tis not so deep as a well nor so wide as a church door; but 'tis enough, 'twill serve."

Marshall was the first Vice-President re-elected since John C. Calhoun and the first to serve two terms under the same President since Monroe's administration. If his first term had been exciting enough for a man of his placid disposition, his second one was to be practically revolutionary. He was to be presented with situations almost unique in vice-presidential history with little in the way of precedent to guide him. While these new events and situations would make his incumbency miserable, he would grow simultaneously in public esteem and no longer face the editorial and senatorial barbs which had heretofore plagued him.

When the United States became a World War I belligerent, Marshall was a conscientious speaker, especially popular during the various

Liberty Loan campaigns. He loyally explained and defended the administration's policies.

Marshall was one of the first to be apprised of Wilson's plans on how the midterm 1918 elections were to be fought. Called on to open the Democratic State Convention at Indianapolis, he conferred with Wilson, as he put it, "to consult him whether I should not make a speech announcing that the only question before the American people was winning the war and standing behind the president. Should I not propose that both Democrats and Republicans nominate men pledged to these two objects and let the people make a choice. . . . I also suggested proposing to the Republican party to close up all political headquarters and to expend the money saved thereby in Red Cross and other war activities."

This radical solution was promptly rejected by Wilson. He told Marshall he "expected to issue a call shortly before the election for a Democratic Congress, and had no doubt that the people would give it to him because they had refused him nothing so far." Here the two men had changed their usual roles; Marshall the politician wanted to put the 1918 elections above politics; Wilson the idealist was out for a partisan campaign and victory. Marshall asked, "Is it your desire for me to make an old-fashioned Democratic speech at the convention?" He said: "Yes. I told him he was my commander-in-chief, and his orders would be obeyed."

Thus was a crucial decision taken. Marshall's approach might have averted the debacle that occurred in November and prevented the last half of Wilson's second term from being a nightmare for the administration. More important, Marshall's patriotic and non-partisan approach might have saved the League of Nations and allowed Wilson to organize the peace.

Meanwhile, Marshall carried out his assignment. At the state convention in June, he recalled how Roosevelt in 1898 had appealed to the people to support President McKinley at the polls. Roosevelt then had said a refusal to sustain the President would look to foreign nations like "a refusal to sustain the war, and the efforts of our Peace Commission to secure the fruits of the war." To Marshall, this was good advice. His shrewd move to quote the greatest living Republican in support of Wilson excited the White House. Joseph R. Tumulty, the President's secretary, felt it important enough to send an excerpt to Wilson, who asked that the whole speech of Roosevelt be looked up for whatever else it contained that might be useful. Marshall had scored a bull's eye, but its effect was dissipated by the October intervention of Wilson. The Vice-President felt "it was perfectly apparent" from then on that Wilson would have "a rocky road."

When Wilson decided to leave the country to attend the Paris Peace Conference, the Republicans had a working majority in both houses and he was in fact a repudiated man. But one reads the record in vain for any move by Colonel House to transfer power to the Republicans. There was a world to remake and neither man was primarily concerned with the implications of the partisan shift, aggravated after election by Wilson's failure to include among his entourage abroad any significant Republican members of the House or Senate.

Wilson's decision to go to Paris against a great deal of Democratic advice broke a precedent; he became the first President to leave the country. To earlier Presidents, this would have seemed highly improper. George Washington, for instance, in his New England tour of 1789 was careful not to touch any part of Rhode Island because, since it had not yet ratified the Constitution, it was "foreign soil."

The President's decision came as a complete surprise to Marshall. The first he heard about it was when the *New York Times* phoned him in Boston the night of the announcement (November 26, 1918). Taft's Attorney-General, George W. Wickersham, had already raised the question of whether Marshall would not properly be acting president while Wilson was abroad and the newspaper wanted the Vice-President's attitude. Apprised of all this by the press, Marshall in private "completely lost control" of his temper. He felt a "deep resentment" and thought the President had been "very unkind" not to have informed him beforehand. However, his wife soothed him back to equanimity and he was able to make proper replies to the pointed queries of the *Times*. Wilson, a few days later, came to visit Marshall. It was not in the former's nature to apologize, but one can believe that this rarity of a visit from him was the equivalent. The President had also another favor to ask his Vice-President. He wanted Marshall "to preside over the Cabinet" while he was abroad, the idea having been "concurred in by the Cabinet." With unspoken misgivings, the Vice-President consented.

Wilson left the country with his Secretary of State on December 4, 1918, and at a cabinet meeting on the 10th, the first Vice-President since John Adams in 1791 was present. Marshall read a statement in order that "my conduct may not be misunderstood nor misinterpreted." He wanted it clearly understood that he was present only "in obedience to a request," was "here informally and personally," and would "preside in an unofficial and informal way." Marshall was not at all convinced that he was doing right, and, lawyer that he was, disavowed any responsibility for what might ensue. He presided over such additional meetings as there were and, when in February Wilson returned and called a meeting of the Cabinet, the Vice-President was invited "as a special . . . courtesy."

Marshall felt the Vice-President was a "member of the legislative branch" and thus should not be engaged in the activities of an executive body. To the argument that he was a potential successor and thus should be informed of the President's policies, Marshall's rebuttal was: "A Vice-President might make a poor President, but he would make a much poorer one if he attempted to subordinate his own mind and views to carry out the ideas of a dead man." Marshall once said that if he had ever succeeded by accident "he would not" have announced "an intention to continue the Wilson policies" for "he would change many things."

Marshall might have expected that his closing years in the vice-presidential office would be routine and without surprises. He was to discover that the age of global strife was upsetting fixed patterns of existence everywhere, even in the vice-presidency. He was to be involved in situations not of his own making that were on the very shadowy frontiers of the Constitution. None of this would be pleasant to a man of his placid disposition.

When the Republican Senate showed no disposition to accept the Versailles Treaty as negotiated, Wilson took his case to the country. He wore himself out, fell ill and had to abandon his tour on September 26, 1919. A few days after his return to the White House he had a stroke of paralysis (October 2) that precipitated the second and more serious crisis relative to the applicability of the disability clause. A chain of communications was established that began with Secretary Tumulty who passed on what papers he felt needed action to Doctor Grayson, who passed on what he felt the President could safely know of to Mrs. Wilson, who presented them, if she thought proper, to the President for action. These channels also worked in reverse.

Since this procedure lasted well into 1920, it appears indisputable that Woodrow Wilson was disabled in both the physical and constitutional sense for a considerable period of time. As in Garfield's time, the pertinent constitutional clause requiring the accession of the Vice-President had become applicable.

At the beginning of the illness, Mrs. Wilson seems to have contemplated the President's resigning. She implied that Dr. Francis X. Dercum, "the great nerve specialist of Philadelphia," told her it was not necessary.

Dercum, after his examination, informed Mrs. Wilson that recovery

"could not be hoped for . . . unless the President were released from
every disturbing problem." Mrs. Wilson protested the impossibility
of this treatment for a President "whom the country looks to . . . as
the leader. . . . Had he better not resign, let Mr. Marshall succeed
. . . and he himself get that complete rest that is so vital to his life
. . . 'No,' the Doctor said, '. . . For Mr. Wilson to resign would have
a bad effect on the country, and a serious effect on our patient. He
has . . . made his promise . . . to get the Treaty ratified. . . . If he
resigns, the greatest incentive to recovery is gone; and as his mind is
clear as crystal he can still do more with even a maimed body than
any one else.' "

Doctor Dercum was here mixing politics with medicine and presum-
ing to treat the country's health as well as Wilson's. At any rate,
Mrs. Wilson became a sort of acting President. While admitting the
seriousness of the situation for those who said they must see the
President, Mrs. Wilson refused, saying "I carried out the directions of
the doctors. . . . Wilson was first my beloved husband . . . after that
he was the President of the United States." All of which was perfectly understandable in a wife, but to the nation and its people,
Woodrow Wilson was first of all President.

Since the implied basis of the decision to continue Wilson as President was that his resignation might prove fatal to him, it is interesting
to note that when he was informed that the Treaty had failed of ratification on November 19, 1919, he stated: "All the more reason I must
get well and try again to bring this country to a sense of its great
opportunity and greater responsibility."

The "palace regency" under the generalship of Mrs. Wilson told
only selected cabinet officials what the specific trouble was. It never
officially informed the Vice-President or the public.

On the day after the stroke Secretary of State Lansing notified the
Cabinet that there would be an extraordinary meeting on October 6th
"to consider the situation." At it, Lansing said it was necessary to
decide whether the Cabinet should "continue to carry on the government—that there was nothing to guide us as to who should decide
the question of the ability of the President to discharge the duties
of his office." It was decided to consult Grayson. He stated the
President was suffering "from a nervous breakdown, from indigestion
and a depleted system." The situation was curious. Certain members of the Cabinet on that October 6th knew exactly what was wrong
with Wilson and others did not and were not to know. Grayson
added that the President had been much annoyed when he had heard

a cabinet meeting was being held "without a call from him." No decision was arrived at as to what to do.

About this same time Lansing made another effort to implement the disability clause of the Constitution. He suggested, Tumulty writes, "that in view of the incapacity of the President we should arrange to call in the Vice-President." Tumulty "coldly" answered that "the Constitution is not a dead letter with the White House." When Tumulty asked Lansing "who should certify to the disability," the latter "intimated that that would be a job for either Doctor Grayson or myself." Tumulty's loyalty to Wilson was fierce and unquestioning. He spoke bitterly of the attempt to supersede Wilson while he was "lying . . . on the broad of his back." But that, of course, was precisely the point of the disability clause, that *because* he was on his back with paralysis he should be replaced under the Constitution. Tumulty then told Lansing "if anybody outside of the White House circle attempted to certify to the President's disability, . . . Grayson and I would stand together and repudiate it."

This ended the effort in the Cabinet to ensure the continued uninterrupted functioning of executive government. The Secretary of State paid dearly for these moves and for continuing to call Cabinet meetings. He was rebuked by letter by President Wilson on February 7, 1920 for his most serious breach of "the Constitutional system." Lansing's resignation followed.

On December 4, 1919, the Senate Foreign Relations Committee created a subcommittee to interview the President. Though apparently to confer on Mexican affairs, it was "really to find out if possible the extent of . . . incapacity." The Senators emerged satisfied "that his mind is vigorous and active." Finally, Colonel House—no longer inside the White House circle—wrote the President to resign his office "using ill-health as the excuse." This, he felt, would give the Versailles Treaty a better chance to be ratified and would "prove that personal ambition" was not the President's motive. House's letter was never acknowledged and it proved to be the last communication that ever passed between them.

Wilson slowly recovered to the point of being able to go out riding occasionally. He met his Cabinet on April 13, 1920 for the first time since his illness and quite regularly thereafter, but he never recovered his old vigor nor complete use of his left arm. He seems to have been a little out of touch with reality for the rest of his term. Wilson's retirement from public view aroused congressional attention. Four measures were introduced on the question of implementing "disability" but they never got out of the House Judiciary Committee. One viewed the question as requiring a constitutional amendment and thus proposed empowering the Supreme Court to determine disability when requested by a concurrent resolution of Congress. It also provided that if Congress were not in session, the Vice-President upon the Cabinet's recommendation could call it into special session. The other measures sought to handle the matter by legislation, one by giving the fact-finding job to the Supreme Court on call by either House and, by its certification either alone or again on call, to determine whether inability had been removed. The final two measures made the Cabinet the most competent judge of disability; one of them even defined inability as illness for thirty days or absence from the continental Unitel States for a like period. However, nothing definite was done, and the matter of how the disability clause operated was still unsolved when President Eisenhower fell ill in 1955.

During Wilson's illness, Marshall tried to thread his way equably. Approaching the Secretary of Agriculture on October 5, 1919, he expressed his "regret that he was being kept in the dark about the President's condition. . . . that he ought immediately to be informed." He then confided under emotional stress that "it would be a tragedy for him to assume the duties of President, at best; and that it would be equally a tragedy for the people; that he knew many men who knew more about the affairs of the government than he did; and that it would be especially trying for him if he had to assume the duties without warning." It would be a tragedy for him to succeed because many men "knew more about . . . affairs" than he, yet he had already rejected the plan of sitting in the cabinet and thus overcoming that lack. While not afraid to succeed, he did not want any more surprises and did not want to take over "without warning."

Perhaps it was Houston who got the "palace regency" to send indirect word to the Vice-President of Wilson's real condition. At any rate, a newspaper correspondent of the Baltimore *Sun*, J. Fred Essary, was commissioned by the White House for this purpose. The reporter "entered the Vice-President's office, sat beside the desk" and told him that Wilson's illness was such that "the President might die at any hour." Throughout, "Marshall sat speechless, staring at his hands." Essary finished, went to the door, and left the Vice-President who never once spoke or "even looked up."

Unlike the previous occasions of illness when both Arthur and Roosevelt were periodically informed through official sources of the condition of the ailing Chief Executive, this is the only time of record that Vice-President Marshall was approached. Moreover, the channel was an unofficial emissary, whose word, if necessary, could be repudiated should the episode be publicized by him or Marshall. The inner circle at the White House had canvassed all angles of the situation to prevent nominal power from falling from the paralyzed hands of Wilson.

Marshall was gradually to get used to the idea that he might succeed by death, but he resolutely refused to fall in with any of the proposals to succeed by inability. Unidentified Senators of both parties tried to persuade him "to assume the presidency." One such group of "four leading Republican Senators informed Marshall that he could have the support of the Republican majority" if he did so. But Marshall had no taste for crisis, nor could he know whether the President's disability was total and permanent. Mrs. Marshall says he once told her: "I could throw this country into civil war, but I won't." On one occasion he did go to the White House to see Wilson, but he never got beyond the petticoat president who refused either to admit him to the President's room or to discuss anything fundamental with him. Thus was he denied access to the facts on which he could base an intelligent course of conduct.

Thereafter, Marshall merely presided in the Senate. He once confessed to his secretary, Mark Thistlethwaite, why he had been publicly silent on the disability question and the various proposed solutions. He said he "would assume the presidency only upon a resolution of Congress and the approbation in writing of Mrs. Wilson and of the President's physician. . . . I am not going to seize the place and then have Wilson—recovered—come around and say 'get off, you usurper.'"

There the matter was to rest. Marshall finished out his term without ever hearing a word "from Woodrow Wilson after that day" he had tried to visit him.

Marshall, indeed, was now a harassed man. He could find no peace even in presiding over the Senate. Wilson's illness coincided with the long, tedious debate on the League and the Treaty. Feeling was intense both on the floor and in the public gallery and Marshall was at his wits' end trying to keep order. He often had to rap the gavel, warn the galleries, call on the doorkeepers to perform their function and threaten to clear the hall (which, however, he never did).

Unlimited debate was a traditional right of the Senate, with its corollary, the filibuster. When the Armed Merchant Ship bill was talked to death in 1917 at the close of the 64th Congress, the Senate finally altered its Rules to allow cloture. On November 15, 1919—two and a half years after its adoption—the Senate voted cloture for the first time on the Versailles Treaty debate. Accordingly, Thomas

Marshall once more faced an unprecedented situation. At first he was successful in piloting the Senate along the path of closing debate prior to a vote on the various ratification resolutions.

On the 19th the Senate was ready to vote on Lodge's resolution as a whole. The crisis of the whole debate was at hand, and the Vice-President now had to play the role planned for him in Democratic strategy. "The Democratic senators would unite to vote down the treaty with the attached Lodge reservations. Then through a favorable though questionable ruling by Vice-President Marshall, they would carry a vote to reconsider, and move for the treaty without reservations or with the Hitchcock (Wilson) interpretative reservations . . . This scheme would work if enough 'mild reservationists' and others came over to make a two-thirds vote. But if it did not work, then there would be deadlock, and the heat of public opinion (so Wilson hoped) would beat so . . . on . . . reservationists that they would bolt to the Democrats."

Marshall loyally played his part, but it was to be of no avail. Three times did he rule in accordance with the plan, but three times the Senate overruled him on appeal. As Professor Bailey has pointed out, the Democrats were: "taking much more than a chance in counting on favorable rulings by Vice President Marshall. The presiding officer, no matter how sympathetic, could be overruled by a simple majority vote—and the Republicans commanded such a vote." With the Treaty and the League rejected out of hand, the Senate adjourned *sine die* at 11:10 p.m.; no one was more weary than Vice-President Marshall.

Bailey's judgment on this fiasco was that the greatest tragedy was that Wilson did not die "that night on the platform in Pueblo," Colorado, in September 1919. For then "Much of the partisanship would have faded, because Wilson as a third-term threat would be gone, and Marshall . . . was not to be feared . . . [he] probably would have recognized the need for compromise and . . . have worked for some reconciliation of . . . points of view." There can be no doubt that Marshall would have so acted — and perhaps succeeded.

CHAPTER 8

Spokesman of Normalcy

When Vice-President Marshall adjourned the Senate after its refusal to accept the Treaty of Versailles, it marked the end of an era. The country was or seemed to be utterly tired of crusading both at home and abroad. It had been agitated at home since the dawn of the twentieth century by Bryanism, muckraking, the Square Deal, Insurgency, Bull Moose Progressivism and the New Freedom. More recently, it had been harnessed to a crusade abroad "to make the world safe for democracy," to engage in "a war to end wars." When it seemed that, under the Treaty, its world responsibilities would continue indefinitely, it rebelled and decided to stay home.

The new mood of the United States was most specifically illustrated in the party situation in 1920. The great exponent of Progressivism within the Republican party, Theodore Roosevelt, was dead. The Democratic national and later international saviour, Woodrow Wilson, was physically finished, a hollow shell of his former vigorous self, speaking fitfully of "a solemn referendum" on the League in 1920 which was never to be. The Progressives and Insurgents were now older, disillusioned, still going through the motions, but lacking the fire and sense of dedication that had once been theirs.

The Democrats, meeting in San Francisco on June 28th, began to show those divisions that would dissipate their strength through three national elections. The South and the Middle West (under McAdoo and Bryan) wanted to make Prohibition the cardinal issue; the big city delegations of the North (exemplified by Boss Murphy of Tammany) wished to make the party "wet." As crown prince of the Wilson forces, McAdoo was also the symbol for the internationalism explicit in the Treaty and the League. However, the northern city bosses sensed the public's indifference and wanted to avoid the League as an issue. The platform that emerged was essentially a straddle of both the League and prohibition, and the ultimate choice, Governor James M. Cox, progressive Governor of Ohio, was a compromise between the McAdoo-Palmer nominations on the one hand and New York's Governor Alfred E. Smith on the other. It was the shift of Smith's strength (about 100 votes) on the 44th ballot that had led to

Cox's selection. Thus Cox's support came, in Josephus Daniels' words, mainly "from delegates anything but Wilsonian, including nearly all the city political . . . bosses."

In other words, those elements which in 1916 had had to fight to prevent Wilsonians from replacing Marshall in the second place, succeeded four years later—or so they thought—in preventing the naming of a Wilsonian for the first. Franklin D. Roosevelt was given the second place on the ticket to appease the defeated group. As a New Yorker with a magic name, who was personable, young (38 years old), and a veteran of the Wilson administrations, he was a natural choice.

The future, however, rested in the hands of the Republicans who had already met in Chicago (June 8th to 12th). The leading contenders were General Leonard Wood, deemed the heir of Theodore Roosevelt's policies; Governor Frank O. Lowden of Illinois, a safe and sane middle-of-the-roader, and the 1912 Bull Moose vice-presidential nominee Hiram Johnson, the personification of "radical" progressivism. Johnson had no chance himself because of the dominant conservatism of the Convention, but he had the power to destroy Lowden's chances.

Probably none of these leading contenders could have been nominated anyway, for the convention was dominated by a Senate junta under the leadership of Lodge. On the floor of the Senate, they had fought against "executive domination"; at the Republican 1920 convention, they sought to name one of themselves, and thus end the primacy of the President over the legislature. The Senatorial clique wanted "to nominate a man who, as one of them cynically said, would, when elected, sign whatever bills the Senate sent him and not send bills to the Senate to pass."

Their choice fell on Senator Warren G. Harding of Ohio, handsome, affable, tractable. In the famous "smoke-filled room" of the Blackstone Hotel in Chicago, the selection was agreed on and put through next day. However, Harding's selection was not the hurried affair it so often is made to appear. Mrs. Longworth recalled that in December 1919 Senator Lodge told her "he thought the nominee would probably be Harding." While the convention was in progress, Johnson had been approached by emissaries of all the candidates to take the second place, but refused. Since he was polling up to 150 votes he still had hopes he might be a compromise choice, but if he was not, he preferred to remain in the Senate. As he said regarding one such offer: "There isn't a thing under the sun that I haven't been offered during the past week. It is singular that the very gentlemen who have been equally insistent on my taking the Vice-Presidency had been equally insistent that I was utterly unfit to be President, although there is only a heart-beat between the two." Johnson well-appreciated the senselessness of concentrating all attention on the presidential choice and then filling the second place with careless abandon.

The senatorial junta finally settled on another member of their august body, Irvine H. Lenroot of Wisconsin, for the second place. Lenroot would give the proper shading of progressivism and withal would be no maverick. For though he had started as a follower of La Follette, he had broken with him, and had maintained a "sturdy liberalism" of his own within the framework of the Republican organization. Unapprised of his selection for the second place, which he "did not want any part of," he was put into nomination by fellow Senator Medill McCormick of Illinois. But the Senators were to be disappointed. In an unexpected revolt against dictation, the convention nominated the Governor of Massachusetts, Calvin Coolidge, on the first ballot. Coolidge himself explained his selection in these simple words:

"The convention of 1920 was largely under the domination of a coterie of United States Senators. They maneuvered it into adopting a platform and nominating a President in ways that were not satisfactory to a majority of the delegates. When the same forces undertook for a third time to dictate the action of the convention in naming a Vice-President, the delegates broke away from them and literally stampeded to me.

". . . I received about three-quarters of all the votes cast.

". . . I was pleased to accept, and it was especially agreeable to be associated with Senator Harding, whom I knew well and liked."

While Coolidge's own version is basically accurate, it is incomplete. To be sure, not since Garfield was nominated in 1880 had there been an uprising so entirely from the floor. But it was an uprising hoped for and planned by Coolidge's backers, led by Boss Murray Crane of Massachusetts who ruled the non-Lodge dominated areas of the State, and the Boston merchant, Frank W. Stearns, a fellow alumnus with Coolidge of Amherst College.

Having coralled "two or three other Amherst men," Stearns proceeded to have printed during the early part of 1920 "seventy thousand copies of a book called *Have Faith In Massachusetts*." This publication was a collection of Coolidge's speeches designed to dramatize his plodding career and capitalize on his brief appearance in the national limelight when he had so acted in the Boston police strike of 1919 as to give the impression he was a strong man. His statement, "There is no right to strike against the public safety by anyone, any-

where, anytime," was hailed as the ultimate in labor relations by a
nation suffering the dislocations and wage-struggles of the transition
from war to peace, magnified by the foolish fear of Bolshevism. The
book of speeches was scattered broadside "to every important leader
of public opinion in the Republican party," including every possible
delegate to the forthcoming convention. The name of Coolidge would
not be unknown at that meeting if Stearns could prevent it!

Coolidge had been proposed for the presidency along with many
others, but this was never meant to be taken too seriously. Calvin
Coolidge had always made one cautious step upward after the other
and his backers were content that his name had been entered at all.
They were interested in the second place for him.

Going to the offices of R. R. Donnelly and Sons with a copy of
Have Faith In Massachusetts and a new photograph early one morning, the spokesman for the Coolidge group said: "We want this in
book form, with an illustration made from this photograph . . . bound
in limp leather. But it must be delivered to every delegate and alter-
nate by 11:00 o'clock tomorrow morning. Can you do it?" The company made the printing and delivery on schedule and added the personal touch that each recipient had his own name embossed on the
cover.

Modern advertising principles of repetition and mass distribution
account as much as anything for the selection of Calvin Coolidge.
During Senator Medill McCormick's speech nominating Lenroot, he
was interrupted at every pause by shouts of "Coolidge." But the
culminating episode was the strategic bawling of Wallace McCamant
of Oregon "who climbed on a chair and began speaking"; then, being
ignored, "clamored for recognition," and finally managed to shout the
single word, Coolidge, which created pandemonium.

It is ironic that, whereas the main efforts in both 1920 conventions
had been put into presidential selection, it would be the two after-
thought vice-presidential nominees who would loom large in history.
Calvin Coolidge was to be the symbol of "normalcy" and "business
civilization" in the next decade, and Franklin D. Roosevelt, when
older, more serious, steeled by his poliomyelitis and resulting partial
paralysis, would personify the return to domestic reform in the
thirties and international responsibility in the forties.

Harding, as President, would be remembered as an unworthy, weak
man, suitable as a poker companion, but hardly qualified for the
exacting role of the presidency. Illustrative of his dependency on
others to do his thinking for him, was the occasion during the campaign when, in making a speech, after two stumbling attempts at

reading a puzzling sentence, he said aloud: "Well, I never saw this before. I didn't write this speech and I don't believe what I just read." It was little wonder that he was advised to wage a front porch McKinley-type campaign and leave the burden of carrying the message of the "return to normalcy" to Taft, Lodge, Root, Hughes and others.

As for Calvin Coolidge, Republican politicians were not sold on his vote-getting qualities. They saw in him a man who "had never been out of New England; had never slept in a Pullman berth, knew no national politicians, had no sense of the country that comes from even New York or Washington contacts with the country and was as cold and as dumb as an oyster. As a popular speaker in the West the party managers felt that Coolidge would fail. They were correct. . . . Coolidge went to Minnesota and the crowd left the meeting. . . . [The managers] sent him campaigning in the South, talking to the hillmen of Tennessee and of Georgia, the unschooled poor white Appalachian cousins of the sturdy Green Mountain boys."

Thus was Vice-President and President-to-be Calvin Coolidge shunted from the main roads to the back roads while Harding himself was kept at home. For whatever it may signify, Tennessee was won by the Republicans but whether this was due to Coolidge's tour there, no one could say. In all he had spoken in "about a dozen states" as he put it, pointing out mainly "the wish of our party to have our country associated with other countries in advancing human welfare. . . . This was not intended as a subterfuge to win votes, but as a candid statement of party principles." By such "candid" statements was the Harding-Coolidge ticket to be swept into office in the landslide of 1920.

Meanwhile, Franklin Roosevelt went to Columbus, Ohio, in July "to discuss the character of the campaign" with Cox. It was then that Cox informed him that "he was going to see President Wilson the next week." Roosevelt, still Assistant Secretary of the Navy, went along too and, on July 18, the famous meeting occurred from which came Cox's courageous decision to make League entry an issue in the campaign. Roosevelt recalled the scene:

"We saw the President in a wheel chair, his left shoulder covered with a shawl which concealed his left arm . . . paralyzed, and the Governor [Cox] said . . . 'He is a very sick man.'

". . . [Wilson's] utter weakness was startling and I noticed tears in the eyes of Cox. A little later Cox said, 'Mr. President, we are going to be a million per cent with you, and your administration, and that means the League of Nations.' "

Wilson answered, "I am very grateful," and the meeting was over. The Democratic nominees left through the Executive offices where Cox, sitting down at one of the desks, took paper and pencil and "there he wrote the statement that committed us to making the League the paramount issue."

Roosevelt's acceptance speech summarized the issues of the campaign. He lashed out at the already publicized "back to normalcy" slogan and denied that that was the people's wish. Instead, asserting that the age of reform was not over but merely interrupted by the war, he called for the nation to "go forward or founder." That speech was a prescient overture to the essence of the 1932 and 1936 F.D.R. Was there ever a more vivid contrast in vice-presidential candidates than in 1920! Though the American people did not know it, their future was before them that summer in the persons of Coolidge and Roosevelt.

In the last election before radio, Roosevelt — who was to become noted as the first American politician to acquire a radio voice and personality—campaigned by train. In all, he made about a thousand speeches and numerous impromptu talks. The returns showed that the Democratic party had undergone its worst defeat since the Civil War. F.D.R. wrote Stephen T. Early, who had just received a new assignment as congressional correspondent of the Associated Press: "One of us at least has landed in the Senate Chamber, though I think your job will be more interesting than the one I was after. At any rate it is fine to know that the A.P. has you to cover the story of that Den of Thieves. . . . Perhaps in this life things have to be evened up in the end, at least you will have nice 'chatty' times with V.P. Coolidge. . . . Thank the Lord we are both comparatively youthful!"

Harding had plans, though somewhat nebulous ones, to increase vice-presidential responsibilities. After the usual conference between party standard-bearers, he issued a press summary which said: "The Governor and I each served as Lieutenant-Governors in our state, and . . . have learned . . . how possible it is for a second official . . . to be . . . helpful . . . in a party administration. I think that the Vice-President should be more than a mere substitute in waiting. . . . I wish him to be . . . a helpful part of a Republican administration. The country needs the counsel and the becoming participation in government of such men as Calvin Coolidge." These were excellent sentiments, but what did they mean? How could the Vice-President do more to be "helpful" than others before him had done? How was he to give "counsel" in any different way than the usual one of conferring to the extent the Chief Executive would permit? Did "becoming participation in government" mean his active participation in the Cabinet? The statement could mean much or little, but was generally thought to be a belated nod of approval at the action of the Republican convention in selecting a man who had not been "officially" presented. Harding reverted to the idea on July 10, when in one of his front porch talks, he said he would, if elected, bring his running-mate "into the councils" because of his "experience as an executive." As a general proposition, Harding felt "the Vice-President can be a most effective agency in keeping the executive officers in touch with the legislative branch of the Government."

On December 17, Coolidge again visited the President-elect and was orally invited to sit in with the Cabinet. It was at this meeting too that "We discussed at length the plans for his administration. The members of his Cabinet were considered. . . . The policies he wished to adopt . . . reducing taxes and revising the tariff were referred to more casually."

Three days after the inauguration, memorable only for Coolidge's inaugural speech to the Senate (the briefest on record for such an occasion), he received the following formal invitation from President Harding: "I have asked the Members of the Cabinet to meet with me for the first time on Tuesday morning at eleven o'clock, and I shall be very greatly pleased if you can arrange to meet with us. Several months ago I said publicly that I thought the Vice President ought to be called into the conferences of the official family of the Administration and I very much hope you will find it possible and agreeable to accept. It has seemed to me that the second official of the Republic could add materially to the fullness of his service in this way. I am quite well aware that there is no constitutional or statutory provision for such participation, but cabinet councils are wholly of an advisory nature in any event and I am sure your presence and your suggestions will be welcome to the members of the Cabinet, and I know that they will be gratefully received by me. I shall look forward to your coming with a very great satisfaction and I hope you will find it possible to arrange to be present on all such meetings."

On that Tuesday morning, March 8, 1921, the new policy of "activating" the vice-presidency went into effect and Coolidge took his position at the foot of the table, next after the Secretary of Labor. True to his own hitherto private views, ex-Vice-President Marshall publicly announced that Coolidge was making a mistake. If so, it was one he would continue for over two years until June 15, 1923, the last Cabinet meeting before Harding's ill-fated Northwest trip. Concerning that experience, Coolidge later wrote: "If the Vice-President is a

man of discretion and character so that he can be relied upon to act
as a subordinate in that position, he should be invited to sit with the
Cabinet, although some of the Senators, wishing to be the only advisers of the President, do not look on that proposal with favor. He
may not help much in its deliberations, and only on rare occasions
would he be a useful contact with the Congress [House], although his
advice on the sentiment of the Senate is of much value, but he should
be in the Cabinet because he might become President and ought to be
informed on the policies of the Administration. He will not learn all
of them. Much went on in the departments under President Harding,
as it did under me, of which the Cabinet had no knowledge. But he
will hear much and learn how to find out more if it ever becomes
necessary. My experience in the Cabinet was of supreme value to
me when I became President."

It was commonly agreed that Coolidge was not voluble in the
Cabinet sessions; in fact, "never once in two years, except when some
one asked a definite question of the Vice-President, did Coolidge open
his mouth." This did not mean that he was stupid or overawed at his
role. Coolidge was a listener and an absorber, but "no innocent. He
could not have sat in the Cabinet and in the Senate . . . for two years
without sensing what was going on under the Harding administration.
. . . Why then . . . did not Vice-President Coolidge act?" The only
possible answer is that Coolidge was neither a crusader nor an activist;
he could not be expected to be one in this situation. All he could do
short of resigning was to keep his own skirts clean and await developments. When he says in his *Autobiography* "much went on in the departments . . . of which the Cabinet had no knowledge," perhaps he
was pleading ignorance. At any rate, he walked in the sun during
those years, the incorruptible amid the corrupted, in the Harding
administration, but not of it. His knowledge of current affairs was
necessarily increased by his auditing the sessions; his acquaintances
with the officers of the Departments rendered the transition from silent
member to leader of the cabinet easier.

Far more important than the official cabinet was the "poker cabinet"
of Harding's time. The Vice-President was not a member of the Ohio
Gang, that influential brotherhood with its hierarchy of regulars and
associates. Nor was his counsel sought in any real emergency. When,
after the mid-term elections made alarming inroads on Republican
majorities, Harding called "a secret emergency meeting of trusted advisers to bring about better teamwork," Coolidge was not invited.
Only the Senatorial junto and the House leaders were included for
this war council.

To a man of such frugal habits as Coolidge there were compensations. He, who still rented a two-family attached house in Northampton, Massachusetts, could luxuriate in his $12,000 a year salary, free automobile with chauffeur, secretary, page, clerk and private telegraph operator. He enjoyed the additional perquisites of a room in the Senate Office Building and one in the Capitol off the Senate Chamber. Practical man that he was, Coolidge desired but one additional emolument, a residence. In his opinion, the Vice-President "is not lacking in dignity but he has no fixed position. The great office should have a settled and permanent habitation and a place, irrespective of the financial ability of its temporary incumbent. While I was glad to be relieved of the responsibility of a public establishment . . . it is a duty the second officer of the nation should assume. It would be much more in harmony with our theory of equality if each Vice-President held the same position in the Capital City."

For a time it seemed that Coolidge would get his wish. In 1922 a home was offered the Government, but Congress refused to accept it. The Vice-Presidents were to remain responsible for their living quarters.

Coolidge, like other Vice-Presidents, had to take part in the Washington social whirl. This was practically a nightly occurrence and often involved dining out. The social elite were treated accordingly to a rare sort of social lion who sat silently through meals, impervious to persiflage and small talk. In answer to one hostess' remark about the Vice-President's "hard lot in having to attend so many official dinners," the practical-minded Coolidge responded "Have to eat somewhere."

As a presiding officer, Coolidge was competent and laconic. Having a wide political background that included most of the elective offices in city and state, legislative bodies were not strange to him, and he experienced little difficulty in discharging his narrowly defined duties. Press reporters thought that the parliamentary aide at his elbow knew scarcely more than the Vice-President about the *Rules*. His impassiveness was illustrated when, on one occasion, Senators McCumber and Reed were yelling at each other, other Senators were crying "order, order," and visitors in the galleries were contributing to the confusion. The parliamentarian pleaded "Use your gavel! Use your gavel—restore order." Coolidge sat calmly watching the fracas, and to a repetition of the plea, answered solemnly: "Yes I shall if they get excited."

Coolidge had been installed as presiding officer only four months when he earned the undying distrust of the nascent farm bloc. Post-war reconversion for the American farmer was a painful process that led throughout the "Golden Twenties" to a rural clamor for assistance. However, the congressional representatives of the agricultural areas would make small headway in a government controlled by industrial groups and the urban middle-class. The first concrete farm relief legislation of the "normalcy" period was sponsored by Senator George W. Norris, the progressive Republican. It sought to give relief to Europe by diminishing "the paralyzing surpluses that depressed farm prices and created a very critical emergency for farm people." The Administration, pressed by the shipping interests, drew up a substitute measure that provided no real solution. This new measure was to be introduced by Senator Frank B. Kellogg at a strategic moment in the debate.

Tipped off as to the plan, Norris went to Coolidge and asked him to recognize Senator Ransdell first when the Senate next reverted to the bill. Coolidge agreed, according to Norris, and the latter primed Ransdell to be ready and on his feet to demand recognition. But at the time appointed, Coolidge departed from the Senate and turned the chair over to Charles Curtis of Kansas, stalwart of stalwarts. With Ransdell "clamoring at the top of his lungs for recognition," Curtis kept saying: "The Chair recognizes the Senator from Minnesota." Kellogg of Minnesota was not even standing and it was only after being called on three times that, confused or absent-minded, he rose to introduce the substitute administration measure that killed the chances of the Norris bill. Relates William Allen White: "Vice President Coolidge, who had remained outside the chamber while Curtis played his hand, coolly appeared . . . and sat him down . . . This marked Coolidge for Progressive wrath."

Norris ultimately collapsed from his efforts to retrieve the situation in the age before air-conditioning. The July heat and his intensity of effort sent him to the hospital. Looking back after a long, fruitful legislative life, Norris would say in 1946, "the defeat of that legislation was the greatest single disappointment of all of my public service in Congress."

Coolidge's comments on presiding in Senate obliquely referred to the agricultural bill affair: "The President of the Senate can and does exercise a good deal of influence over its deliberations. The Constitution gives him the power to preside, which is the power to recognize whom he will. That often means that he decides what business is to be taken up and who is to have the floor for debate at any specific time."

In these quiet ways, more influenced than influential, Coolidge spent

two years as Vice-President. He had "made little headway in political
Washington, and outside . . . in the country he had attracted no
interest."

In the summer of 1923, this atypical Vice-President, summering at
his father's Vermont home, succeeded to the presidency. During the
night of August 2nd, a telegram arrived informing him of the President's death in San Francisco, followed by one from Attorney-General
Daugherty asking him to take the oath at once.

In the most dramatic incident of Coolidge's life, he took the oath
in a farmhouse by oil lamp, repeating the words after his father, John
Coolidge, notary public of Vermont, who officiated. In after years
when Coolidge was sitting for a portrait, the artist, at wits' end, was
trying to find some facial expression to record. Hoping to catch the
President off guard, he asked him what was the first thought that
flashed through his mind when he received the news that he was now
President. Coolidge's answer, uttered with no change in dead-pan
expression, was "My first thought was that I could swing it."

With the incidents of Coolidge's first term we are not concerned,
but we are concerned with his concept of the task. Unlike Theodore
Roosevelt who conceived of himself succeeding just as if elected,
Coolidge felt "it is a sound rule that when the President dies in office
it is the duty of his successor for the remainder of that term to maintain the counsellors and policies of the deceased President." Much
more then than his predecessors by accident did Coolidge accept the
"caretaker" status of succession. This, probably unconsciously, laid
the groundwork for that interpretation of the famous 1927 message
"I do not choose to run for President in 1928" which claimed that his
reelection then would not violate the two-term tradition because he
had been only the administrator of Harding's presidential term from
August 1923 to March 1925. If this was the true meaning behind his
1927 withdrawal, Coolidge would be posthumously vindicated by the
ratification of the 22nd Amendment in 1951 which considers succession for a period of less than two years to be not a term and thus
allows a Vice-President-successor to be eligible for two full terms.

Coolidge had a tactical approach of his own to presidential decisions. Discussing some matter on which he had been urged to "take a
position," Coolidge said: "I wouldn't take it. The situation had not
developed. Theodore Roosevelt was always getting himself in hot
water before he had to . . . Public administrators would get along
better if they would restrain the impulse to butt in or be dragged into
trouble. They should remain silent until an issue is reduced to its
lowest terms, until it boils down into something like a moral issue."

In other words, his "action" in the 1919 Boston police strike was a good enough method as a principle. The Coolidge method, basically, was to sit tight when problems loomed ahead, hoping that most of them would be dissolved or shunted away from his path.

At least the theory was unique, and apparently successful, for Coolidge prosperity became a byword and "Keep Cool with Coolidge" satisfied the American electorate in 1924, when with seeming effortlessness, he repeated Theodore Roosevelt's precedent of winning a term in his own right. He saved the Republican Party from the follies of the careless Harding and distracted public attention so that the party could enjoy eight more years of presidential control. Normalcy meant passivity and quietude during which business could operate in a favorable political climate and Coolidge was in perfect harmony with the dominant political and economic trend. He was the politician without an organization whom the rank and file wanted and whom the Old Guard had had to take in expiation for their sins.

CHAPTER 9

Last of the Old Guard

Only ten months before the Republican National Convention was to meet in 1924, Calvin Coolidge became the sixth successor by death. Even Theodore Roosevelt had had over three years in the White House to build political power and be the unopposed choice of his party. In addition, Roosevelt had a colorful personality and a mania for action. With none of these advantages, Coolidge nevertheless was quietly and unanimously nominated in 1924 for a term in his own right.

Alice Longworth, visiting the White House after the succession, had noted "the atmosphere was as different as a New England front parlor is from a back room in a speakeasy." That explained as well as anything why Coolidge suited Americans in 1924. By being his own puritanical self, he gave the impression that he was cleaning up the Augean stables, and the country applauded him. The political leaders (the Senate junto of 1920) had "for an extremely brief period . . . hopes . . . that there would be an open field for the nomination. The extraordinary way in which the country took to Mr. Coolidge closed the door." And at the Cleveland Convention affairs were so cut and dry that only three days were required to complete all business. Coolidge controlled the convention in every respect except the vice-presidential selection. In a curious inversion of the delegates' revolt that had resulted in his own selection in 1920, Coolidge's spokesman in 1924, William M. Butler of Massachusetts, was unable to put across the President's choice—William E. Borah, who was to serve as foil for Coolidge's conservatism.

Borah was complete anathema to the old-line leaders whose favorites were Lowden and Curtis. Though Lowden had insisted he did not want the second place, the convention nominated him on the second ballot. This official nomination was formally rejected and again the leaders consulted. Senator Charles Curtis of Kansas, the Republican floor-whip; Herbert Hoover, the Secretary of Commerce, and Charles G. Dawes, then being acclaimed for his chairmanship of the German reparations commission that had come up with the "Dawes Plan," were all considered. On the third ballot Dawes was picked, 682½

128

votes to Hoover's 334½. Curtis was not significantly supported.
Dawes' own opinion was: "I was nominated . . . notwithstanding the
efforts of the Chairman of the Republican National Committee who
finally endeavored to unite his followers for Hoover." The significant
fact was that Dawes was not blessed by President Coolidge; already
distant, if not hostile, relations were presaged between the Republican
standard-bearers.

The Democrats met at Madison Square Garden in New York in a
convention that still stands as the longest on record. Whatever high
hopes they had had that corruption would be a sure-fire winning issue
went glimmering in the unseemly wrangle that ensued over the presidential nomination. The bitterness engendered by 103 ballots before
a compromise presidential choice, John W. Davis, emerged, left a disgruntled party seriously divided for the race ahead. Under the circumstances, no interest at all was taken in the selection for the second
place. Hatch's story by an "unidentified leader" is probably true.
After the choice of Davis, a conservative Morgan lawyer, the Convention recessed till 8 p.m. Two score or so leaders caucused in a room
beneath the platform and decided on Senator Thomas J. Walsh of
Montana, the Convention's Permanent Chairman. Walsh declined,
after which an Iowan, E. T. Meredith, was agreed on. At seven forty-
five, Meredith's refusal to run was in hand, and the leaders became
"confused, not knowing what to do." Someone said to Bryan, who
was making his final appearance at a Democratic convention: "Why
not persuade your brother to take the nomination?" Bryan replied,
"It might not take much persuading." Charles Wayland (Charlie)
Bryan "readily acquiesced" with no one voicing objections. At that
juncture, presidential candidate Davis appeared. Bryan introduced
Davis to "Charlie" as his running-mate. Davis accepted the selection
then and there and it was put through a few minutes later.

A more unplanned, casual vice-presidential choice apparently has
never been made. Yet on the surface at least it was not too bad a
one. The name Bryan on a Democratic ticket was an assurance of
liberalism to offset the Wall Street connections of Davis. Many voters
might think Bryan was "W.J." himself. Geography was served, West
Virginia and New York balanced by Nebraska; an out-and-out dry
second place candidate would be popular in rural areas. Unfortunately, "Charlie" was considered ludicrous because he wore a skull cap
and his explanation that he needed it to protect the sensitive veins of
the head under his bald pate from the sun's rays did not help him.

The decision of the two major parties to accent conservatism and
stability in their choices caused the first significant third-party move-

ment since the Bull Moose campaign of 1912. Once more LaFollette
led the call to progressivism and this time was nominated at Cleveland. At his request, the Convention chose the Democratic junior
Senator from Montana, Burton K. Wheeler, who was assisting Walsh
in the Teapot Dome oil investigations. The Progressive Party of 1924
scared the major parties. The Republicans feared 1912 all over again.
The Democrats feared that enough liberals would follow Wheeler's
bolt to throw the choice into the House. These fears were to be
unfounded.

The apparent nonchalance with which the vice-presidential nominations were made in 1924 was explained by Dawes as due to the fact
that the vice-presidency:

". . . is the office for which one cannot hope to be a candidate with
sufficient prospects for success to justify the effort involved in a long
[pre-convention] campaign. One's political availability . . . cannot
be determined until the nominating convention has in effect decided
upon the head of the ticket.

"Geographic considerations — sectional political situations which
continually change, combined with the controlling fact that the
nominee . . . must fit into a picture dominated by the Presidential
nominee — make early quest . . . too dangerous to attract public men
of sufficient stature to justify a serious aspiration for it. Nevertheless it is regarded at its real value by public men, whatever may be
their assumed attitude."

Dawes himself was easily the most commanding figure of the two
major party nominees. With a record of party regularity that dated
back to the first McKinley-Bryan campaign, he had been an intimate
associate of William McKinley. The assassination of that President
altered the course of Dawes' public life. Committed to a senatorial
race while McKinley lived, he was defeated after he died. For the next
twenty years Dawes concentrated on the managerial and counselling
aspects of the Illinois party and built up a considerable banking business in Chicago. During World War I he was a member of Woodrow
Wilson's "war cabinet" which included such figures as Hoover and
Bernard M. Baruch. He went overseas as General Purchasing Agent
for the army in France with the rank of Brigadier-General.

Dawes' experiences made him agree with the Wilsonian stand on
the League and the Treaty of Versailles, and he publicly espoused
ratification in 1919. A friend of Harding's, he was the first man considered for Secretary of the Treasury. However, when Andrew Mellon's
name was suggested, Dawes heartily concurred. He first came under
the national spotlight when he testified to a congressional committee

investigating wartime expenditures. By his vigorous defense of his activities, punctuated by profanity, and his recurring use of the expletive "Hell and Maria," he became a national figure, and also ended what he deemed persecution of honest administrators who had not counted the cost in view of the overriding necessity for victory. Harding called him into his administration to set up a more business-like fiscal management. Dawes agreed on condition that he should stay just a year to get it adequately started. The resulting Bureau of the Budget still operates under the general framework drawn up and implemented by Dawes in 1921-22.

It was during that year that Dawes became an associate member of the Harding poker cabinet, which meant that he was an occasional visitor to the bi-weekly poker sessions that went on in the White House or in the notorious house on K Street. However, he was not part of that sordid segment of the Harding administration.

After leaving Washington, Dawes took up the cause of civic reform in his home town of Chicago. He opposed Mayor Big Bill Thompson for reelection because of his tie-up with gangsters and racketeers in the nascent Al Capone era. He became the moving spirit in organizing (April, 1923) "The Minute Men of the Constitution," a society of all those opposed to "radicalism" in or out of politics. As it developed, the Minute Men group operated chiefly against labor unionization and sponsored the open shop as the "American system." Lumping political radicalism, gangsterism and labor unionization together as group manifestations of the same "un-American" principles, Dawes was to earn the undying hatred of organized labor. At its height, this labor-baiting society grew to more than 25,000 members in about 30 towns and cities of Illinois and adjacent states, and flourished until Dawes quit when nominated Vice-President. After that it "virtually ceased to exist."

Appointed by Coolidge to work with Owen D. Young as the American delegation to the forthcoming Experts Committee on Reparations, Dawes was elected chairman of the group which from January to April 1924 worked out the report which embodied the plan for German reparations payments which has ever since borne his name. Dawes always insisted that it was a group effort and once during his 1924 campaign protested it "makes me sick" to have it repeatedly said "I did it alone." Dawes thus was riding the crest of publicity in connection with an internationally significant problem when he won the Republican vice-presidential nomination.

The Republican nominees conferred in Washington with Chairman William Butler on July 1 and roughly outlined campaign strategy.

Coolidge was to stay close to home, either the White House or Vermont, while Dawes was to do most of the travelling. Dawes' essential independence was shown in his acceptance speech. "I announced," he recalled, "the constitutional issue precipitated by Senator LaFollette as the dominant one. Chairman Butler was adverse to this course, feeling that . . . economy should be . . . stressed. I sent my speech before delivery to President Coolidge, who returned it without suggestion as to change, except that he substituted 'an important issue' for the 'predominant issue' as a caption to that portion . . . devoted to the LaFollette position on the Constitution."

Dawes' biographer, who was then a reporter attached to the vice-presidential campaign tour, attested that his acceptance speech was "his principal and almost his only" one, for he "deviated very little from it in subsequent appearances."

Reflecting the dissatisfaction of many people, LaFollette had proposed that the Constitution be amended to give Congress the power to override judicial vetoes on legislation. This was in effect Roosevelt's "recall of judicial decisions" which had so alarmed conservatives in 1912, and was still to alarm them in the tranquil twenties. Taken in conjunction with the endorsements LaFollette had received from the Farmer-Labor Party, Socialist Party, the executive council of the American Federation of Labor and the Railroad Brotherhoods, it seemed to Dawes that his "Minute Men" idea now needed to be proclaimed nationally, and he was more than willing to do so. Coolidge, who had stood for law and order ever since the Boston police strike of 1919, was not adverse to the issue either. Dawes wrote: "I travelled fifteen thousand miles . . . and made one hundred and eight speeches. I endeavored to keep that issue [LaFollette's proposal] in the minds of the people."

Dawes was able to strike terror in the hearts of Americans by prophesying: "The bill of inalienable individual rights, the general recognition of which is the foundation of civilizaton, would be, under the LaFollette proposition, at the mercy of Congress." Reporters heard this variation on a theme so often during the tour that they "were sick of it and asked if he couldn't alter it since they had difficulty writing any copy." But the General would not step out of character; he answered: "There is one issue in this campaign, and only one. That is whether you stand on the rock of common sense with Calvin Coolidge, or on the sinking sands of socialism."

It was certainly a peculiar campaign! With Dawes making the third-party candidate the issue and with LaFollette's cohorts replying in kind, Davis and Bryan seemed to be campaigning in a vacuum.

At one point, Davis quite rightly exploded: "The Republican campaign is a vast, pervading and mysterious silence, broken only by Dawes warning the American people that under every bedstead lurks a Bolshevik ready to destroy them."

Additional confusion was added when once during the campaign Dawes, a native Nebraskan, visited the capital at Lincoln, and called on Governor Charles Bryan, the Democratic vice-presidential candidate. After a short but "entirely friendly" chat, Dawes emerged to tell the press "Charlie Bryan's all right! . . . We don't agree politically but he is square."

As the campaign drew to a close, liberal Democrats like Roosevelt, nourished illusions in order to sustain themselves through this sterile era: "I have a hunch that Davis' strength is really improving, but I still think the election will go into the house. Anyway I am philosophic enough to think that even if Coolidge is elected we shall be so darned sick of conservatism of the old money-controlled crowd in four years that we [will] get a real progressive landslide in 1928." But the elections were another Republican landslide—a seven million plurality, 382 electoral votes to Davis' 136. LaFollette, though receiving four-and-a-half million votes, had carried only his own state. Progressivism just could not exist, seemingly, in the climate of normalcy and Coolidge prosperity.

Two more personally incompatible men than Coolidge and Dawes are hard to find in the history of presidential-vice-presidential relations. It was temperamentally impossible for Coolidge to be cordial with anyone and even his friendship with Frank W. Stearns was more one of repression than of demonstration. The President let it be seen that he had small regard for his running-mate. As Ike Hoover put it: "I feel sure he [Coolidge] did not want Dawes at all. I heard him mention Borah or Hoover [for the nomination] . . . Never for a moment would he listen to Dawes and even after the nomination . . . and election . . . he had no patience with him. He was never taken into the fold."

Yet, with it all, no public wrangle or unseemly private quarrel ever developed. It was never Coolidge's way to precipitate matters. Thus, at least on the surface, their relations were always correct and on occasions the two could work together if they had the same views on the question. Where no such parallel interests existed, Dawes went his own gruff, voluble way, as often as not blocking the President and adding to the stockpile of Coolidge's frigid dislike.

Four episodes stood out that accounted for Dawes being "never taken into the fold": his gratuitous remarks concerning a seat in the

Cabinet, his stealing the show on Inauguration Day, his failure to be on hand in the Senate at a crucial time when his casting vote would have saved a presidential appointment and his anti-administration views on the agricultural problem. These not only illuminate the nature of Dawes' relations with the President, but also point up the inherent freedom of action in the vice-presidency when a man of strong opinions and explosive energy occupies it.

Dawes, like Coolidge, was to deny any ill-will, and was never to "pop off" in public. Rather, Dawes' view was: "The busybodies and mischief-makers, of which Washington has its full quota, . . . have said much of unpleasant relations between Coolidge and myself; but I have paid little, if any, attention to them and if Coolidge has, I am mistaken. Nevertheless, the official relations of the President and Vice-President lend themselves to the encouragement of misapprehensions which are easy to create. I have always sensed the inherent embarrassments involved in the plan of having the Vice-President sit in the Cabinet . . . After my election, not knowing how Coolidge felt about it, I wrote him stating my views on the subject."

This was not quite the whole story. Dawes did not merely write personally and privately to Coolidge to head off an expected but as yet non-existent invitation; he gave his opinions in a press interview in a boorish manner that would have offended even a thick-skinned party hack. He said:

"Long before I had any thought that I would have an individual interest in the question, I said the plan . . . was unwise. The Cabinet and those who sit with it always should do so at the discretion and inclination of the President. Our Constitution so intended it. The relationship is confidential and the selection of a confidant belongs to him who would be injured by the abuse of confidence, however unintentional. No precedent should be established which creates a different and arbitrary method of selection. Should I sit . . . the precedent might prove injurious to the country.

"My friendship and high regard for President Coolidge are such that it would be personally a pleasure to sit . . . but I will not do so because, in my judgment, it involves a wrong principle. With it fixed, some future President might face the embarrassing alternative of inviting one whom he regarded as unsuitable into his private conferences, or affronting him in the public eye by denying him what had been generally considered his right."

A more gratuitous slight had seldom been made to a President by a Vice-President. Surely plenty of opportunity had existed in prior meetings with Coolidge to have thrashed the matter out in private.

It was a gruff rejection of an as yet unproffered invitation and took the iniative away from the person to whom it properly belonged, the President of the United States. Examining Dawes' reasoning does not build up his case any. Granted that those who sit in the Cabinet should always do so at the President's "inclination and discretion," should not the Vice-President allow the President to exercise that "discretion," and, if exercised positively, to accept it as a way of building up his knowledge of Administration affairs and policies? The assumption always has been that Coolidge would have done for Dawes no less than had been done for him by Harding, which had not harmed Harding and had helped Coolidge. Dawes' argument based on "our Constitution" can be dismissed since the existence of the Cabinet is unknown to the Constitution. Also, his statements that if he sat "the precedent might prove injurious to the country," and a principle would be "fixed" that might embarrass a future President were without substance. By worrying about the embarrassment that might occur to future Presidents Dawes was wholly forgetful that he was embarrassing President Coolidge. His bumptious declaration of vice-presidential independence quashed for the rest of the "Age of Conservatism" the effort to lift the office of Vice-President from its slough of despond. The matter of a proffered Cabinet seat would not even arise during the succeeding Hoover-Curtis administration.

Coolidge, following his custom of silence, held aloof at the time from the one-sided controversy precipitated by Dawes, but meaningfully gave his views when as a private citizen he wrote: "If the Vice-President is a man of discretion and character, so that he can be relied upon to act as a subordinate in such position, he should be invited to sit . . . he should be in . . . because he might become President and ought to be informed on the policies of the administration. He will not learn all of them." The implication was clear that Dawes had not been asked to sit because he was indiscreet and insubordinate.

Inauguration Day, March 4, 1925, was to be notable for the address of Dawes rather than of Coolidge. To Coolidge, it was the high point of a 30-year political life and the glamorous capstone and climax of a career mostly humdrum and unglamorous. Yet he was to be denied his day in the sun. The Vice-President as usual captured the headlines.

A Vice-President's remarks to the Senate made after being sworn in are generally a tame preliminary to the main attraction. But in 1925 Dawes used the occasion to give the Senate a tongue-lashing because of its archaic rules. One would have to go back to Andrew Johnson's inauguration in 1865 to find an equally sensational parallel.

Senators and reporters could think and talk of nothing else but Dawes' laying down of the law to them, with the result that Coolidge's oath-taking and inaugural address were quickly forgotten.

Excitement was still rife over the Vice-President's declaration of war on the Senate when a batch of Coolidge appointments was sent over for confirmation. Only one was questioned, that of Charles Beecher Warren of Michigan as Attorney-General. Democrats called him an attorney for the sugar interests and denied he could be trusted to prosecute the anti-trust laws vigorously. Argument became heated and prolonged. The Vice-President had a long-standing practice of napping after lunch whenever circumstances permitted. On March 10th, with the debate on Warren continuing and with Dawes having on his speaker's list the names of six Senators who wanted to be heard, he believed that no business would be decided that afternoon. After checking with both party floor leaders, Curtis and Robinson, who assured him that no vote would take place that day, Dawes went to the home of Vice-Presidents, the New Willard Hotel, and slept.

But in the Senate, Curtis, believing that the savage Democratic assaults on Warren were taking effect, decided to press for an immediate vote. As the roll call progressed it became apparent that the result would be close. Dawes was requested to return to the Senate in case there should be a tie. Meanwhile, the roll call was completed. It showed a 40-40 tie. Parliamentary maneuvers to waste time proved unavailing. The *coup de grace* was given when Lee S. Overman of North Carolina, the lone Democrat who had voted for confirmation, announced a change of his vote. Dawes arrived, but too late. There was no longer any tie to break. Coolidge's appointment had been defeated, a rarity in cabinet nominations since Jackson's time. When submitted by Coolidge six days later in an unusual show of Jacksonian temper, Warren's name was again rejected, this time 46 to 39. Rumor had it that though Coolidge "never said a word . . . for publication" he held Dawes responsible. Dawes' own explanation was that the "regrettable incident" was due to his "inexperience with the explosive nature" of the Senate: "Later I came to know better the uncertainties of the Senate . . . The Gridiron Club has never had a dinner since . . . without reminding me of this event, at one time bringing in an alarm clock four feet high . . . However I was in no danger of forgetting it." Unlike his previous inept actions, this one had made Dawes look ridiculous. The national laughter that followed could hardly have been enjoyable to him, though he seems to have taken it in good humor.

The final source of irritation between Coolidge and Dawes arose over the plight of American farmers and what should be done by government in the matter. Perhaps because of his Nebraska upbringing and early association with the Bryan brothers, Dawes' conservatism did not extend to the farm question. Or perhaps he was merely building good-will among the farming areas with an eye to the 1928 presidential nomination. At any rate he espoused the farm point of view. By contrast, Coolidge's indifference or hostility to farm relief was not to change substantially over the years.

The Republican platform of 1924 had recognized the existence of a farm problem and in usual platform verbiage had pledged its study and solution. At a meeting of the two running-mates in Vermont after Dawes' speech at Augusta, Maine, on August 23, Coolidge had confided that he intended to appoint a Commission "to make suggestions" in the matter. Dawes suggested a three-man committee, known for "its constructive ability," to be comprised of Owen D. Young as representative of the Democratic and industrial points of view; Frank O. Lowden for the Republican, agricultural interests, and a Harvard University economist as specialist. Ultimately Coolidge was to appoint a commission of "a more or less political complexion," as the Vice-President phrased it, which came up with a loan plan palliative.

Apparently believing that his August 1924 suggestion would be acted on, Dawes continued campaigning and deviated so far from his LaFollette phobia as to announce in a speech at Lincoln, Nebraska: "We make but one promise—that the Republican party, utilizing the best minds and those by training best fitted for the task, will bend every effort to the study of our agricultural problems, to the end that through legislation, or other means, its solution may be accompished."

Meanwhile, the farm bloc retained its initiative and bedevilled the Coolidge administration with the McNary-Haugen Bill, which was to become almost a creed in pre-New Deal days. It had as its central idea the restoration of "the purchasing power of farm commodities to a prewar level by segregating exports from domestic supplies and dumping the exports at a surplus-disposal price abroad." Since this was a scheme not unknown to centralized industry, the farm bloc felt the decentralized farm industry would need Federal governmental assistance in putting it into motion. Once fairly started, outlay by government would be minimized "for the farmers with domestic prices so sustained could afford to split between themselves the loss taken on their dumped exports, by payment of an 'equalization fee.' "

Dawes, without publicly proclaiming his assent to the legislation, did register his objections to the Administration's counter-measure, the Curtis-Crisp bill. Drawn up by Secretary of Commerce Hoover, this measure would have set up a loan fund of from $100 to $400 million at low interest rates and encouraged the formation of farmers' cooperatives. Dawes accepted the farm bloc view that this type of measure was no answer, and that the basic principle in farm relief should be to help the farmer get out of debt rather than to increase his indebtedness.

Once in 1926 when Senator James E. Watson of Indiana was making a pro-McNary-Haugen speech in the Senate, he produced "a single sheet of typewritten manuscript outlining the [equalization] fee in principle." Sending it on to the reading clerk to be read into the, *Record* as part of his remarks, Watson said: "This explanation . . . was prepared by the Vice-President, who is a supporter of the McNary-Haugen bill." Immediately aware of his slip, Watson had his damaging admission expunged from the *Record*, but it was too late. The press gallery had heard it and the President would hear of it.

In another rare outburst of repressed feeling, Coolidge soon after replied to a mid-western visitor who had characterized Dawes as potential presidential timber and popular among the farmers, "Yes . . . I have noticed that the McNary-Haugen people have their headquarters in his chambers."

The zenith of this running-battle between the running-mates of 1924 was reached in February 1927 when by Dawes' intervention the McNary-Haugen Bill was successfully brought to a vote, passed, and sent on to the White House for the inevitable veto. A veto was action, and Coolidge hated to act, especially when the senators, "a lot of damned cowards," as he termed them to Chief Justice Taft, "passed the buck" to him in order to take the heat off themselves.

Such then were the Coolidge-Dawes relations that saw them in periodic opposition on basic items of presidential policy.

The main outlines of Dawes' relations with the Senate have already been indicated. Dawes was a businessman—methodical, efficient, a man of action and accomplishment. Like his predecessor he started to study the Senate *Rules* after he had been elected, but unlike Coolidge, who had experience in presiding and hence a large amount of resignation to things as they were, Dawes had presided only over boards of directors and an international conference. He thought Senate proceedings outlandish and unworkable. He therefore decided to try to streamline them. His remarks at inauguration were his opening artillery barrage in "Operation Streamline." Concentrating his fire on Rule XXII, he castigated the undemocratic procedure whereby a special two-thirds majority was required even to limit, not shut off, debate. Even if applied, cloture still allowed the minority to forestall vote taking if the time of session was running out. In view of the fact that cloture had been applied only once since its adoption in 1917, it was apparent to Dawes that a minority even of one had the power to stop government from operating if his legislative wishes were not met. "That rule . . . places in the hands of one or of a minority . . . a greater power than the veto exercised . . . by the President of the United States." He added: "Reform . . . is demanded . . . by American public opinion."

The spectacle of Dawes "shouting at the Senators, shaking his finger at them and banging the desk for emphasis" was not a pretty one. As for the Senate, it "glared back at Dawes." Perhaps the most balanced comment on the whole proceeding was Chief Justice Taft's remark to his son: "Dawes made an excellent speech but he disgusted a good many people. But the matter was true in every respect."

Reporters flocked around senators at the first opportunity for their comments on the "dressing down." Typical was the minority leader's opinion (Joseph T. Robinson of Arkansas): "Dawes showed as little knowledge of the Senate's rules as he did good taste—not quite as little, but nearly." Majority leader Charles Curtis of Kansas maintained a discreet silence. Reporters, running to inform Dawes of the senators' blistering comments to get his reaction, had to wait till he woke up from his post-inaugural nap. Then he remarked: "What Senators think does not make any real difference. . . . I am going over the heads of the Senators anyway on the issue . . . Unless this . . . goes to the people the fundamental institutions of the country will suffer."

He kept his word. Though subjected to an inordinate amount of invective, ridicule, parody and satire by senators during the early days of his incumbency, he campaigned throughout 1925, trying in vain to arouse public opinion in a matter impossible to dramatize effectively. Articles flowed from his pen, but it was all in vain. The rule stood (still stands as a matter of fact substantially as it then was), and Dawes ultimately relaxed and resigned himself.

Slowly senatorial opinion toward him changed. He became a competent president and took great pride in the fact that never once in four years was a ruling of his overturned by the Senate. Senator Joe Robinson admitted that as far as he knew this set a precedent. Dawes attributed this record to the fact that he never knowingly decided a point of order from the viewpoint of partisan advantage and also to his reliance, which he freely admitted, on the journal-clerk, Charles Watkins, an accomplished parliamentarian. In his curious, unblushing manner, Dawes never minimized his own prowess, yet shared credit with others: "Perhaps it would be unfair to me to say that the reason I have never had a point of order sustained against any ruling of mine . . . is wholly due to Watkins—but undoubtedly it is chiefly due to him. Senate precedents are almost always conflicting, and when Charley Watkins gives me a choice . . . I sometimes make my own decision. But it is chiefly upon his advice that I act—and when I have done so, on several occasions, Senators versed in the rules and precedents have strongly combated his reasoning as expounded by me; but the Senate has never sustained the opposition."

In such ways then did Charles G. Dawes retrieve his sorry beginnings, and gain the respect of the Senate both as a body and, in good part, individually. His *Notes as Vice-President* bear abundant evidence of his ability to work with Curtis (administration leader), Robinson (Democratic leader) and Borah and Johnson (Insurgent leaders). He was the funnel through whom Coolidge and Secretary of State Kellogg worked to get the Kellogg-Briand Peace Pact ratified without reservations in 1929. His office conferences with administration floor leaders, irreconcilables and Democrats and his plain all-around hard work are frankly detailed in his diary.

Cloture was successfully invoked twice during Dawes' tenure, but more often, as he ruefully admitted, the Senate gave in to a threatening minority in order to avoid a filibuster. As it was, frequently sessions wound up in a filibuster and required extra sessions being called in order to put through necessary legislation. Certain routine business was altered for the better, thus saving an hour or more at the opening of the daily session. By 1928, a typical procedural opening was: a sharp tap of the gavel at noon, followed by the Chaplain's invocation. Then the Vice-President's announcement: "Reading of the Journal." The reading clerk would begin: "Monday, January 30—." Senator Curtis interrupting, "Mr. President, I ask unanimous consent that the reading of the Journal be dispensed with and that the Journal stand approved." Dawes would intone: "Without objection, agreed to," and tap his gavel. Again, if the Senate were dealing with uncontested measures, Dawes, after each one was given its first reading (by title only) would announce "Without objection the measure will be considered as having passed through various parliamentary stages to final passage . . . and without objection the bill is passed," and "bang" would go the gavel.

As the 1928 convention aproached, it was apparent that Herbert Hoover was in the lead for the presidential nomination. However, a considerable group was involved as it soon became apparent that the President, *if* he was not to be a candidate for a "third" term would present no choice of his own. Among the declared presidential aspirants were Old Guarders Charles Curtis and Frank O. Lowden. Undeclared, but doubtless willing, was Charles G. Dawes. Coolidge stuck by his original terse statement, issued in 1927 on the fourth anniversary of his succession, that he did not "choose" to run. "Draft Coolidge" movements sprang up, mainly in the East, but he neither encouraged or discouraged them.

Until his nomination on the first ballot, Hoover posed as the administration candidate but got no blessing from it and was unsupported by the Old Guard organization leaders, who had no confidence in his Republicanism or his practical political ability (he had never run for an elective office). As Alice Longworth pithily put it: "Offhand I can't think of any big league politician who was enthusiastic for Herbert Hoover." The Old Guard's sentiments were epitomized by their Senatorial leader, "Charlie" Curtis, when, two days before the nomination, he said publicly, "Why should we nominate a man for whom we will have to apologize throughout the campaign?"

Yet, when the platform refused to endorse McNary-Haugenism, it demonstrated that Hooverites were in control. Lowden, in disgust, released his delegates and Hoover won overwhelmingly, 837 votes to Lowden's 74. Curtis received 64; Coolidge, 17; and Dawes, four.

It was significant that Dawes appeared in the balloting for the presidency at all. He had had some possibilities for 1928, but he had never actively exploited them. He alone among the Big Three possibilities was supported both in Wall Street and on the farms. Big business, as indicated by the "Draft Coolidge" movements, was apathetic to Hoover and opposed to Lowden. The agricultural areas were opposed to Hoover. Thus Dawes was a possibility. But he had no intention of trimming sails to catch every favorable wind. On September 10, 1927 he had publicly commended the "courage, conviction, and action" of Woodrow Wilson with regard to the League of Nations. In other words, he was defending his own record of support of the League, in an age when such support was not orthodox Republicanism. Moreover, Dawes had been a Lowden supporter for President since 1920, and on November 30, 1927 announced "I am not a candidate. . . . I favor . . . Frank Lowden, assuming that President Coolidge is not a candidate." Thus, his attitude toward the presidency was that if lightning should strike him, he would be happy, but he would not work to corral delegates for himself. A worse choice than Dawes could have been made in 1928, and secretly many Republicans thought it had been.

Dawes also figured in the 1928 vice-presidential selection which ultimately went to Curtis. It was agreed by the organization leaders that Dawes should have a chance to qualify for renomination. When questioned as to his views on the farm relief problem, Dawes agreed to view Coolidge's vetoes as having shelved the McNary-Haugen bill for the next four years. But when the leaders asked him to make a public declaration, his hackles rose and he refused. His name was thus eliminated.

Curtis, who might have been considered unavailable because of his active participation in the stop-Hoover movement, was agreed upon largely because of Senator Borah's insistent demand. The selection of Curtis could not be very palatable to Hooverites, but with Borah threatening a floor fight, no one desired to rock the boat and he was accepted. Put in nomination by Borah, he won 1052 of a total of 1089 votes.

In view of the fact that Hoover was supposed to be a liberal, the ticket of 1928 was comparable to the previous Republican selections from 1904 through 1916; a balance of opposites. The Old Guard, submerged under Coolidge, again had a party hack in the second position. When some leaders had raised the point that the vice-presidential nomination might better have gone to an insurgent like Norris, he "indicated my distaste far more forcefully than the circumstances justified." To a fighting liberal like Norris, Hoover was no kindred spirit, and Norris was to support the Democratic ticket that year for the first time in his stormy career.

The Democrats had learned the lesson of 1924. Pondering the statistics of that vote they had seen that the combined Democratic and Progressive vote had run ahead of the Republicans in 27 states totalling 248 electoral votes. They thus buried the hatchet elsewhere than in each other and went overwhelmingly to Smith who was publicly endorsed for the third time in a Democratic national convention by Franklin D. Roosevelt.

Two names stood out for the second place: Senators Joseph T. Robinson of Arkansas and Alben W. Barkley of Kentucky. As minority leader in the Senate, Robinson had seniority and he also had the practical advantage of being supported by Smith. Smith would give more than enough progressivism to the ticket. Consequently, Barkley's farm and labor support was discounted. Moreover, his sponsorship of the Railway Labor Board bill would raise serious doubts in big business circles. Robinson, it was felt, was just the proper shade of liberal-conservative who would be unobjectionable from every standpoint. Though it was argued he might cause some difficulties among the Negroes of the northern cities and would also face some deep-South animosity where the Klan exerted strength, he was chosen on the first ballot by 1035 votes out of 1100. For the first time since the Civil War, a Southerner was on a national ticket, and for the first time in vice-presidential history the majority and minority leaders in the Senate opposed each other.

The Vice-President, after listening over the radio to the proceedings of the Democrats at Houston, confided to his diary: "Listened . . . to . . . the speech of the Permanent Chairman, Joseph T. Robinson. He is a man of great ability. . . . It seems tonight that he will be nominated to succeed me. . . . If he is elected, the place will not submerge him. I regard him as a statesman of high rank." Dawes was less enthusiastic about the nominee of his own party. His only comment on Curtis' nomination was, he "is certainly qualified to make a fine presiding officer."

CHARLES CURTIS

Charles Curtis has appeared in these pages often enough to need little further identification. Part Kaw Indian, his political life went back to the 1880s when he was county attorney of Shawnee, Kansas. By dint of hard political hack work and fighting the Farmers' Alliance, he was rewarded with the organization nomination for the House in 1892 and, despite the Populist and Democratic tide, was elected. For the next forty years, except for one break, 1912-14, he was to be in Congress (as a Representative until 1907 and a Senator until 1929). Nor was he ever to be essentially different from the way William Allen White, a co-worker then, remembered him in 1891:

"His politics were always purely personal. Issues never bothered him. He was a handsome fellow, straight . . . with an olive skin . . . a gentle ingratiating voice, and what a smile! . . . He won his way by his smile and hard work. . . .

"I never saw a man who could go into a hostile audience, smile, shake hands, and talk . . . so plausibly that what he said . . . was completely eclipsed by what he was as a human being."

When Curtis made his bid for the Senate in 1903, he was opposed by another Representative, Chester I. Long, and by Governor Stanley in the Republican-dominated legislature. The railroads controlled the legislature and were themselves divided. The basis of the railroads' power was their issuance of passes. The Republican caucus deadlocked for a week until "the Missouri Pacific moved its cohorts from Curtis to Long, on the promise that Long would support Curtis in the next senatorial campaign, with all the railroad attorneys concurring and affirming the bargain."

Charlie Curtis knew what it meant to have to wait his turn, but by the same token if one played the stalwart game honorably, one's turn would come. Thus had his entrance into the Senate in 1907 been fixed since 1903. He entered the Senate as "a Gould man," just as Senator Long was known as "a Morgan man." In the Taft regime, he was "the President's Kansas mouthpiece."

Temporarily shelved when he lost the primary nomination in 1912, he thus avoided the stigma of defeat that beset the Republicans when Wilson captured the state by 15,000 votes and the Democratic senatorial candidate won. He captured the next Senatorial primary in 1914 from the incumbent Bristow (who had been insurgent) and went on to beat the Progressive Party nominee. Bull-Moosers could not understand how Curtis had managed it.

Though returned to power, Curtis had to content himself as a member of the Republican minority for the rest of the decade, but under Lodge he advanced to become minority whip. He had found his niche, just as he had in the House where he had been close to Reed and Cannon. Placed in the Senate Committee on Rules, he was rapidly amassing those strategic positions from which, when his turn came, he would advance to full leadership.

As a member of the Senate junto, Curtis played a strategic role in the nomination of Harding. When the cabal decided on Harding, it was Curtis who was to give the tip-off as to when the break should be made in the balloting. In this sense, the Convention was just another Senate session, with the Republican state leaders waiting for the sign from their party whip as to how to proceed. Curtis played his part to perfection, going among the Kansas delegation that Saturday morning to tell them the decision that on the next ballot or two they would break for Harding. Early in the afternoon, "Curtis came [again] . . . and told us that now was the time to break." Kansas marched to Ohio, and the bandwagon commenced. Two ballots later Harding had his majority.

By 1923, Curtis was Chairman of the Committee on Rules. On Lodge's death, he succeeded to both titular and actual leadership of the Senate. Curtis was a tactician, a manipulator. With no interest in issues, his policy was "you boys tell me what you want, and I'll get it through." As a workman, Curtis excelled. His first year as Senate leader saw him close that body "without all-night sessions for the first time in forty years."

During Coolidge's elected term, he was overshadowed by ex-Chairman (now Senator) William M. Butler of Massachusetts, the White House spokesman. Thus Curtis was chagrined at the Warren nomination and pleaded for its withdrawal. Coolidge was adamant—and it was defeated. Such episodes made it plain to Curtis that he was still only a legman and messenger boy. It could not have been too unpalatable to him therefore to allow the McNary-Haugen Bill to be passed twice in the Senate (he voted for it himself) and to put Coolidge "on the spot" and force him to veto.

Thus by 1928 Curtis and other regular Republicans could feel it was his turn for advancement. By pleading with the party to choose a real Republican for President, Curtis damned Hoover and indirectly offered himself. Denied the first place, he was resigned to the second. As for his past cutting references to Hoover, they were water over the dam to Charles Curtis and he felt no embarrassment at the necessity of praising Hoover to the limit in the campaign. Nor did Hoover fail to reciprocate.

Both vice-presidential nominees campaigned actively, Robinson concentrating on the South and border regions, Curtis on the Middle and North West. Curtis did not have to talk on issues. Like the rest of the Republican orators, he "unceasingly praised the Coolidge administration," attested to Hoover's "regularity," and in general gave the impression that "Republican victory with Hoover would mean a continuation of the famed Coolidge prosperity." In truth the Republicans did not have to be positive, and Hoover did not propose to debate Smith. He accepted Coolidge's strategy of silence, and held himself "aloof, except for occasional 'dignified' appearances." When he did speak, it was to condemn water power development as "socialistic" and farm relief as un-American. The Republican victory was so complete, questions began to be raised as to the ability of the Democratic Party to survive.

During the campaign, Curtis found himself in Evanston, Illinois, and called on Vice-President Dawes. Dawes wrote: "He referred . . . to the vice-presidency as amounting to nothing. . . . But when I find him tired, with a husky voice and bandaged arm, resting after a 5,000 mile trip and preparing to start on 10,000 miles more, I am inclined to think he places quite a high value on the office."

Curtis' openly deprecatory attitude to the office he was seeking was at variance with Dawes' philosophy:

"The office is what the man in it makes it — which applies to all public offices. The fact that the Vice President in the Senate Chamber cannot enter into debate is considered a disadvantage, yet for that reason he is removed from the temptation to indulge in the pitiable quest of that double objective so characteristic of many Senate speeches—the placating of general public opinion and of an opposing local constituency at the same time. For his prestige as a presiding officer, it is to his advantage that he neither votes nor speaks in the Senate Chamber. Outside . . . his position as Vice President gives him a hearing by the general public as wide as that accorded any Senator, other things being equal. If he lacks initiative, courage, or ideas, he of course will be submerged; but that is true also of a Senator or any other parliamentary member.

"Whatever may be said to the contrary, as anyone discovers who occupies the office, the people hold it in great respect. While I shall serve eight months more . . . and may make future mistakes, I see the prospect of closing my public career at least without discredit. The occupancy of a public office, unless decorated with public respect, is a curse to anyone."

Dawes was to avoid such "future mistakes." On occasion, he relinquished his seat to Curtis "so that the people could see their next Vice-President." Dawes was sent into exile by Hoover who appointed him Ambassador to Great Britain, but was brought home in 1932 to head the new Reconstruction Finance Corporation. Resigning under somewhat of a cloud after six months, he went into political retirement until his death in 1951.

Of Curtis as Vice-President little need be said. He was the product of forty years of political maneuvering and would so use his four years of incumbency. Not being of Hoover's calibre, he was not his intimate. Not being an idea man he could not be a counsellor. Thus he was left, as Dawes had prophesied he would be, an effective presiding officer, loyally upholding whenever possible the Administration's program (as when he used his casting vote on May 20, 1930 and July 13, 1932) and for a pastime wondering what would be his future after 1932.

When the Dolly Gann-Alice Longworth social precedence feud broke out, he could hardly be neutral. Since Theodore Roosevelt's daughter was the wife of Speaker Longworth, she claimed precedence over Curtis' half-sister, Dolly Gann, whom he had made his official hostess. The age of wonderful nonsense was coming to an end, but the amount of public notice and interest given this tempest in a teapot indicated it was not yet over.

Unaware of the deep impact the stock market crash of '29 would have politically, Curtis publicly announced as early as August, 1930 that he would seek re-election as Vice-President in 1932. The results of the midterm election, however, effectually destroying the Administration's control in both houses, made it necessary for Hoover to calculate carefully his own chances for re-election. (The Republicans had a nominal majority of one in the Senate, rendered meaningless because of six Progressives, and a slim hold on the House that was lost in 1931 due to deaths and by-elections.) This meant that Curtis' future was in doubt. After a conference with Hoover in March, 1931, the Vice-President had to backtrack. He now announced that he was undecided whether he would run for the vice-presidency or for his old Senate seat. Hoover would give him no assurance, merely telling reporters that no decision on a running-mate had been arrived at.

With political survival at stake, both President and Vice-President acted in self-defense. Just as the Chief Executive wanted to throw him over for an Easterner like Ogden Mills, so Curtis appears to have undercut the President. Charley Michelson, chief publicity man for the Democrats, put it this way: "Having concluded that Mr. Hoover's race was run, they [Republican standpatters] became bears in Republican stock. Hence . . . [they] including the most astute politician of the lot, Vice-President Curtis, lent aid and comfort to the enemy. Publicly, of course, they did lip service; but every one of them let it be seen that they had not departed from the frame of mind they were in at the Kansas City convention of 1928, when most of them were assuring whatever audience would listen that Hoover could not be elected."

The effect of this reciprocal "knifing," reminiscent of Taft-Sherman activities before 1912, led to the same result in 1932. Both Hoover and Curtis were renominated. The 72-year-old Curtis campaigned actively once more, like the trained politician that he was, went down to defeat, and was heard from no more. He lived out his remaining three years of life in Washington, D .C., close to those haunts which were his lifeblood.

With the departure of Curtis from the national scene, an era had come to an end. Normalcy, Coolidge prosperity and political passivity had been shattered by the impact of the crash of 1929. Wise men had heard its premonitory rumblings. And whereas normalcy's President, Calvin Coolidge, could issue soothing statements in 1927 whenever the market started to shake out the speculators, statements which had the effect of zooming stock prices up again in a new frenzied high, his Vice-President, more truly conservative and a business man, could confide to his diary (July 10, 1928) his fears: "The business situation . . . points to a coming business change. The credits of the country which, under natural laws, eventually grow beyond a proper proportion to the cash in which they are redeemable, give evidence . . . of reaching that situation before many months. Will it, when reached, make . . . the American people . . . suddenly turn over in bed—that is, wake up some morning changed from an optimistic to a pessimistic view of the future . . .? Such action might mean political revolution."

One is left with the impression that Dawes was a towering figure in the vice-presidency, the most positive, competent, idea man since Theodore Roosevelt, one who was on top of his times. He was of course a conservative, even a reactionary in things like labor unionization, but how many national figures were pro-labor during the twenties? Alone among the Presidents (or Vice-Presidents) during his era, Dawes was a progressive in farm relief, a major item of action in the New Deal age that would follow. His very stubbornness made him unwilling to make prosperity pronouncements when he sensed how weak the underpinnings were. As a methodical business man, he used the business approach of study by experts. He urged action based on fact-finding at a time when it might have done some good. These had been his characteristics as Budget Director, Reparations Chairman, and on the farm question. He was to work in the same way on the first task he undertook after leaving the vice-presidency, a study of the Dominican Republic's finances in order to regularize them. When he accepted the Dominican government's offer he immediately called in experts to assist him.

CHAPTER 10

Conservative Among Revolutionaries

The stock market crash of 1929 and the ensuing economic collapse brought a changed political and economic climate that gave high hopes to the Democrats when they met in Chicago. Their indicated choice for the presidency in 1932 was the ex-vice-presidential nominee of 1920, Franklin D. Roosevelt. After his brief appearance as a national figure then, Roosevelt had suffered his crippling illness in 1921, and except for his "Happy Warrior" speeches placing Al Smith's name in nomination for the presidency in 1924 and 1928, had avoided public appearances. However, Smith had prevailed on him to run for Governor of New York in 1928 and, in the ensuing Democratic debacle, Roosevelt had carried the state for himself, while Smith lost it. By being re-elected in 1930 by an overwhelming majority, Roosevelt had clearly made himself a logical contender for the presidential nomination in 1932. By dint of good organization, Roosevelt came into the 1932 Chicago convention with the majority of the delegates pledged to him.

Since the Democrats operated under the two-thirds rule, the situation was ripe for a trade, as in the case of Wilson and Marshall in 1912. Although Smith was a candidate and felt he was deserving of renomination, it was not to be. Also in the race was the veteran Representative from Texas, John Nance Garner, Speaker of the House since 1931. Newton D. Baker, the Wilsonians' choice to replace Marshall in 1916, was looked upon by many as a dark horse compromise choice. Of all the main presidential contenders, Garner seemed the most unlikely to be chosen. He had only two state delegations, his own and California, with a total of 90 votes. Although more than a favorite son, he had little national backing. Since Smith had about 200 solid votes for him, it was clear that the early ballots would be indecisive. James A. Farley frantically sought to devise some method of ensuring Roosevelt's victory, first by proposing that the lowest men be eliminated, thus freeing their votes for use elsewhere, and then by having the two-thirds rule abolished after the sixth ballot if no choice should be made by then. All these proposals were thwarted, since obviously Roosevelt would be the strategic gainer.

After three ballots had been taken (with 770 votes necessary for choice), the count stood Roosevelt 683, Smith 190, Garner 101 and a trailing field of six others with Baker, 8 votes, as anchor man. Speaker Garner was in Washington during the convention. After analyzing the third ballot returns, he phoned his campaign manager at Chicago, Representative Sam Rayburn: "Sam, I think it is time to break this thing up . . . Roosevelt is the choice of the convention. He has had a majority on three ballots. We don't want to be responsible for wrecking the party's chances. The nomination ought to be made on the next roll call." Rayburn went to work; he found "Smith's bloc . . . firm," some Roosevelt state delegations "about ready to desert him," and the California delegates willing to go to Roosevelt if Garner would release them. Texas refused to break "unless [Garner] went on the ticket" as Vice-President. Rayburn's final judgment was that "if Texas and California did not go to Roosevelt on the fourth ballot . . . the convention was in for a deadlock." Garner gave the go-ahead signal: "I didn't like the thought of taking the Vice-Presidential nomination. But I wanted another 1924 . . . even less. So I said . . . 'release my delegates . . . I'll do anything to see the Democrats win one more national election.' " The Californians shifted their 46 votes "jubilantly," the Texans their 44 "sullenly." Roosevelt won easily on the fourth ballot with other states breaking to him after the California bolt. Garner's nomination as Vice-President "by acclamation" followed in due course.

Garner's version of the selection of the fateful Democratic ticket is, like most authorized recapitulations, incomplete. Nowhere does he indicate the influence of William Gibbs McAdoo who, as Hearst's spokesman, controlled the California delegation. Garner would not have been in his strategic position if it were not for Hearst and McAdoo. As 1932 approached, Hearst sought to be a President-maker through his national chain of newspaper holdings. Already rebuffed by Hoover on the federal sales tax issue, and an old enemy of Al Smith, he was against Baker because of the latter's staunch support of the League of Nations. Roosevelt took too long to repudiate the League (February 2, 1932). Accordingly, Hearst settled on Garner in January, building him up as a "Texas Coolidge." There is no evidence that Garner would otherwise have even considered himself as a presidential candidate. He often said the Speakership was the limit of his ambition, the thing he had always wanted since he became a fixture in the House. But by the same token, once Hearst had put the Presidential bee in Garner's bonnet, it buzzed around there frantically. It was Hearst's ability to carry California for Garner by some

45,000 votes over Roosevelt in the May primaries that had whetted Garner's appetite and also made certain that Roosevelt could not walk off with a first ballot Convention nomination.

When it became evident at the convention that the vice-presidency was quite clearly for sale to whomever could lead the decisive break to Roosevelt, Garner turned out to be the first one amenable to giving up his own non-existent chances for first place by accepting the second. When the all-night session had recessed after the third ballot, the decisive Rayburn-Farley conversations took place which settled the selections for both positions. Farley clearly indicated that the vice-presidency was for sale throughout the convention: "I was cautiously tendering support for the vice-presidential candidacy in return for delegations. I offered to support Ritchie for the second place if he would withdraw his name. . . . We offered the same post to Governor Byrd."

After Rayburn had agreed to the arrangement, he had no difficulty getting McAdoo to agree. Both these gentlemen were more anti-Smith than pro-Roosevelt, but Hearst was compensated because he had forced F.D.R. to state that American participation in the League of Nations was no longer an issue.

There is no reason to accept Garner's sentiment: "I wish I had not felt obliged by party loyalty to go on the ticket with him, but I did." As John Hay had told T.R. in 1900, there was no instance on record of a Vice-President being elected by force. Farley stated that "no one but Speaker Garner himself was in a position to release either the Texas delegation or the California delegation." Garner did not have to take the vice-presidency if he did not want to, his party loyalty could still have been served by making a free offer of either state's delegates to Roosevelt.

Roosevelt broke precedent by flying to the convention and accepting his notification in a speech pledging "a new deal for the American people." In a more dignified manner, Garner spoke a few words to the convention by means of a telephone-amplifying system and—as if to point up the validity of tradition—requested his formal notification by letter, and accepted it in like fashion. Though he breathed confidence that 1932 would be a Democratic year, Garner took no chances. He ran again for Congress from his "pocket borough." To all cynical remarks, the answer was that Texas demanded his re-entrance.

In the campaign, Roosevelt repeated his strenuous tactics of 1920. Garner, on the other hand, was a reluctant campaigner who caused considerable trouble by his tendency to stay in his Uvalde, Texas, home. Garner's defense was that the Democrats did not have to talk, that the Hoover administration was done for and that too much volubility might lead to vulnerability. However, there was more to it than that. As Democratic leader, Garner had be-devilled the conservative administration by his advocacy of a sales tax, direct unemployment relief, a public works program and enlarged capitalization of the Reconstruction Finance Corporation—all of which were heretical in a time of national election, would have increased taxes and led to extensive deficit financing. The Republicans "decided they could defeat Mr. Roosevelt by quoting Mr. Garner." They felt he would frighten business into voting for Hoover. The anti-Garner angle was "the psychological mate of the whispering campaign about Roosevelt's reputed ill health." The idea was that Roosevelt "would die soon," Garner "would make a dangerous President," and therefore it was "safest" to vote for Hoover and Curtis.

Aware of these potentialities, Garner thus had an additional reason for silence, and it was only with the greatest difficulty that Roosevelt got him to come to Hyde Park for the usual campaign conference. Here Roosevelt mapped out for him a rigorous regimen, especially in the East where he was to win over workingmen as a sort of "Texas Al Smith" by reason of his direct, homely manner and humor. During this time Roosevelt would campaign in the West, after which they should meet again, compare notes and change places.

Garner was unenthusiastic. He did stop off in New York on his way back to Texas to try to get Al Smith's support for the ticket (it ultimately was given), but beyond that he appeared to want to hibernate in Uvalde. Roosevelt again managed to get him up to Kansas for his own opening speech at Topeka in September, but Garner himself spoke only briefly and went back to Texas. After several weeks, Roosevelt again prodded Garner to come to Albany for another conference, insisting he had to make some speeches, and urging him to answer Ogden Mills (Hoover's financial expert). Garner agreed and was accompanied to New York City to confer with Louis M. Howe and Charles Michelson, ghost writers for the emergent New Deal, who prepared a speech for a nation-wide broadcast. Garner almost got away on an afternoon train for the South, but was held virtually incommunicado until after the broadcast. Then he was allowed to go his way.

As Vice-President, Charles G. Dawes had served as a link between the action era of the New Freedom and that of the New Deal, an oasis of positivism in a static age. So John Nance Garner was to serve as the bridge between the conservative twenties and the revolutionary thirties. It was not so much that Garner was a reactionary (his legislative program was considered ultra-liberal in some quarters before Roosevelt came along); it was more that, as the New Deal gathered momentum, it went much farther afield than he had ever contemplated or desired. Conservatism in politics is relative. Whereas he could have been considered "sound" or "radical" during Normalcy by merely shifting ground slightly, he came to be the party's drag anchor on the New Deal during his eight years as Vice-President. His comments on Republican Presidents of the twenties under whom he served in the House are revealing: "Coolidge was very kind to me. . . . I liked to go . . . to have breakfast with him. . . . I had nice visits with Coolidge . . . Coolidge seemed to have an unerring judgment of people. . . . He could spot a gold-bricker quicker than anyone I ever saw."

As for Hoover: "I fought [him] with everything I had. . . . But always . . . according to the rules. . . . I never reflected on the personal character or integrity of Herbert Hoover. I never doubted his probity or his patriotism. In many ways, he was superbly equipped for the Presidency. If he had become President in 1921 or 1937 he might have ranked with the great Presidents."

In other words, there were no absolute ideological barriers between the Republican Chief Executives and the Democratic House floor leader and Speaker during Normalcy. There were merely differences as to specific solutions or emphasis.

Hoover had sensed more than Garner the true meaning of Roosevelt's nomination in 1932 as he brought out in his closing speech of the campaign at Madison Square Garden, "This campaign is more than a contest between two men. It is a contest between two philosophies of government." Garner, the "Charley Curtis of the Democrats" as one writer termed him, could no more be really at home in the New Deal climate than Calvin Coolidge.

The new Vice-President had been born in 1868 in Texas. He had only four years of primary education but, by self-application in law, he was admitted to the Texas bar at the age of twenty-one. Being in ill health, he removed to the Rio Grande region in the dry, southwest area, and began to make good. In the course of time, his holdings included three banks, many business houses, residences, farms and ranches. The ranches totalled 46,000 acres in three counties and were potentially oil-bearing. Chosen as a member of the Texas Legislature in 1898, he served two terms in it and was chairman of the Redistricting Committee which detached his home county from an already existing congressional district and combined it with other counties, in some of which he owned property, to form a new Fifteenth Congressional District. Promptly nominated as its first Representative, he was elected in November 1902 and served continuously for the next 30 years.

His Congressional career Garner summed up frankly: "For my first five or six years . . . I just answered roll calls, played poker and got acquainted. . . . I got just as ambitious as anyone. I believed that even if I did not have as much genius or talent as some . . . I . . . [had] more energy . . . The Speakership was the highest thing in the House and I aimed at it. I tried to represent my constituency, but that representation had to fit in with what I considered the national good."

Critical observers of Garner's career in part agreed with his estimate and in part dissented. As one caustic commentator observed: "Garner is living proof . . . that you can travel a long way if only you stand still long enough. His career is based upon the obituary column and the power of inertia. He got into Congress by creating his own Congressional District. . . . kept his mouth shut, eyes on the pork barrel and thereby stayed in Washington. . . . He came from a district where the Democratic nomination was equivalent to election and where he was the Democratic party. . . . By the law of seniority and the principle of the survival of the survivors, he eventually became an important man."

Garner soon found it unnecessary to campaign for reelection. By 1932, he had not made a campaign speech in twenty years and his reticence and strategy of silence in that presidential campaign was partly due to plain fear that he had forgotten the art of political oratory.

Garner's independence of his constituents' wishes did not necessarily reflect great moral courage for they were "largely Mexican, who didn't bother with reading . . . [and] few . . . ever came to Washington." He first became nationally prominent when in 1924, as ranking member of the Ways and Means Committee, he opposed the Mellon tax bill with its reduction in the higher brackets only. By championing the smaller income group Garner became labelled as a liberal and attracted Roosevelt's attention. In 1928, he succeeded to the floor leadership of his party. His rise to the Speakership in 1931 saw his dream of a quarter-century come true. Now, two years later, a wholly unanticipated vista had opened before him.

Only once before, in the case of Schuyler Colfax (1869-1873), had a Speaker been elected Vice-President. Garner was to continue to preside over the House until March 4, 1933, when he assumed the duties of presiding over the other branch of Congress.

In 1920, Franklin D. Roosevelt had written a campaign article entitled "Can the Vice-President Be Useful?" and had answered his own question in ways much as Theodore Roosevelt had in his 1896 article. Now, in 1932, F.D.R. was impressed with the necessity of molding a team to handle the vast problems his administration would face. With an honored, organization man like Garner as Vice-President, a man whose knowledge of the men and ways of Capitol Hill was legendary, Roosevelt felt it was necessary that he be included in the councils.

It seems probable that in the pre-inauguration period Roosevelt felt that Garner was both personally and politically consonant with him and that therefore no considerations of intra-party factionalism would be involved by his sitting with the cabinet.

Garner accepted the invitation, subject to three conditions: "I did not feel I should make public statements. . . . I would not make any recommendation for public office unless I was asked for a recommendation. . . . I would not make any recommendation as to national policy—unless I was asked." On this basis, Garner became a regular participant in cabinet sessions from the beginning.

The Vice-President did not allow his conditions to hold him back in the cabinet (or out of it). While he did refrain in the main from public policy statements, points two and three were at least occasionally forgotten. Farley, who regarded Garner as "one of the truly great public men of this generation," recollected that in the cabinet he "has the habit of waiting until the conversation lags and then expressing his views in quick, short sentences, . . . hard for those who disagree with him to answer. Garner is . . . stubborn . . . in hanging on to his views and he never hesitates to speak up, even if everybody else at the meeting holds views exactly opposite to his own."

Farley recounts that at one cabinet meeting, apropos of a presidential jest "about an old flame of Jack Garner's," the Vice-President made a plea, after the laughter had subsided, for the appointment of a Miss Margy Neal to the Social Security Board, "detailing her qualifications." In other words, patronage would be asked for by the Vice-President, whether the initiative came from the Administration or not.

Even before his inauguration Garner recommended a national policy (government guarantee of bank deposits) which was not only unsolicited, but against Roosevelt's opposition. Garner's newspaper friend, Timmons, recalled a post-election dinner at which he heard Roosevelt answer Garner's latest arguments: "It won't work, John. . . . You had it in Texas and it was a failure, and so it was in . . .

other states. The weak banks will pull down the strong. It's not a
new idea, and it has never worked." There was no animosity in the
disagreement—Garner called it "amiable"—but it was a running difference of opinion just the same. (Garner's insurance idea was incorporated in the Glass-Steagall Bill of 1933 as the Vandenberg Amendment, and became the F.D.I.C.) Garner interpreted his self-imposed
conditions to sitting in the cabinet liberally.

Roosevelt wrote or phoned Garner frequently in the months before
inauguration, seeking his views on problems or requesting his assistance. In January, for instance, he wrote from Warm Springs,
Georgia: "I have been discussing government reorganization, etc.,
with Swager Sherley, and we are trying to set up a definite but informal study. . . . You and I have talked about this before. . . . You
might care to select a member. . . . Talk it over with Swager."

For the first term, Garner was a major figure in the Democratic
Party and worked faithfully to ease the path of the many bills that
came over from the White House. Not only did this mean presiding
in the Senate, and privately conferring with doubtful senators, but
often inviting balky House members to his "Board of Education" (as
his office in the old Supreme Court Chamber was called) to be persuaded to vote "correctly." A typical "education" talk to a Southern
Congressman was the following one of April 20, 1933: "Sometimes
conditions in a country justify temporary violations of deep principles of government. If there was ever such a time it is now. . . .
Roosevelt is traveling one of the roughest roads any President ever
traveled. . . . The last thing I would want to do would be to even lift
a straw that would hinder his progress. . . . Now this bill you are
talking about isn't going through as it was proposed. I told the
President it could not be justified economically. . . . as to your vote
. . . the South has been mighty proud to have a Democratic President. They want you to support him . . . to yield something . . . in
times like these when none of us know just what will work. If I were
you I would vote with the President on this and everything else I
could. . . . You are young enough to be my son. If I had to campaign I would stake my chances on supporting the President."

Garner did most of his work in his three offices: a new four-room
suite in the Senate Office Building (presided over by Mrs. Garner who
continued to be his secretary), the usual Vice-President's room off the
Senate Chamber (for quick Senatorial conferences), and the "Board
of Education" (a plain small room where he kept his private stock of
liquor as oil for the legislative machinery). Jonathan Daniels says

that Senator Truman "enjoyed gathering in Garner's sanctum . . . to strike a blow for liberty."

But the Garner method could also be employed right on the Senate floor if need be. Garner would call upon somebody else to preside and then "wander around the Senate Chambers during a zigzaggy debate . . . and sit down in the seat next to a wavering Senator at exactly the right time to come up with that Senator's vote on the subsequent roll call."

The effectiveness of such tactics was reflected in the relative ease with which the early New Deal program went through in the Hundred Days of the special session (March 9—June 16, 1933). Because of his power and efforts, "the Administration consulted him about everything." Garner did not himself approve of all the basic legislation, but, if he could not get it withdrawn or altered, he supported it loyally. His justification for so acting was: "I sat in on conferences both at the White House and with Congressional leaders on these bills. On some of them I got modifications. When you do these things in party government you have to take some parts you do not like. . . . There must be discipline and responsibility and when a program is decided on everybody has to fall into line."

Senators sometimes criticized him for pushing through legislation so rapidly it took away their "breath." He outspeeded Dawes and would state directly after the second reading: "The question is: Shall the bill be engrossed, read the third time and passed. There being no objection the bill is passed." Garner maintained he was acting "strictly according to the rules." If the Senators were not alert "that is their hard luck. . . . If a bill is pending and there is no objection to its passage, why shouldn't the Vice-President say . . . 'the bill is passed.' " One can imagine how these tactics would have fared had the Vice-President been a less powerful figure or the times less receptive for action—any action.

Within a year Garner made the grade with the Senate and was commended for his presidency of that chamber in a resolution introduced by Borah. Such Bipartisan moves were rare at the outset of any incumbent's tenure, but the resolution was adopted "by a unanimous rising vote and . . . an ovation." It read: "Resolved: That the Senate hereby expresses its profound appreciation of the vigilance, impartiality and distinguished ability with which the Vice-President, Honorable John N. Garner, has presided over the proceedings of this body during the eventful session now drawing to a close."

Even in the cabinet, Garner's influence was early used effectively. When the Hitler regime began its "persecution of the German Jews at

the beginning of the Roosevelt Administration, Garner . . . tartly reminded his colleagues that the internal policies of Germany were no
. . . business of the American government and . . . suggested that the
hotter the Nazi excesses, the sooner they would burn out." No Administration stand was then taken on what would later be generally recognized as the beginning of genocide.

Outside the Cabinet, Roosevelt also conferred with him on matters
of foreign policy. The only serious disagreement Garner admitted
having with Roosevelt after the bank deposit scheme (which had resulted in the President's capitulation) was over recognition of Russia.
The United States was the last of the world powers to withhold recognition and, though it has been discussed periodically during the twenties, nothing had been done. Roosevelt "broached the subject" to
Garner in June 1933. The Vice-President was emphatic: "I'd hate to
see you get off on the wrong foot. . . . I'd bide my time on it. I think
the country and the bulk of the Democratic party are opposed to it.
What support there is . . . seems pretty tepid, and the opposition . . .
are hot against it. But regardless of the sentiment . . . I don't think
it is right. If this outfit has kept its word to anyone or done anything in good faith I have not heard about it." But this time Roosevelt did not heed Garner's advice. Negotiations began on his initiative, and by the Vice-President's sixty-fifth birthday, November 22,
1933, recognition was an accomplished fact. Garner told Timmons:
"I hope it turns out better than I think it will . . . In time of a
depression such as this, when millions of people are out of work, it
looks like a poor time to invite in organized and disciplined agitators."

Meanwhile the Vice-President had been permitted to help shape
the delegation to the ill-fated London Economic Conference of 1933.
Due to his recommendation, Roosevelt appointed "R. W. Morrison,
a wealthy Texan . . . the day before the delegation sailed." Raymond
Moley, the chief economist of the first brain trust, did not think much
of the appointment. Morrison's "views on tariff and money were unknown to the President."

Garner retired to Uvalde for a well-earned rest after his special
session labors. Roosevelt phoned him about the Cuban situation
where, after the fall of Gerardo Machado, near anarchical conditions
prevailed. The President feared the United States might have to intervene militarily. He was afraid an American citizen might be shot—
and then what? Garner answered: "I think I'd wait and see which
American it is." Garner urged a hands' off policy, which was followed.

Garner's role in the Administration had thus been well staked out in
his first vice-presidential year. He was a combination presiding

officer, Cabinet officer, personal counsellor, legislative tactician, Cassandra and sounding board. On occasions, too, he would be called on to help keep Congress in line when the President was not on hand and undesirable legislation seemed in the offing. Such was the case in April 1934 when Representative Lemke of Minnesota reintroduced the Frazier bill, providing for government purchase of all farm mortgages as the alternative to foreclosure.

Garner and other cabinet members were to put pressure to prevent this bill from being brought to the floor. F.D.R. armed Garner with a telegram denying he had approved the bill during the campaign: "tell Vice-President . . . I . . . never endorsed Frazier or Lemke bills. . . . also that if this type of wild legislation passes the responsibility for wrecking recovery will be squarely on the Congress." The President's repudiation did the trick, and the measure stayed in committee.

Garner had developed his own philosophy of the office of Vice-President by mid-1934. In a magazine article, he stated that the office was "almost entirely unimportant." The Speaker had "more power in shaping the legislative policy of the government than any other officer." During this early period at least, many wondered if he was not still performing the role of Speaker without the title. Garner acknowledged the "new dignity and importance" with which Roosevelt had imbued the vice-presidency by having him sit in the cabinet and making him "a party to the discussion of problems, the formulating of policies." Personally, he would have preferred just to "preside . . . and go fishing," yet it was "gratifying to share in the councils and . . . return to the Capitol from the twice-weekly meetings and report directly on the views of my chief." Not even the Speaker nor the majority leader of the Senate did this, so that Garner felt he was a means of keeping "the executive and the Congress acquainted with each other."

As far as reforming the Senate was concerned, the Vice-President saw only "one glaring need"—fewer committees with smaller memberships. In this regard, the House was "much better." But "I offer all this merely as an observation. It is not my place to advocate reform. . . . The Vice-President can only observe." Taking it all in all, Garner found the Vice-Presidency " a lot of fun" but he was "conscious of the obscurity and unimportance" of his office.

Garner drew the line on social affairs. He performed the minimum duty in this respect and early got the reputation of retiring at nine o'clock. From 6 P.M. to 7 A.M. it was his practice to receive no telephone calls, saying these hours "are my own." He felt it necessary to dress formally only about once every six weeks "when the Chief invites us . . . or especially wants me to attend some function." It was also his habit to get out of Washington as soon as possible whenever a session was over, and to return for the re-opening as late as possible. Thus was it said of him that he had "converted the vice of laziness into political virtue." In 1934, the President tried to cajole "Dear Jack" into coming north for a visit: "You must be an awful trial to your wife! She must be mighty tired of seeing you just 'settin round' . . . If she sweeps you out some morning . . . come and stay with me for a few days in Washington. . . . In any event, I wish you would give me your slant on conditions politically. I am working hard on trying to cut costs of running things. . . . I . . . believe that the voters . . . are pretty well satisfied . . . and . . . still want action. . . . I would like to have your slant . . ." Garner, however, had no intention of giving up his practice of 30 years for such transient things as the first New Deal mid term election. He predicted the Democrats would get a vote of confidence, as they in fact did.

The year 1935 was pivotal for Roosevelt-Garner relations. The first rifts in their close liaison appeared and, though no break occurred, each began to suspect the other's motives. Early in May, Farley and Garner discussed the soldiers' bonus bill with Roosevelt on an auto ride from Maryland. The Vice-President offered the opinion that Roosevelt should "veto the bonus, in temperate language, so as not to incur the ill-feeling of veterans, explaining that he had to maintain the credit of the nation." Furthermore, he felt that it would be best for the party if Congress re-passed the bill over the veto. Roosevelt was agreeable for he did not think the bonus really would impair the national credit and it would have a good "pump-priming" effect on the economy. It was so planned. But after the President had vetoed the bonus bill, he heard that Garner was telling Senators about the plan. Farley found the President "fuming" at the Vice-President: "Jack Garner has been talking too much. . . . He's got me in a spot where I can be accused of bad faith if the bonus is passed over my veto." Farley was incredulous: "I can't believe Jack let it out." The President was sharp: "It's out. . . . I want you to contact Robinson and work with him to get enough Senators to uphold my veto." The veto was sustained (as was Roosevelt's good faith), but the President had been put in a bad light. Clearly Roosevelt's belief in the Vice-President as a tactician had been weakened. Though he never was to say anything to Garner, the first storm warnings had been posted.

Miss Frances Perkins, Secretary of Labor, says Roosevelt told her that Garner "leaked" official information and thus altered the nature of cabinet sessions from one of policy discussion and formulation to one of staff reporting. Thus because of Garner's presence, cabinet members "got into the habit of staying behind to talk privately to the President." Garner called the new practice "staying for prayer meeting." Unfortunately, the Secretary does not date her information, though from the context it is clear that she is speaking of the first term.

Regardless of whether Garner acted innocently or maliciously in the bonus matter, he began about this time to have his doubts concerning the general trend of the New Deal. He was of the opinion that the immediate crisis that had warranted special legislation was over and that from then on "there could be a little more deliberation in the passing of legislation."

That some 1933 legislation had been ill-advised was attested when the Supreme Court unanimously invalidated the NRA on May 21, 1935. Roosevelt was so angered that he made his famous remark, "We have been relegated to the horse-and-buggy definition of interstate commerce." Garner, like Raymond Moley, was alarmed at the implications of Roosevelt's anger and favored "frankly putting a constitutional amendment through Congress" that would enlarge its "powers to regulate industry." Though the President seemed interested at first, nothing came of the proposal. The passage of the Wagner-Connery (Labor Relations) Act of July 5, 1935 deepened Garner's misgivings. It was "one sided, makes government a partisan of labor, and in its effort to stop the exploitation of labor has in it the seeds of exploitation of capital." However, since he knew "it will be tested in court," implying that it would fall as the NRA had fallen, he was willing to "give it its day in court and in experience." He told Timmons: "I don't want the Democratic party to be an organized labor party or an organized capitalists' party, and this law can be administered in a way to make our party" the former.

Other Texans, too, were irate at the pro-labor law. John H. Kirby, a wealthy Texas lumberman, wrote Garner the day the bill became law: "How long are you going to tolerate the apostasy of the Roosevelt Administration to the cardinal principles of the Democratic Party and the notorious contempt for the plain terms of the Consitution?" Garner answered: "You can't do everything you want to and I can't do half what I would like to do. You can't control everybody you would like to and I am in a similar fix. I think that answers your question." (This exchange first came to light in the spring of 1936. Garner's letter was a sensation because it was the first public inkling that he was not wholly sympathetic to the New Deal.)

It was probably with some pleasure that Garner went with a congressional delegation to the Philippine Islands for the installation of Manuel Quezon as first President. The trip took him away from a political climate that was growing distasteful. It was, incidentally, the first instance of a Vice-President travelling abroad. In Japan, Garner was received by Emperor Hirohito—and balked at taking off his high-laced shoes. The Philippine ceremonies came off without difficulty or speechmaking by him and he returned with a new outlook on the pleasures of travel. (Garner did not represent the President or the United States; Secretary of War George H. Dern did. Garner was there as President of the Senate.)

He had not been back in this country very long when he took a presidential foreign assignment, this time to promote the "Good Neighbor" policy at the opening of the Mexican section of the Inter-American Highway. He acquitted himself well. Josephus Daniels reported to the President: "I doubt if any public man has ever visited Mexico who was more warmly received . . . than . . . Garner. His address on the Laredo bridge was a gem . . . But even better . . . were his brief talks . . . He represented our country in a manner that would have made you proud."

On the whole, Garner's first term had been a huge success. He was influential, esteemed, versatile, and had a position with the President no twentieth century Vice-President had ever achieved. Roosevelt, forgiving him his one lapse, had taken to referring to him as "Mr. Common Sense," and Garner, for his part, felt Roosevelt had "been a good President. . . . He's got too much power. Some . . . is no longer needed. The other can be worked into the framework of the law. He has been matured by four years in office. With good administration of the laws . . . his second term should be an Indian summer."

The 1932 ticket was renominated by acclamation at Philadelphia. Farley felt that convention "was more of a family reunion than anything else. We could have completed our work in one day and gone home."

Battered by the defeats of 1932 and 1934, the Republicans offered a ticket that stressed economy (Governor Alfred M. Landon of Kansas) and Roosevelt Republicanism (Frank Knox of Ohio). The choice of Colonel Frank Knox, publisher of the Chicago *Daily News*, an old Rough Rider and Progressive, was explained in terms of the need to give representation to the defeated point of view. He was a disappointed aspirant for the presidency and so was selected to maintain harmony. Garner felt these Republican choices had "set the stage for a party debacle" and thought the opposition would have been much better off by giving "Herbert Hoover a Grover Cleveland try." Though he felt that no Republican could have won, he thought the ex-President "would carry more states than anyone else . . . [and] carry a number of other Republican candidates to victory." The 1936 Republican ticket was strange indeed. Neither man had ever held any federal office, and Knox had never even held a state office.

Though Roosevelt intended to make no major campaign, just "a number of short talks," he wanted Garner's participation. The Vice-President could see no point in campaigning himself and would not commit himself. He told Farley: "The personality of the Chief is the principal issue in this campaign. . . . If your organization . . . gets our votes to the polls, the 'Boss' is going to be elected by a larger vote than . . . '32." He finally yielded—to Farley, not Roosevelt—and delivered one speech in New York. While he was in the North, Garner began to plant seeds of doubt in Farley's mind. Telling the campaign manager how he had recently been praising him to the President, Garner said the Boss "appreciated . . . my frankness . . . but he said no more. Could it be he's a little jealous of your popularity in the party?"

These jarring notes were as yet in a minor key; they were temporarily drowned in the smashing November victory that saw the Democrats capture every electoral vote but the seven of Maine and Vermont. The Democratic sweep of 1936 was the nearest approach to electoral unanimity since Monroe's reelection in 1820. Some 60.7% of the popular votes went to the Roosevelt-Garner ticket.

The Twentieth Amendment, ratified in 1933, had changed the inauguration day to January 20, and was first applied to the second inaugurals of Roosevelt and Garner in 1937. This innovation was accompanied by an omission of the ceremonies for the Vice-President in the Senate Chamber, and so both President and Vice-President were sworn in on the portico in front of the Capitol. For Garner, the most memorable part of the whole day's proceedings was when "Roosevelt told him he never would run again for public office." Garner replied: "Neither will I . . . I am going to . . . do some traveling." Through all that was to follow, Garner would maintain that Roosevelt should have acted in accordance with that unsolicited expression of intent.

Garner was relieved by the belief that there would be a terminal day in sight for the disturbing innovator. He also had the organization man's distaste for "political castoffs from other parties" — like Ickes and Wallace—who "admitted to no Democratic party loyalty, [and] regarded themselves merely as coalitionists." The term New Deal Party, rather than Democratic Party, became progressively annoying to him.

Feeling as he did, Garner saw the second term as a major debacle. As Frances Perkins put it, Garner's "principal advice" after 1933 was, "Mr. President, you know you've got to let the cattle graze." Roosevelt, however, drove ahead with new controversial items of legislation or tactics that abruptly ended Garner's hopes of a tranquil, "digesting" term. Four developments in 1937 disrupted Democratic Party unity and the Vice-President inevitably became identified with the anti-Roosevelt wing. These were: the wave of sit-down strikes, continued deficit financing, the Supreme Court bill and the Senate majority leadership contest.

As 1937 began, auto workers occupied the strikebound plants of the industry. This was a wholly new tactic in American labor history and pressure mounted in the country for the President to act. Within the Administration, Garner "hotly debated" with the President. Though the Vice-President got Roosevelt to agree that the sit-down strikes were neither "right" nor "legal," still no condemnatory pronouncement was issued. Garner returned to the attack at a legislative conference, called by F.D.R. with Senate majority leader Robinson. The conference lasted nearly three hours, and by Garner's own admission "It was the hottest argument we ever had. . . . We went at it hot and heavy." Never before had the differences of opinion between Roosevelt and Garner been less than "amiable." This time they had a "brawl," as Garner later reported. To Roosevelt's view that he "couldn't get those strikers out without bloodshed," Garner answered: "Then John L. Lewis is a bigger man than you."

No administration attitude was ever forthcoming on the sit-down strikes, and though Senator James F. Byrnes of South Carolina sponsored a resolution of condemnation, it was defeated, 48 to 36. Robinson, spokesman for the White House, told Byrnes "I am for it, Jim, but I will have to oppose it." As for the Vice-President, "It was common knowledge that Garner favored the Byrnes resolution." (Freshman Senator Harry S. Truman voted for the resolution.)

The news that the Administration would ask for an appropriation of one-and-a-half billion dollars for relief in the next fiscal year likewise nettled Garner and the conservative wing. To them, as Garner told Relief Administrator Harry Hopkins, "relief was becoming a way of life" for part of the population and ought to be curtailed. On the general question of continuing unbalanced budgets, his viewpoint was blunt: "We have tried everything in the economic cookbook and are at a point where the country knows better what to do for itself than Washington. . . . I never heard of any other great nation trying to spend itself into prosperity by going into debt."

All previous differences between the "new deal" and "straight line" Democratic wings paled into insignificance when the court plan was announced by the President on February 5. Sent to Capitol Hill without warning, it seemed the most basic piece of legislation yet proposed, because it sought to reorganize the judiciary system, including even the hitherto untouchable Supreme Court. Unlike other basic measures, for which pre-planning and conferences with the legislative leaders occurred, Roosevelt had "sprung a surprise" by sending over a completed bill. In the uproar that greeted the measure, Garner early drew the conclusion that it "never . . . had any chance of passage." His greatest worry was that the proposal "threatened party harmony." For months to come, the Court fight split Congress wide open, with the President (like Wilson in the matter of the Versailles Treaty) rejecting all overtures to withdraw it or tone it down. When the Supreme Court itself (April 12, 1937) upheld the constitutionality of the Wagner Act, many Congressmen felt there was now little point in the "court-packing" plan. Then in May, one of the anti-New Deal justices, Van Devanter, resigned, thus allowing the President to make his first appointment to the Supreme Court. Many loyal Roosevelt supporters now felt that he could with grace accept a workable compromise that would heal party rifts. Roosevelt, however, continued to drive ahead, and in the midst of the continued wrangling, on June 11, the Vice-President departed for Texas. Since he had never before left on a vacation while Congress was in session, the move was sensational. It gave added point to the gossip that the President and Vice-President were quarreling (which was true) and brought the ideological schism within the Democratic Party into the limelight. Roosevelt was "smoldering" over Garner's departure. He barked at Farley on June 18: "Why in hell did Jack have to leave at this time for? . . . I'm going to write . . . him . . . and suggest he come back. This is a fine time to jump ship. What's eating him?"

Farley defended his friend's actions and got the President to agree to let Garner stay away a "couple of weeks" more before writing him. Farley wanted to use the period to inform Garner of the situation and to suggest that "he return." It was Farley's considered judgment that Garner's "walk out" was the turning point in presidential-vice-presidential relations: "I don't think the President ever forgave Garner. I believe this marked the beginning of coolness on his part. In the past he had accepted criticism from Garner good-naturedly, evidently aware Jack would finally support him even against his own judgment. Thereafter things were never the same between them; so I judged from my seat at the Cabinet table."

Garner had overstepped the allowable bounds of opposition. His "jumping ship" was a public act that dissipated the impression of executive harmony that the President placed so much importance on maintaining. Marvin McIntyre, the President's secretary, phoned Garner to tell him that his act had "annoyed" the President. Garner seemed to be a little taken aback at the violence of the reaction and insisted he had not meant anything by it. As he wrote Farley, "If he [Roosevelt] had told me [I should stay on hand], at any cost I would have made other arrangements. I plead for his unlimited confidence since he has mine to the fullest extent. I am subject to his call at any moment."

Garner wrote the President along similar lines and, on July 7th, Roosevelt wrote "Jack" a long and very appealing and revealing letter:

"Frankly, I honestly think you ought to be coming back pretty soon, timing it so that it would not be said that you were rushing back to . . . call off a filibuster . . . It would be fine if you would come back . . . in a week or ten days. Then there is . . . the really continuing comment on your absence. . . . I was sure there would be the usual deliberate mis-construction . . . and I have consistently said that it was all nonsense and that you were coming back soon.

"If Congress does not run wild . . . you will be glad to know that the Budget for the coming year [will be balanced].

"On . . . labor . . . the past two weeks have brought . . . the right psychology on . . . the public. . . . They are pretty sick of the extremists . . . in the . . . unions and also of . . . Girdler and some of his associates. . . . The point is that if the Administration had made pronouncements last winter . . . the . . . people would not have had certain examples . . . which have taught them to take a pretty sound view. . . . And finally, . . . I miss you because of you, yourself, and also because of the great help . . . you . . . give to the working out *peacefully* of a mass of problems."

Thus seeing the abyss of estrangement and an open break yawning before them, both President and Vice-President attempted to minimize their differences. It is instructive to note that of the two points that so far divided Garner from the second phase of the New Deal, the labor question and unbalanced budgets, Roosevelt had finally acted during Garner's absense on the former and now held out the hope of favorable action on the latter. On June 30, in reference to the Little Steel strike, Roosevelt had said "A plague on both your houses," which was interpreted to mean he had little sympathy for either the Republic Steel Company or the union. The significance was that it implied a non-pro-labor attitude, his first. The balanced budget continued to be an ideal, for "recession" set in as the summer ended, causing relief rolls to climb. For his part, Garner had signified his personal loyalty to the "Boss," always a major point with Roosevelt, and had indicated that there was nothing separating them that a little party regularity and a legislative breathing spell would not cure.

Roosevelt had, as a matter of fact, already been compelled to yield in the court reorganization plan, and was in the process of having Senator Robinson get the Senate to agree on the amended bill. His hopes for a face-saving compromise were destroyed on July 14 when Robinson was found dead in his apartment "clutching a copy of the Congressional Record." The majority leader had overtaxed himself trying to do a tremendously difficult job.

Senators tended to blame the President for his stubbornness in not seeking a compromise earlier when it could easily have been had. With Garner away and Robinson dead, the President seemed to be losing his political touch. The Senate was leaderless. While Senators were discussing the succession, Roosevelt intervened by sending a letter to one of the contenders, Alben W. Barkley of Kentucky, telling him to see the unfinished court fight through to the end. This seemed to the Senate to be a presidential intrusion in the competition between Barkley and Pat Harrison of Mississippi.

In the midst of this seething complex pattern of politics, emotion, loyalties and ideologies that intertwined the court and the Senate leadership fights in July, Vice-President Garner—out of direct touch with the events of the past month — came back into the picture. Roosevelt designated him to be his representative at Robinson's burial in Arkansas. On the trip back to Washington, with a cross-section of the Senate aboard, Garner made his drawing room a temporary office, "took off his coat, loosened his belt" and told the porter, "Bring me some branch water." One by one, every Senator was called in to the emergency "Board of Education," and Garner got "an accurate line on how the vote stood" on both the court and the leadership questions. On the former, as he later said, "the fate of the bill was settled by Senators on the train coming back from Little Rock"; on the latter question he publicly declared his neutrality, telling newsmen: "I shall not by the nod of the head, the wink of the eye or the use of the vocal chord indicate any preference."

On July 20, after the funeral party had arrived in Washington, the Vice-President went to the White House. Roosevelt asked him for his estimate of the court situation. Garner's answer was unvarnished and ungrammatical: "You are beat. You haven't got the votes."

Roosevelt commissioned him to make the best settlement possible. Within two days the Roosevelt-Robinson bill was dead, the Senate voting 70 to 20 to send it back to committee. The President blamed Garner for the defeat: "He didn't even attempt to bargain. . . . If Garner had put up any kind of a fight, the thing could have been worked out differently." Actually, Garner seems to have been blameless in the matter, for, as Farley admitted, "He didn't have a winning hand." It is true that Garner was not in sympathy with the Court bill, but he was not as emotionally upset about it as many other loyal Democrats. He felt that the House would have sat on the bill and, even if it had not, "No President can control that court. Those black robes and life-tenure appointments have their effect on men." Garner felt that whatever slim chance he might have had to save face for the President was lost when Roosevelt applied pressure to ensure Barkley's selection as majority leader. This pressure succeeded in getting a previously declared Harrison adherent to switch his vote in the Democratic caucus of July 21. Barkley thus won by 38 to 37.

Both Farley and Garner believed Roosevelt acted in violation of a promise not to interfere in the leadership question. Senator Truman said (while President) that the only time his political friend, Boss Tom Pendergast of Kansas City, ever tried to influence his vote was then. Pendergast was unsuccessful for Truman insisted on voting for Harrison. The interesting thing here is that in 1950 President Truman attributed Pendergast's phoning him to the "White House" and in 1952 to "Jim Farley." Ex-President Truman does not discuss the matter in his *Memoirs*.

Party harmony had been irretrievably wrecked by these four events of 1937 and the legislative program had lagged. The President felt it was time to go to the people by means of a radio address: "And I want to tell them that some Senators and Congressmen and the Vice President, too, are more or less antiquated in their thinking. We can't proceed, as they would have us, on the theory that we should let well enough alone." Undeclared war now began between President and Vice-President. Though Roosevelt never publicly pinpointed Garner as the apotheosis of the conservatism he felt he had to oppose, their relations became more and more distant.

Garner did help to bring about one last innovation to improve executive-legislative liaison. In the fall of 1937, he got Roosevelt to agree to hold conferences every Monday with Congressional leaders in order to go over the legislative situation. Attended by the Vice-President, Speaker of the House, and Senate and House majority leaders, these meetings began in January 1938, and have continued as a practice in the federal government to the present. As to their utility, Garner was disappointed. His final opinion was that the conferences "were satisfactory to a degree only." The President "talked the legislative leaders into a lot of things and we seldom talked him out of anything permanently. He would come back in another direction to accomplish his desires."

Whatever harmony the legislative conferences were meant to effect between President and Congress was vitiated by Roosevelt's attempt to "purge" conservative Democrats in the elections of 1938. The Vice-President opposed the plan as soon as he heard rumors of it. His whole being rebelled at the idea—not only because of the natural affinity he had with those selected for removal, but also because to one of his organizational loyalty it was monstrous that anything should be done that might return Republicans to Congress instead of Democrats. Roosevelt's reported answer was that he preferred a liberal Republican to a conservative Democrat, but intended to replace conservative with liberal Democrats.

Referring to those Senators who had been against the Court plan, Garner told Roosevelt: "I don't think you ought to try to punish these men . . . You may have reason to be provoked at them, but you can't defeat the Southern Senators, and if you defeat the Democrats in the North you will get Republicans instead." The President remained unconvinced, campaigned for his favorites against those marked for destruction and went down to overwhelming defeat in the primaries and fall elections. The net result was one success in a New York Congressional contest, many failures, and an increase of Republican Congressional strength for the first time since 1930.

In 1938 Congress had passed a "Monopoly Investigating Bill" which called for a joint Congressional committee to look into the degree of corporate concentration in the United States. Some thought it was the committee's purpose to see to it that the blame for the continuing recession (depression) be laid at the door of private business in an election year. At any rate, the President had his views as to which Senators Garner should select for membership on it and wrote the Vice-President accordingly. By the terms of the bill Garner was given the power to select three Senators for this Temporary National Economic Committee, as it came to be called. But he was also beyond the stage of catering to Roosevelt's desires. Roosevelt kept telling him, "Jack, you ought not to appoint our enemies on these committees," whereas Garner felt that if he kept off publicity seekers that was enough. "I never gave much attention to his [a Senator's] party politics and none to his shading within a party." Garner felt he "had to treat the Senate with dignity. If I had not it would have been up to the Senate to take the power of committee appointments away from me."

On this point Garner was setting up a weak defense. The Senate was not a homogeneous whole, it was a bipartisan body, and it hardly seemed likely that it would alter the presiding officer's power in this respect because he loaded special committees in favor of the majority party. What really was at stake here was the intra-party split. By mid-1938 Roosevelt's enemies were not Garner's and so Garner appointed as few ardent New Dealers to committees as he could with safety. Of the three Roosevelt names suggested for the TNEC, Garner appointed only the old Republican war-horse, Borah. For the other places he appointed Joseph C. O'Mahoney of Wyoming and William H. King of Utah. O'Mahoney's appointment was justifiable, indeed mandatory, because he was the author of the investigation resolution. Senator William H. King of Utah, a conservative, seems to have been appointed because of his seniority in the Senate.

Roosevelt's qualms about Garner's use of his appointing power went back to the Nye Committee investigation of munitions makers (1934). Garner had appointed as chairman Senator Gerald P. Nye, Republican of North Dakota, who had proposed the investigation. "This was a blunder of major proportions," Secretary of State Hull said; Nye was a deep-dyed isolationist and a member of the minority party. As it turned out, Nye's group had a "most unfortunate effect on our foreign relations," and laid the groundwork for justifying the Neutrality Act of 1935 and for the persistent cynicism of Americans toward responsibility abroad. Hull, however, exonerated Garner of blame and placed it on Key Pittman, chairman of the Foreign Relations Committee, for not giving the Vice-President a recommendation. Garner, understandably, did not refer to this blunder anywhere in Timmons.

By December, 1938, the political air had become thick with talk of a third term. As the rejuvenated Republican Party flocked back to Congress, the Vice-President returned bearing the unanimous endorsement for President of the Texas Democratic state convention. Another point of estrangement. Roosevelt had already written Garner to cut short his vacation for the usual pre-session conference, but made no reference to the favorite-son endorsement. The easy informality was still present, "Dear Jack" and "Affectionately yours" opened and closed the missive, and the President still wanted the Vice-President's "judgment" on the "many problems arising." Garner obliged and visited the President on December 18, for what was to be their "last long private discussion." Thereafter, Garner was never again to see the President alone. The experiment at making the Vice-President useful as a partner had smashed on the rocks of ideological incompatability.

In fact, the last Roosevelt-Garner private conference hardened the difference between their views.

Roosevelt's summary of the conference to Farley was: "I'm afraid we didn't get anywhere. Jack is very much opposed to the spending program . . . tax program . . . and . . . relief program. He seems to be pretty much against everything and he hasn't got a single concrete idea to offer. . . . It's one thing to criticize but something else again to offer solutions." The result was that in the new Congress there began that loose coalition of conservative Democrats and the enlarged Republican representation which effectively brought to an end the New Deal as a program of domestic reform.

During the last two years of the Roosevelt-Garner association, they were in almost constant disagreement. This opposition finally took the form of an anti-third term coalition between Garner, Hull and Farley, whereby each denied presidential aspirations for himself and encouraged them in the other two. In this, Garner was undoubtedly a prime mover. As early as November 1937 he had begun to build up in Farley's mind the belief that the latter was "big enough to be President." By 1939, Farley believed that of the three likely successors to Roosevelt if he should step down from the presidency, "I don't think he would have taken Garner under any circumstances, . . . he would have preferred Hull to Garner, although he believed Hull would have made a poor Chief Executive." For himself, Farley felt Roosevelt thought "my religion and my background" were handicaps.

At the Jackson Day dinner on January 7, 1939, the President, flanked by Farley and Garner, started a discussion with them about Martin Van Buren. Roosevelt's view was that Van Buren, the last Vice-President to have been elevated directly to the presidency by election, had been a failure because he had not been a true Jacksonian liberal. From this one could infer either that Jackson should have run for a third term himself or else picked a truer liberal than his Vice-President. Roosevelt was clearly telling Garner he would not get the chance to be a Van Buren! On July 6, Garner invited Farley to lunch and with "tears in his eyes and . . . voice charged with conviction," outlined his position: "I can't support a third term and will fight any third term bid. . . . I don't want to be President . . . [but] I feel I'm the only one who can head up any opposition. . . . The two of us can pull together to stop Roosevelt."

Farley would not definitely commit himself then, but Garner got the chance to indicate again that the basis for Roosevelt's "jealousy" of himself and Farley was, on the one hand, the Vice-President's popularity "in Congress," and on the other, Farley's popularity "in office and before the country." Garner also indicated that he had already been in contact with Cordell Hull on the matter. He said that Roosevelt was "jealous of Hull for his standing before the public. Cordell and I have talked that over." The reason why Garner felt he was "the only one" to "head up" the anti-third term opposition was because of the independence of his office from the President. Hull and Farley were after all cabinet appointees of the President whose hands were tied unless they resigned, which would have been politically unwise for them. Cordell Hul maintained a discreet silence in his *Memoirs* about any relations with Garner during the jelling period of the coalition (1938-1939).

The outbreak of World War II in September introduced a wholly new factor in the third term equation. Garner again called in Farley on October 20. According to Farley's testimony, the Vice-President reacted as if the European War were not of prime importance. He was worried more about the non-organization men around the President who he felt would influence Roosevelt to run again because he was their "meal ticket." The Vice-President vowed he had "more honest affection" for Roosevelt in his "little finger than they have in their whole bodies." Furthermore, he hoped to "God . . . nothing happens to him. . . . I don't want to have to go down there." Finally, Garner said "I don't want him to run, whether we are at war or not." In other words there were no conceivable circumstances that warranted a departure from the two-term tradition. Garner thus laid bare his whole position during the post-Polish campaign lull of World War II, and he was never to depart from it, even though the cataclysmic events of May and June 1940 would see all western continental Europe at Hitler's feet and only Great Britain left in the field against him as a shield to American security.

On December 8, 1939, the opposition triumvirate was completed when Farley told Hull to start getting delegates for himself, as he was going to do and as "Garner should do. Then the three of us can sit down and determine what is best for the country and the party."

A few days later at Uvalde, Garner formally announced his candidacy for the Presidency: "I will accept the nomination for President. I will make no effort to control any delegates. The people should decide. The candidate should be selected at primaries and conventions as provided by law, and I sincerely trust all Democrats will participate in them."

An editorial note by Elliott Roosevelt in the *Letters* says that "up to late 1939 there is no indication . . . in these papers that FDR himself was . . . actively considering a third term. Only in . . . a letter . . . to Frank Knox in December, when he contemplated the possibility of a Russo-German victory, did FDR indicate that such a crisis . . . might justify setting aside political . . . traditions." Unfortunately, neither the text nor the date of the letter to the Republican Knox is given, but it is probable that it was that of December 29, 1939. If so, the President first intimated he might have to run on the heels of the conservative-isolationistic Garner's announced candidacy. Farley followed suit in January, but Hull decided not to announce his candidacy. On the Vice-President's candidacy, Roosevelt's reaction was that "the whole thing is just balmy." The President maintained public silence on the issue of his own candidacy and the Farley-Garner declarations caused no particular ground-swell. Garner despaired: "Hell, he's fixed it so nobody else can run now." But the two agreed not to back down, and Garner likewise agreed not to run again as Vice-President if Roosevelt should ask him. Garner's excuse for the failure of his primary efforts was the presidential silence on the various declared candidates. Without the President's support no candidacy was better than "a can of stale beer."

At the convention, the two anti-third term candidates for the Democratic nomination held their ground and refused to take themselves out of the running. The President was overwhelmingly renominated on the first ballot Wednesday, July 17. Garner's spokesman, Timmons, refused to release Garner's votes to make the nomination one "by acclamation."

Thus the most impressive bid of a twentieth century Vice-President to capture his party's nomination for the first office of the land came to an inglorious end. Garner remained silent in Texas throughout the campaign, returned to Washington doggedly to preside over the Senate for his last few months and received right up to the end of his term "the regular invitation to the Cabinet meeting" which he faithfully attended.

The story of Garner's bid for the Democratic presidential nomination in 1940 raises as many questions as it answers. Was his action really anti-third term (as he consistently said) or was it anti-Roosevelt? Would he have felt the same way under all possible circumstances? He once told Timmons: "I would be against a third term on principle even if I approved every act of Roosevelt's. . . . I would

oppose my own brother for a third term." Since the chief justification
for violating the tradition was the unprecedented international situation, one is left with the impression that Garner had no real appreciation of the meaning of Hitler's near victory in the spring of 1940.
In the mid-summer of 1939 before war began, Garner said that if war
came: "Of course, it would furnish the needed talking point for the
people . . . trying to win a third term for him. . . . I don't think war
is inevitable. I have never heard Roosevelt or anyone else say that
it is. . . . I am against a third term whether there is war . . . or not
. . . Any President . . . can be effective [in bringing about a just peace,
if the United States keeps out of war]. . . . If we go to war, whoever
is President, the nation will commit its total resources . . . to . . .
bring it to a conclusion as quickly as possible."

This reasoning is only speciously plausible. In essence, Garner
denies the importance of that democratic leadership which is unques-
tionably the most significant attribute of a President of the United
Sates. Would it have made no difference if during the American
Civil War James Buchanan had been President rather than Abraham
Lincoln?

The committing of total resources is no guarantee of their effective
use; the vital spark of any war effort is executive leadership. Can one
imagine that Great Britain's war effort would have been the same
if Neville Chamberlain had remained in power after Dunkerque? Or
that there would have been no difference in the American effort if a
Garner had grappled with such problems as Lend-Lease, the atom
bomb and the United Nations?

Garner's essential conservatism was illustrated by his Borahesque
views about World War II. One feels that he was living in a tight
little world where party politics and the rules of the game were un-
alterable. By these rules, he was to feel that his turn had come for
the Democratic nomination in 1940. Thus to the original question
whether Garner's attempt to become President in 1940 was more anti-
third term than anti-Roosevelt it is most probably correct to state it
was a combination of both factors, a large third component being his
own personal desire to fulfill the unrequited dream of 1931-2 when
Hearst had first mesmerized him.

However, candor requires the mid-century observer to note that
Garner's declared reason for opposing Roosevelt in 1940 has been
vindicated in constitutional law. The Twenty-Second Amendment
forbids any future president from doing under any circumstances
what Franklin D. Roosevelt did in 1940. It is now the declared sover-

eign will of the American people that "No person shall be elected to the office of the President more than twice."

A less publicized fact about the 1940 situation is its bearing on the two-term tradition for Vice-Presidents. Garner, paradoxically, was upholding this less significant but nevertheless real custom while seeking to promote himself for a presidential nomination. And again, his position has been vindicated by the latest constitutional amendment. All former parts of the Constitution treating of executive election problems include both President and Vice-President, but the Twenty-Second Amendment prohibits a third term for Presidents *only*, and avoids any mention of a similar restriction on Vice-Presidents. The inference is that the "danger" for the latter office never having arisen it need not be guarded against. The "culprit" was Franklin Delano Roosevelt and him alone.

Would Garner have been available for a third vice-presidential term? It is clear that he would not be with Roosevelt. Timmons was authorized to tell the Democratic convention if need be that "Mr. Garner would not again take the vice-presidency in any circumstances." Since there was no possibility that anyone but Roosevelt would be the presidential choice, the phrase "in any circumstances" only had practical applicability to running with Roosevelt. That personage just ten days before his own nomination had asked Farley directly: "Jim . . . do you think Jack would run again?" Farley admitted his "surprise" in view of all that had transpired and felt Garner "would not." Whether this was a *bona fide* offer or just a "feeler" one cannot categorically say, but a short while later in the same conversation, "The President said flatly he would not take Jones, Garner, or Rayburn." Garner said that he, too, received pleas to make it the "same old team" again, but could not say whether they were official or not. It seems probable that if Garner had intimated his willingness to accept a second renomination, it would have been his for the asking. Garner's presence on the ticket would have ensured that party harmony would prevail at least through the election. Roosevelt's frenzied efforts to get Cordell Hull to run with him indicate that Garner would have been acceptable in the first instance.

Garner was undoubtedly the most powerful of the twentieth century Vice-Presidents. He himself denied this, distinguishing between "a great Vice-President" and "a great man as Vice-President." He felt the former was an impossibility because the office in itself was unimportant: "The Vice-President has no arsenal from which to draw power . . . no offices to bestow or favors to extend. He can make power for himself sometimes by his personality and ability. Only if

. . . men . . . have friendship for him and faith in . . . his judgment can he be influential."

Garner's sources of power and influence were two-fold, Roosevelt's very real desire to make the Vice-President "useful" and Garner's own senior position in the party and among Congressmen and Senators. On the whole, the former source outweighed the latter and when it was withdrawn by the middle of the second term, Garner was merely an obstruction to the President, not a positive power in himself.

It is clear that the life-giving element to a Vice-President's positive power is the President's initiative. What would be the case when a President desired to make "useful" an incumbent who had neither a party position nor legislative experience would be demonstrated in the case of Henry Agard Wallace which follows.

CHAPTER 11

Left Versus Right

The question of the vice-presidential running-mate for Roosevelt's third term was an acute one. Considerations of domestic and international policy were involved. The strangeness of the times was reflected in the ultimate choice. Just as the vigor and strength of the conservative Democratic wing had led the President before 1938 to favor the liberal Harry Hopkins to succeed him, so the all-engrossing foreign situation and its complications led Roosevelt after the Munich Pact of September 1938 to favor the conservative but internationalist Secretary of State Cordell Hull. In other words, as long as the paramount issue seemed to be the continuation of the New Deal, Roosevelt would favor a New Dealer; but when the international situation became primary, Roosevelt would turn to a man experienced in international affairs. Hull himself admits that "from the end of 1938 until July, 1940, President Roosevelt expressed himself to me as definitely in favor of my being his successor in 1940." But Hull consistently refused to organize his own candidacy and Roosevelt neither endorsed him publicly for it nor spoke for anyone else. The way was thus prepared for the third term draft.

By mid-1940 the practical problem was to find a vice-presidential running-mate with political appeal who would help to dramatize the basic issue of the time: democracy vs. dictatorship. The President rejected all candidates of the Garner stamp (Farley, Jesse Jones, Sam Rayburn) as either isolationists or domestic conservatives or both and sought to induce Cordell Hull to be the vice-presidential nominee. Hull could emphasize the moral basis of American foreign policy since 1933, the good neighbor policy, reciprocal trade agreements, the rule of international law and order. Though conservative on domestic issues (except the tariff), he was not identified with the anti-Roosevelt blocs in Congress or with Big Business. He was acceptable both to anti-New Deal Democrats and to the internationalist wing. New Dealers would be satisfied as long as Roosevelt himself headed the ticket.

However, Hull felt he "could render far more valuable service in the troublous days ahead by staying at the State Department." On three

177

separate occasions after July 3, 1940 did the President seek to persuade
Hull. Calling him to the White House, Roosevelt "pleaded with me
for some two hours and forty minutes"; several days later he "pressed
his proposal on me most earnestly." The third time was "a night or
so later" when Roosevelt telephoned Hull at his apartment and sought
to get Mrs. Hull on the wire to "convince her" to "convince you" to
run. When Hull declined, Roosevelt closed their conversation with
the remark: "If you don't take it, I'll have to get Henry Wallace to
run."

Though the Secretary of Agriculture was relatively unversed in foreign affairs, he was alive to the menace of Nazism. In no uncertain
terms Wallace declared on February 12, 1939: "Superior ability is not
the exclusive possession of any one race or . . . class. It may arise
anywhere, provided men are given the right opportunities." Ed Flynn,
Democratic Boss of the Bronx in New York, told Roosevelt: "Wallace
had a quiet but strong following." Secretary of Labor Perkins felt
that Wallace would strengthen the 1940 ticket because "he had a following among farmers," was "comprehensible to the industrial working
people of the country", and "had a real following among the liberal
thinkers in every section." Such encomiums had their weight with
Roosevelt and caused him to intimate to Madame Perkins that Wallace "might strengthen it [the ticket] politically, and one has to think
of it, he would be a good man if something happened to the President.
He is no isolationist. He knows what we are up against in this war
that is so rapidly engulfing the world."

However, when the Democratic convention opened on July 15, 1940,
Roosevelt had committed himself on no vice-presidential candidate.
Though Farley believed Roosevelt was already decided on Wallace
and remained quiet until the last minute "in order to keep the field of
vice-presidential candidates in line for the third term," it is clear that
as late as July 17 (the day before Wallace's nomination) Roosevelt
was still pleading with Hull to accept. Meanwhile tension mounted at
the convention. The supporters of the 15 or so candidates for the vice-
presidency were trying to corral delegates while the President's managers (Harry Hopkins and James F. Byrnes) were uninformed as to his
real wishes. Secretary Perkins cut through the indecision by calling
Roosevelt and insisting that he intervene by giving direction to the
convention. Roosevelt's reply seemed to be almost a soliloquy—as if
he was thinking through to a conclusion over the phone. With Hull's
latest refusal still ringing in his ears, he told Madame Perkins: "I
think Wallace is good. I like him. He is the kind of man I like to
have around. He is good to work with and he knows a lot, you can

trust his information. He digs to the bottom of things and gets the facts. He is honest as the day is long. He thinks right. He has the general ideas we have. He is the kind of man who can do something in politics. He can help the people with their political thinking. Yes, I think it had better be Wallace."

Roosevelt's choice of Wallace nearly wrecked the Democratic party. Opposition was intense on the part of most organization Democrats and even some New Dealers felt it a bad selection. Ickes, for one, felt it "a damned outrage" and threatened to bolt. Even the President's sons (Elliott and Franklin, Jr.) were reportedly displeased. One delegate seized the convention microphone to bawl: "Just because the Republicans have nominated an apostate Democrat, let us not for God's sake nominate an apostate Republican." Mrs. Roosevelt, defending the choice, addressed the delegates before the balloting: "If Franklin felt that the strain of a third term might be too much for any man and that Mr. Wallace was the man who could carry on best in times such as we were facing, he was entitled to have his help: no one should think of himself but only of the job that might have to be done." (Farley attests that Mrs. Roosevelt was also against Wallace's nomination and phoned her husband to back Jones, but she denies this, saying "I expressed no preference for any candidate.")

The convention uproar so angered the President that he contemplated rejecting the third term nomination just extended to him. After writing a refusal he ordered his chief ghost writer, Judge Samuel I. Rosenman, to put it in shape. The news of Roosevelt's intentions were evidently relayed to his Chicago managers, for Farley admits that when the balloting for the vice-presidential nomination finally got under way during the evening of July 18th Byrnes "went weaving in and out the delegations on the floor pleading, 'For God's sake, do you want a President or a Vice President?'"

The convention was told to take Wallace or lose Roosevelt. As a device (if it was only a device), it succeeded. One by one the more than 15 vice-presidential candidates dropped out; only House Speaker William B. Bankhead of Alabama opposed Wallace in the balloting. The latter was nominated on the first ballot, receiving 627 out of the 1,100 votes cast—hardly a landslide. Wallace, who had been attending the convention, was on the platform after his nomination; he was ready to make his acceptance speech but "because of the temper of the delegates" he was prevailed upon not to talk. The embittered convention came to an abrupt close after hearing only the President's acceptance of a third term nomination, highlighted by a slip of the tongue when in referring to Wallace's candidacy he said it was for "the

high office of President of the United States." The error would be remembered throughout the ensuing campaign.

There is no direct testimony by Henry Wallace himself in this convention. To all indications he was never directly asked whether he
would accept. "I don't remember," says Madame Perkins, "whether
anybody thought to tell Wallace [he was F.D.R.'s choice] but I think
I finally called him." The symbolism of the choice of Wallace was
indicated in a letter the President wrote after the convention to Senator George Norris: "Wallace is a true liberal—far more so than any
of the others suggested for Vice President—with the possible exception
of Bill Douglas, who would have been harder to get nominated."

Though true liberals were on both ends of the 1940 Democratic
ticket (a rare occurrence in American political history), the left and
right wings of the party were further apart than ever, and even professional Democrats, to whom ideology was less important than victory, were alarmed by the vice-presidential candidate. Wallace was
never to overcome the circumstances of his selection in 1940 and
would be at best tolerated by non-ideologues and at worst anathe-
matized by Southern Democrats.

For their part the Republicans had reversed the Democratic process
in choosing their slate. Whereas Wallace, the "apostate Republican," was no regular Democrat, Willkie, the Republican presidential
choice, was a long-time Democrat. A semblance of sanity had been
preserved in Republican ranks by the overwhelming selection for
Vice-President of Charles L. McNary, minority leader of the Senate,
and veteran exponent of farm benefits.

The storm center of 1940, Henry Agard Wallace, was a native Iowan,
born in Adair County, October 7, 1888. Brought up as a farmer-
student-editor, he combined an agrarian youth with a scientific farming education at Iowa State College. He learned the political aspects
of the farm problem from his grandfather and father (the latter was
Harding's Secretary of Agriculture), ran the family newspaper, *Wallace's Farmer*, and developed a highly successful hybrid corn. During
the 1920s he branched out, participating in the farm-lobbying in Washington for McNary-Haugenism. Though his influence was minor, he
attracted the attention of Rexford Guy Tugwell, the Columbia University economist who passed on Wallace's name to Henry Morgenthau, Jr., the gentleman-farmer neighbor of Governor Roosevelt at
Hyde Park. Through this sequence of events Wallace was weaned
away from his family's Republican political tradition and became a
Roosevelt supporter in 1932. Quite surprisingly to Democratic insiders, he was offered the Secretaryship of Agriculture in the first

Roosevelt cabinet and, with Tugwell, was given *carte blanche* to reorganize the Department "as an instrument of active national planning." For the next eight years Wallace became the focal point of the much disputed complex of New Deal farm policies with their curtailment of surpluses to raise commodity prices, domestic allotments, soil conservation and erosion, rural electrification, ever-normal granary, and farm parity concepts.

Wallace's ideas—proliferated in speeches, pamphlets and books— gave him more than agricultural support. He was trusted by urban workers and minority groups throughout the North and had real (if unorganized) strength when Roosevelt chose him as his 1940 running-mate. This unusual man was an enigma to his contemporaries. Creating strong emotional responses of agreement or disagreement, he seemed unmoved by the storms he engendered. It was clear that he would make an unusual campaigner.

In his opening gun of the 1940 campaign, Wallace gave the Republicans both barrels, using a sentence that would be widely quoted: "Whether it knows it or not, the Republican party is the party of appeasement." Those "who stand for business appeasement with Germany," he felt, were "the most dangerous of all fifth columns." Roosevelt was pleased at this offensive; it kept the Republicans explaining and denying from the outset.

In New Mexico, Wallace delivered a campaign speech in Spanish. It was the type of "queer" thing he was always doing that made him suspect to most down-to-earth politicians. His ultimate reaction to the whole business of campaigning was "It's a funny way to live."

Among the issues centering around Wallace was the threat of publication of the "guru" or "zenda" letters. These letters allegedly had been written by Wallace to a female astrologer. They were couched in the weird jargon of a secret cult and juxtaposed political affairs and the efficacy of Tibetan amulets. Now in the hands of the Scripps-Howard newspapers, the letters threw the Democrats into confusion. The prospect of an infidel-astrologist succeeding to the presidency of the United States could have very serious effects on the November election. This was all the more significant just a year after the outbreak of a war commonly said to have been started after Hitler had consulted his astrologists. The "guru letters" were considered so dangerous that Charles Michelson, director of publicity, reportedly moved the entire Democratic publicity staff to New York City to be ready to counterattack if they should be published. They never were. Roy Howard decided not to take the responsibility involved since the "damaging" letters were not clearly identifiable as Wallace's, though

the "sensible" (non-mystic) ones were. Approached directly on the
subject, Wallace laughed "Are those things still kicking around? She's
been trying to peddle them for years." No sensation ever resulted and
the letters, true or false, never publicly figured in the campaign. Curi-
ously enough, Mrs. Roosevelt in writing of the incident assumes their
validity and merely tries to explain them—and Wallace: "I did not
know Henry Wallace well, but my feeling was that he had simply been
carried away by his intellectual curiosity. He was not realistic enough
to appreciate how these letters would look to people who did not have
the same kind of curiosity. I think that is one of his chief troubles:
he cannot keep his feet on the ground, and therefore cannot gauge the
reactions of the average person. Mr. Wallace is perhaps too idealistic
—and that makes him a bad politician." During the crisis engendered
by the letters, the least ruffled person appeared to be Roosevelt himself. When Anna Rosenberg relayed their existence to him, he retorted with glee, "Hell, couldn't we prove that Henry slept with the
woman?"

As election day approached, Wallace faded into insignificance. "The
Champ," as Willkie goadingly termed the President, dropped all pre-
tenses of aloofness and frankly campaigned. The Democratic ticket
won overwhelmingly in the electoral college and tidily in the popular
vote. Republicans were consoled that with a maverick candidate they
had polled a larger popular vote than ever before in the party's history.

F.D.R.'s victory was complete: he had dared to challenge the anti-
third term tradition, compelled the selection of his running-mate, denied Democratic conservatives any face-saving crumbs, and tested his
popularity with organized labor against that of John L. Lewis.

It was evident that the Vice-President-elect was to be marked for
useful work just as Garner had been in the more halcyon days of his
administration. The State Department announced that Wallace
would go to Mexico City as the President's representative at the inauguration of Avila Camacho. The latter's election victory over General
Almazan had been proclaimed as one of the common man over coun-
ter-revolutionary forces and what better symbol of this was there than
Wallace? On the practical side, it was important also to woo Mexico
in matters of Pan-Americanism and hemispheric defense now that
Nazism was dominant in Europe and significant fifth columns were
already at work throughout strategic areas of Latin-America. Wallace's
visit was the more apropos because of his ability to speak Spanish.
Ambassador Josephus Daniels was ecstatically happy. Wallace was
not merely the representative of the Colossus of the North, but the
spokesman of plain people everywhere, most of whom in Mexico were

farmers. Daniels spoke of how his Embassy looked when Wallace arrived there. It was "more like a county fair than a diplomatic establishment because many Indian farmers had brought their corn to show it to Wallace, not as visiting Vice-President, [*sic*] but as a world-recognized authority on the breeding of corn. During his whole visit he held a sort of corn clinic for all comers."

Wallace was to have an administration unique in vice-presidential annals. Not only would he sit in the cabinet but for his four years he would be the trouble shooter of the third term—with some unforeseen results. In only one area, that of liaison between White House and Senate, would he be deficient. Wallace's wall of impervious silence on the plane of personalities, a silence he has maintained to this day, does not allow one to assess his reaction to the half-tolerant, half-scoffing attitude of the Senate toward him.

Wallace made no inaugural speech to the Senate; he merely began presiding. What might be termed his inaugural was a brief address given to the Electoral College. He quoted Mr. Dooley on the relationship between the Vice-President and the Senate: "Th' Sinit is ruled be courtesy, like the longshoreman's union. Th' Vice-President is not expected to butt in much . . . All that his grateful counthry demands from th' man that she has ilivated to this proud position on the toe iv her boot is that he shall keep his opinyons to himself." Wallace promised to do just that. He thanked the audience for giving him "the opportunity of getting acquainted with ninety-six Senators," and added: "I look on this as my one big job in the months immediately ahead." As it turned out, Wallace neither kept his "opinyons" to himself nor did he win the camaraderie of the senators.

Instead Wallace became the moral equivalent in World War II of Woodrow Wilson in World War I. As the war clouds deepened, Wallace became more and more articulate in pressing a global approach to solving global problems. Meanwhile, the distant relationship between the Vice-President and the Senate was summed up by Wallace's successor, Harry S. Truman, who sat in Senate throughout most of Garner's tenure and all of Wallace's: "While Garner was Vice-President . . . there was hardly a day when at least half of the . . . Senate did not see him in his office . . . or . . . somewhere around the Capitol. In the past four years, I doubt if there are a half a dozen Senators all told who have been in the Vice-President's office."

As one of his first and most unpopular acts, Wallace removed the private bar in the Capitol office. The milk-drinking Vice-President might have realized the magnitude of the human problem he faced had he glanced at the *Congressional Record* for January 20, 1941—devoted to tributes to the outgoing Garner by Democrats and Republicans alike, culminating in a unanimous vote of appreciation and thanks for Garner's "courtesy, fairness, impartiality and ability" during the previous eight years. No Senator would say such things about Henry Agard Wallace.

When the simple inaugural ceremonies were over, and the Senate met the next day under their new President, it immediately plunged into the routine of business. No initial ceremonies signalized Wallace's presidency. It was only toward the close of the brief session that Majority Leader Barkley spoke from the floor: "In due time I shall present him [Wallace] with a copy of Roberts' Rules of Order, Thomas Brackett Reed's Commentaries on Parliamentary Law and Cushing's Rules of Order . . . that he may master the rules which do not apply in the United States Senate." The ensuing laughter was sufficiently voluble to be duly noted in the *Record*.

Wallace had little interest in the Senate. When he was there he often filled the Chair in a relaxed, if not comatose, condition. An admirer explained the Vice-President's lounging as an old newspaper-office habit and affirmed that Wallace "found that tall-backed swivel chair on the Senate dais a comfortable place to rest, and his cultivated practice of half-listening until something vital was said saved him many an hour of utter boredom." However, to an ardent Wallace-hater who observed him both in and out of the Cabinet Wallace "usually dozed in his chair . . . often sleeping fifteen or twenty minutes at a stretch."

The usual vice-presidential method to break the boredom of listening to windy Senators is to call a Senator to preside. Wallace early developed that practice to a fine art, even before additional assignments excusably took him away from presiding. His procedure was to appear for the opening of the daily session and, after seeing the Senate fairly started on general debate, depart for lunch. He might or might not return, depending on circumstances.

Though the new Vice-President was close to the President, he had little desire to influence patronage distribution. Wallace lacked the organizational approach so basic to the professional politician. In patronage questions, he usually stepped aside, but if pressed, he would "as a rule suggest three or four names . . . offhand." Old loyal workers in the Department of Agriculture were hurt by his lack of "natural gratitude"; they felt he should have used his influence to advance them. To the unfriendly Dwight MacDonald this trait was further proof of the Wallace pathology: "Men who have thought they could count on his friendship have found instead, when a test came, egotism and coldness. The friend of humanity in general turns out to be the friend of nobody in particular." However, since the main thesis of MacDonald's book is that Wallace is a conniver for power, deceitful and ruthless in furtherance of his personal ambitions, it would seem contradictory that he should consciously alienate lieutenants as a practice.

In 1920 Franklin D. Roosevelt had felt that a Vice-President could be useful to an administration in four ways—as a member of the Cabinet, as an executive aid to the President, as a policy maker in areas "that do not belong in the province of" any particular cabinet member, and as a liaison officer interpreting administration policies to Congress and the public. More specifically, he felt that the Vice-President could be a roving expediter since he was "not tied down to a desk," and could therefore study overlapping departmental situations and report on them. Such an assignment would make him an "additional set of eyes and ears" for the President, "a kind of super handy man." Roosevelt felt that such a concept in a reorganized government could well have far-reaching effects: "Voters . . . might deem it always . . . wise to choose a man of broad experience for the vice presidency and a President able to direct him . . . to deal with large national policies . . . we should then be on the road to improving . . . the vice presidency and . . . to . . . achieving better mutual relations between White House and the Congress." Roosevelt's 1920 aims envisioned him as the recipient of the renovated office. As President over a decade later, he dealt with his Vice-Presidents in ways conditioned by his own early thoughts. If Garner had been useful in the first and last of the four ways F.D.R. outlined in 1920, Wallace would be given his chance to demonstrate his potentialities as "executive aid" and "policy maker" in supra-departmental matters.

The need for better liaison between the President, his Cabinet, and the executive agencies was especially pressing in the Thirties and Forties as mushrooming New Deal and national defense activities kept enlarging the Federal government. Robert Sherwood summarized the chaotic situation of the Roosevelt office during this period:

"All of the aides on the White House staff were . . . not officers in any chain of administrative command. Thus, the President before 1939 had no real executive organization of his own. There was no one between him and the Cabinet officers through whom he could exercise authority. One might presume that the Vice-President would perform the function of Deputy President or Chief of Staff; the Constitution, however provides that . . . [he] shall serve as President of the Senate

. . . Thus, the innumerable lines of authority . . . ran . . . to the President's solitary person."

To remedy this disorder, Roosevelt tried in 1938 to get a sweeping reorganization bill through Congress. He failed, but achieved a partial success in the spring of 1939. Additional reshuffling was accomplished by executive order on September 8, 1939 on the heels of his Proclamation declaring a "limited national emergency" due to the outbreak of war in Europe. The rest of the needed coordination had to be forgotten or improvised through Harry Hopkins who became a sort of "Cabinet officer without portfolio."

Such were the administrative conditions when Henry Wallace became Vice-President. Freed of Garner's obstructionism, Roosevelt could test Wallace as administrator and policy maker in vital areas of national defense. He wrote Wallace on July 9:

"I have been giving a great deal of consideration in the last few weeks to . . . our economic defense. As you know, several . . . government departments and independent agencies have important responsibilities in this field which are fixed by statute. I have given some consideration to appointing a director of economic defense . . . The more I think of it, however, the more I . . . favor . . . a committee . . . rather than an administrative unit. I had in mind appointing five or six people from various departments concerned, who would consider the broad implications of our economic relationship . . . in the world today and . . . [for] the future. . . . I do want the advice of a competent group sitting constantly . . . I have been wondering if you would take the chairmanship . . . you know more about this field than anybody in town and it is essential that we have someone . . . in whom the various cabinet officers will have confidence."

Wallace was willing. On July 30, 1941 a new era for the vice-presidency began with Executive Order No. 8839 establishing an Economic Defense Board. Its chairman was the Vice President and its other members were the heads of the Departments of State, Treasury, War, Justice, Navy, Agriculture and Commerce. Additional members could be appointed by the Chairman "with the approval of the President." The Secretaries could designate alternatives to sit for them "subject to the continuing approval of the Chairman." All affected departments and agencies were ordered to conform to the Board's decisions. Though the Board was to give "advice and assistance," its Chairman in the final analysis was "authorized to make final decisions when necessary to expedite the work of the Board."

A revolution of the first magnitude in the vice-presidency had been accomplished. Previous tentative moves toward reorganization by

F.D.R. were now broadened, not by specific legislative enactment but "by virtue of the authority vested in me by the Constitution and statutes of the United States, [and] by virtue of the existence of an unlimited national emergency," which he had declared on May 27, 1941. Prior uses to which he and other Presidents had put Vice-Presidents were commonly affairs of a ceremonial nature. Now, by one stroke of the pen, the Vice-President became a super-Department head, a chief of economic defense, the commander of a bewilderingly large array of bureaus, agencies and offices. The concept of economic defense was liberally defined to include imports, exports, stockpiling (including preclusive buying), foreign exchange and property, international investments, credit, shipping, patents, commercial communication, plus the final broad phrase "and other foreign economic matters." Thus, in one way or the other, every single cabinet member was under Vice-President Wallace in some aspect of his duties, as were most important independent agency heads.

Unfortunately, Wallace did not have a political personality commensurate with his intellectual capacities. He was ultimately overwhelmed by his unpopularity with powerful segments of official Washington and with conservative business interests generally. The ultimate dissolution of the Board of Economic Warfare (as it came to be called after Pearl Harbor) was not due to any mistake in elevating the vice-presidential office to a position of great administrative responsibility and power. The failure was a consequence of Wallace's personal deficiencies and radical ideology.

Wallace had no sooner begun the staffing of the Economic Defense Board when another Executive Order, issued on August 28, created the Supply Priorities and Allocations Board (SPAB). (Washington commentators, with some justification, observed that the President's answer to an administrative problem was the creation of another board to solve it.) The SPAB was to assure "effective coordination of the priority powers and supply allocation activities of the Federal Government in . . . conformity with the basic defense policies of the President." Established within the Office for Emergency Management, the SPAB included the two directors of that organization, several cabinet officers, the Administrator of the Office of Price Administration (Leon Henderson), Lend-Lease Supervisor (Harry Hopkins), and the Chairman of the Economic Defense Board. Wallace was designated by President Roosevelt as Chairman of the SPAB, and so was in a position to mesh economic defense in the international field with the domestic civilian situation. The "front-line administrator" of the SPAB became Executive Director Donald M. Nelson, whose efficiency in this post became outstanding. In its three months of peacetime existence the SPAB "set the Nation's sights on full industrial mobilization" and in a series of decisions, "ordered an increase in steel capacity by ten million tons a year" (October 2), "placed restrictions on non-essential building" (October 9), "forbade the use of copper . . . for civilian use" (October 21), and two days later "issued the necessary orders for the allocation of equipment and materials" necessary to fulfill the terms of the Moscow Lend-Lease Agreement.

About a month after Pearl Harbor the SPAB was dissolved, the War Production Board being established in its place, with Donald Nelson heading up the new centralized agency. Harry Hopkins' notes leave little doubt that this plum was avidly sought by others. Henry Morgenthau, Jr., "wanted it worse than anything in the world," and Vice-President Wallace "hoped the President would ask him." Nelson seems to have been chosen because he had the President's confidence and was "the best of the lot." When Wallace and Nelson met with Roosevelt on January 13, 1942, the President "told Wallace that in order to give Nelson the kind of authority he must have, Nelson would have to be Chairman . . . and have all the power." A sufficient reason for the President's passing over Wallace was that the WPB was a full-time job, as Nelson's experience in it soon attested. Not even Roosevelt could have divorced the Vice-President completely from his constitutional duty of presiding in the Senate. Any effort at dividing the Vice-President's time and attention between the two tasks could only have resulted in damages to both and would have impeded the President's one undeviating aim—victory in the war.

The 1941 expansion of vice-presidential functions was climaxed in October when the President established an advisory committee on atomic energy composed of Wallace, Stimson, Army Chief of Staff George C. Marshall, Vannevar Bush and Dr. James B. Conant, president of Harvard. The Secretary of War characterized this committee as the basic agency for making "all major decisions of policy on the development and use of atomic energy." The Vice-President remained a member of it throughout his tenure in office and was familiar with secrets jealously guarded from the Cabinet as well as Congress. The atomic energy committee recommended in June 1942 expansion of activities which led directly to the Manhattan Project.

An enigmatic passage in Frances Perkins' recollections indicates that Wallace may have initiated the American atomic bomb program by convincing the President that the gamble must be taken. She writes: "He [Roosevelt] gave the signal to go ahead on the exploration and development of the atomic bomb because of his hunch that

[Dr. Albert] Einstein, like his fellow scientists, was truthful and wise. He had seen him on Henry Wallace's recommendation, and he knew Wallace, a man of scientific understanding, was also truthful and wise." When sometime between 1946-47 Wallace was queried about this, he said it was "untrue."

In the Cabinet, Wallace espoused a tough policy toward Japan. Relations with that country necessarily worsened with every successive Japanese advance southward in East Asia. Public opinion, however, was dormant to the danger and the isolationist groups were highly articulate in proclaiming that no threats to America existed. Though for a time it appeared that the President would accept a plan to issue joint Anglo-American-Dutch warnings to Japan, he finally decided against this and contented himself with a vague warning on August 17, 1941. At the first Cabinet meeting after this warning, Roosevelt outlined his essentially middle-of-the-road policy toward Japan. Wallace wrote the President that same day: "When you mentioned Japan . . . this afternoon, I had a strong desire to express myself but [decided] to do so . . . privately. I do so hope that . . . you take an exceedingly firm stand . . . the appeasing stand or partially appeasing stand is certain to bring bad results. . . . If we take a strong stand, the entire Axis will be impressed and the psychology of the American people will be strengthened.

"I do hope, Mr. President, you will go to the absolute limit in your firmness . . . such a policy will bear rich dividends, . . . any sign of weakness . . . will be misunderstood by . . . the Axis and will cost us, directly or indirectly, many millions of hours of man labor and much suffering."

Throughout 1941, while the United States stumbled toward war, Wallace was already looking ahead to the post-war era. In April he spoke of this country's "second opportunity to make the world safe for democracy." Now the Nazi threat to democracy had arisen and once again the American heritage was at stake: "In strengthening our youth against the Nazi lie, we must make their faith glow in the truth, which is that the essence of democracy is belief in the fatherhood of God, the brotherhood of man and the dignity of the individual soul. Democracy so defined is almost identical with religion."

For democracy to survive in the period ahead it must have "the Bill of Duties" to make possible the continued privileges of the Bill of Rights. "The battle of the peace will be more difficult to win than the battle of the war. All Europe will be a mad swirl of chaotic forces. Unless we . . . help in the reorganization . . . these forces will leap from continent to continent and destroy even the United

States." The Vice-President's early prescription for successful peace
included the following elements: 1) "an international order sufficiently strong to prevent the rise of aggressor nations"; 2) no economic warfare either by the victors or vanquished; 3) "we cannot
compel a defeated nation to pay . . . high indemnity and at the
same time forbid . . . [her] to export"; 4) "the defeated aggressor
nations" must have "the opportunity to buy raw materials and sell
manufactured goods without discrimination" as long as they behave
themselves. These "second chance" requirements of Wallace in 1941
were generally to be the actual blueprints by mid-century, when
democracy was wondering if it was still in the era of the second
chance—or none.

Here then was the Wallace "new order," the "new frontier which
Americans in the middle of the twentieth century find beckoning them
on." His Economic Defense Board, charged with the function of
planning for the post-war economic situation, had already come up
with tentative blueprints very familiar to the mid-century American,
however strange they were to most Americans of the early forties.
UNRRA, the Marshall Plan, the various foreign aid programs, Point
Four, the "statesman's" Japanese Peace Pact and other facets of
American policy are post-war developments that differ only in speci-
fics from Wallace's early postulates.

At the time of the Pearl Harbor attack, the Vice-President was at
the apex of his prestige and authority. He alone attended both of the
conferences President Roosevelt held that Sunday evening with the
Cabinet and legislative leaders. He was with the President from 8:30
p.m., when the Cabinet was received until 10:45 p.m., when the congressional meeting ended. His dual appearance symbolized his unique
position in the history of the vice-presidency as a personal confidant
of the President, a member of the Cabinet, a coordinating administrator in his own right, a policy maker and the chief ideologist of the
Roosevelt administration in both domestic and foreign policy. His
Achilles heel was that Congress distrusted him and his ideas. Having little influence in the legislature, he could do little in behalf of the
administration program there. Wallace's power derived almost entirely from the President. To the extent that F.D.R. continued to
support him, Wallace would remain a power; when executive favor
was removed, he would sink back to the formal aspects of his office
and ultimately be denied a second term.

The year 1942 saw the beginning of the downfall of Henry Agard
Wallace. When his functions as Chairman of the Supply Priorities
and Allocations Board were terminated on January 13, 1942 he inten-

sified his activities in the Board of Economic Warfare (BEW) and soon ran afoul of Martin Dies, the State Department, the Reconstruction Finance Corporation, and the House of Representatives.

By a series of executive orders, the BEW gradually expanded in powers and functions. However, it ran head on into trouble with the State Department and the Reconstruction Finance Corporation. Those agencies could not in the best of circumstances have viewed favorably the invasion of their functions. The fact that BEW was directed by the liberal, advanced visionary Vice-President made the clash all the more violent. While the BEW pressed for an expansion of overseas procurement and stockpiling of critical war materials, it began to feel itself hamstrung by the activities of the State Department and the RFC in this field. With the former controlling foreign policy and the latter holding the purse strings on stockpiling, the BEW's area of freedom was very narrow. Wallace felt the domestic conservatism he had battled since the Twenties controlled the overseas economic war effort.

A running battle began in 1942 that would be fought on many fronts, foreign and domestic, and would result in BEW's dissolution in 1943. The conflict is most understandable as one between New Dealers and anti-New Dealers, with each attempting to win President Roosevelt to its side.

Wallace opened the battle in a speech at Omaha in March 1942. He said that the American farmers had been ready to "go to town" on agricultural production because they had been preparing to do so for ten years. The case was entirely different in industrial production because "industry did not plan and accumulate reserves." This plea for a planned economy and criticism of the RFC's meager stockpiling program was immediately rebutted by spokesmen of industrial interests who asked how business men could be expected to be prepared for total war when it came when they had been "in the 'dog house' for eight years."

Martin Dies, Chairman of the House Un-American Activities Committee, entered the lists by publicly denouncing certain of BEW's 3,000 employees as nudists, Communists, "pinkos" and "world-savers." Wallace promised to investigate Dies' specific charges but strenuously objected to his effort as he saw it, "to create the impression that the Board . . . is planning a nudist post-war world for the United States."

Smarting under the lackadaisical attitude of the RFC in executing procurement contracts entered into by the BEW, Wallace went to the President for clarification and on April 13 received a new Executive Order. Jesse Jones, head of the RFC, interpreted it in biting terms:

"This order was intended to give Mr. Wallace control of all overseas economic activities of governmental agencies engaged in the importation of the materials of war . . . permitting them . . . to direct us what to buy and where and when, and to pay no attention to the price tag . . . And, what was dear to the ambitions of Mr. Wallace and his reformers, the Executive Order ordained that they should send abroad such technical and economic representatives as they might deem necessary." Jones added: "When we thought their [BEW's] orders were proper, we complied promptly. When we thought the orders were not . . . we tried with great patience to reason with them."

What Jones most strenuously objected to was "work clauses" inserted into the procurement and production contracts made with Latin-American countries. To his way of thinking the insertion of minimum working conditions clauses would "interfere . . . with the sovereignty of those republics, with the eating, housing, hygienic and working habits of their peoples . . . [and] have compelled Latin American producers to pay their employees wages with sufficient purchasing power to equal the North American scale."

It was quite obvious, then, that the New Deal, socially and economically, was being fought out on a world-wide basis, just as before the war it had been fought out on the domestic American stage.

Meanwhile, the State Department moved to protect its bureaucratic interests. It had never resigned itself to the invasion of its policy-making functions by the BEW. Cordell Hull, in estimating Vice-President Wallace felt that "He was so active that his tendency at times was to trench on the jurisdiction of his colleagues, including myself, and to interfere with their policies . . . This became very disagreeable to me . . . when Henry Wallace's Board of Economic Warfare sought to appropriate the chief economic war functions of the State Department and other agencies." Hull's Undersecretary, Sumner Welles, further complained of Wallace's interfering in State's post-war planning: "Work . . . was periodically halted . . . by the squabbles that so frequently broke out . . . The most notorious . . . was . . . caused by a presidential order . . . [giving] the Board full authority to determine American postwar economic foreign policy. It was obviously impossible . . . to plan intelligently, or to recommend specific postwar settlements if it [State] had no authority to decide what this policy was going to be. It was doubly impossible when . . . [the Board] gave every indication of holding views diametrically opposed to those of the Secretary of State himself." (Welles's account is not above criticism. He says a State Department committee began working on "preliminary postwar research . . . exactly three weeks after

Pearl Harbor," and the "presidential order issued at the insistence of Henry Wallace . . . placed at the head of the newly created Board of Economic Warfare . . . gave the Board full authority to determine American postwar economic policy." Thus the implication is clear that Welles's group was first in the field and Wallace's butted in later. Actually Wallace received planning authority months before Pearl Harbor.)

When Hull vigorously complained to Wallace and the President in May, 1942, Roosevelt told his Vice-President "that he would not have signed the original order [of April 13] had he known the State and Commerce Departments were opposed to the transfer." Wallace's answer to Roosevelt was truthful, if startling; he had not asked the approval of these departments because he knew he would not get it. President Roosevelt then issued, on May 20, a statement defining the relations between the State Department and the BEW which left foreign policy in the Secretary's hands and placed all business matters in the BEW's. Where a decision might involve both foreign policy and business judgment, the statement contemplated discussion between Hull and Wallace and "a joint decision, in matters of sufficient importance obtaining direction from the President."

Since both BEW and the State Department had foreign economic agents, a *modus vivendi* was worked out for these, with non-duplication of functions and facilities as the main objective. All BEW field representatives were to be subordinated to the American chief of missions and to report through State Department channels only. Hull was satisfied, Wallace was disgruntled and Welles felt it was only a "paper adjustment." Said the latter: "It . . . never worked out and, as long as the Board . . . continued . . . conflicts with . . . State were recurrent. They hampered inordinately the achievement of the major task that we had set for ourselves."

Though the Undersecretary, who himself was not in ideological agreement with Hull on post-war policy, did not indicate how the BEW interfered "inordinately" after the May 1942 clarification, he may have had in mind the trouble that arose over Vichy policy in that same year.

At the time, no aspect of American foreign policy seemed so contradictory as the maintaining of friendly relations with the Petain government of unoccupied France. Clearly under the domination of Hitler and run by "collaborators" or out-and-out Fascists, it seemed unconscionable that this country should be fighting democracy's cause and at the same time fawning on Petain. The contradiction was justified because of the advantage of having a listening post in

Nazi-controlled Europe, stiffening the back of Petain against Hitler, establishing and broadening contacts with resistance groups and neutralizing French resistance to the North African invasion of November 1942. As an aspect of American friendliness to Vichy, an economic agreement was entered into in 1941 whereby the United States agreed to supply shipments of goods to France and her colonies. When Pierre Laval returned to power as Vice-Premier, the supply program was suspended, but Hull agreed to its resumption in June 1942 and the BEW certified to the release of certain commodities. William L. Langer, the chief apologist of "our Vichy gamble," was unimpressed; the quantity released by Wallace's Board "could be carried in two bottoms."

Admiral Leahy, Chief of Staff to the President and Chairman of the Joint Chiefs of Staff, had to intervene at Roosevelt's direction and make it clear that shipments to North Africa were to be regularly sent with no strings attached, but the "Representatives of BEW at once raised objections . . . Finally the meeting broke up in an almost disorderly way when Admiral Leahy rose and walked out."

Langer hits hard at the BEW officials who appeared "unenlightened and unregenerate" throughout the summer and fall of 1942 despite the general order, repeated in September by Admiral Leahy, that there was an "urgent necessity of pleasing and placating the French in every way possible at this time." By October, all hope of healthy cooperation had come to an end. Assistant Secretary of State Adolf A. Berle went directly to Wallace to iron out the problem. Berle's report stated: "Mr. Wallace said that he understood the situation perfectly. There was certain information available to him and probably available to the Department which had not been, and could not be, divulged to . . . the men lower down." Wallace stated that he had already passed on the word to his assistants to capitulate, but to Langer "even this conversation [between Wallace and Berle] did not really break the log-jam, and . . . not much headway was made with the program." About all that Wallace's last minute intervention had accomplished was to make the last meeting of the committee "fairly harmonious."

It might be urged that Wallace, as titular head of the BEW, was too busy to be aware of these bickerings, but the fact remains that he was the responsible head of the organization. Wallace ultimately moved correctly to subordinate economic warfare to overall political considerations, but he moved tardily and ineffectually and to that extent bears partial responsibility for adverse effects in the area of resistance to the Allied landings on November 9, 1942. The President's estima-

tion of Wallace must have declined during 1942 as these deep and bitter conflicts came to his attention and he was obliged to intervene to
resolve them. Rather than being an executive aid to the President,
lightening his administrative load, Wallace seemed to be adding to it.

As the year closed, Wallace was still periodically expressing his
hopes and fears to the President on various matters—even war strategy—and Roosevelt was warmly replying. One example will suffice.
The Vice-President feared Hitler would counter the Allied North African invasion by moving through Spain to get at Gibraltar and Africa.
Wallace felt England ought to "move with greater speed via Portugal"
to check this. The President airily answered: "You and I think
alike. I told Winston last January to read up on Wellington's Penin-
sula Campaign. We have both done it."

Wallace was periodically speaking or writing things so provocative
that they aroused a barrage of opposition in Congress. He wanted to
see Latin-America again become a great natural rubber-producing area
for the twin purposes of lifting living standards there and providing
a more invulnerable source in time of war. Others felt a synthetic
rubber industry in the United States was the answer Thus when
Wallace wrote an article in which he labelled his opponents "isolationists," he was answered in kind. Representative Grant of Indiana felt
the Vice-President's article presented "a sorry picture" of "the greatest nation in the world . . . strangled under the grasp of Government
control." Representative Gifford of Massachusetts added: "One of
the most remarkable statements made by Mr. Wallace . . . is that he
wants this world built on the exact pattern of T.V.A. . . . the most
perfect example of socialism yet effected in this or any other country."
In the upper chamber Wallace got support in his rubber battle
when Senator Harry S. Truman, Chairman of the War Investigating
Committee, on August 10 read into the record a statement commend-
ing the part played by Wallace from 1938 on in the development of a
rubber program, both natural and synthetic.

Wallace's views on Russia aroused sharp opposition. Before 1941, he
was clearly not a communist or left-winger. He followed no party line
changes at the time of the Nazi-Soviet Pact of August 23, 1939. He
was anti-Hitler before and after the Pact, something no Communist or
fellow-traveller could be. Like most Americans after June 1941 he wel-
comed the participation by Russia against Germany. He also took it
on himself to explain Russia to the American people. The only thing
certain is that, at the expense of historical truth, he sold Russia to
himself. Speaking at Madison Square Garden on November 8, 1942,
he quoted de Tocqueville to illustrate how Russia and the United

States were meant to be harmonious neighbors. What Wallace quoted was correct, but he juxtaposed two sentences and omitted the intervening remarks in which de Tocqueville contrasted Czarist Russian oppression with the freedom of Jacksonian America. Disingenuously, Wallace concluded "Russia and the United States today are far closer than Tocqueville could possible have imagined."

Taking the road of self-mesmerization, Wallace began to go further astray to wind up in 1948 the captive of American Communists and fellow-travellers. Only in the grim period after the Korean invasion of June, 1950, did he take steps to extricate himself from their clutches.

Equating the American and Bolshevik revolutions as twin facets of the onward march of the "common man" was pure fiction. The confusions and contradictions of American foreign policy since World War II stem very largely from the departure from realities during World II as far as the nature and purposes of Stalinist Communism were concerned. No man had greater weight in leading this movement of delusion and perhaps deceit than Wallace and he bears heavy responsibility for its results. In 1943 he wrote on "Three Philosophies" (Prussianism, Marxism and Democracy). Defining the basic Marxist hypothesis as "class warfare is inevitable until such time as the proletariat comes out on top, everywhere in the world," he felt that this philosophy no longer dominated Russia. "Many of the Marxian activities of the last ten years which people of the West have most condemned have been inspired by fear of Germany." The Russian people were "fundamentally more religious than the Prussians;" they hungered "for spiritual food" and "have a better opportunity to find that spiritual food than . . . the Prussians."

In February 1943, Garner, in retirement at Uvalde, Texas, talked with Farley. He was as much against Roosevelt as ever: "Jim . . . it would be a terrible thing to have Roosevelt elected again . . . I hear he is losing ground. The possibility of having Wallace as President is repulsive to me . . . Why, we might have a revolution." Farley was in complete agreement, as was Hull, angry over the criticism "so-called liberals" had been making of his Vichy policy. The anti-third term guard was still in being; it was to give, at the very least, moral support to the Jesse Jones forces during the struggle that removed Wallace from his super-agency, the BEW. Jones's own account of the 1943 fracas illustrated the political purpose of the incident, for his chapter-heading is "How Henry Wallace Missed the Presidency," and he infers that the United States owes him a dept of gratitude for his part in seeing to it that the "miss" occurred. The basis for the Jones-Wallace animosity has already been amply analyzed. Jones places great emphasis on the "arrogant 'Order No. 5' " Chairman Wallace of the BEW issued in January 1943, allocating (usurping, Jones says) to the BEW "all of the powers to buy, stockpile and sell foreign critical materials." Jones felt his RFC powers, congressionally conferred, could not be superseded by a mere order of Wallace. Thus "we did not obey the order to the letter." Since Wallace felt Order No. 5 was a logical specification of the broad grant of power given to him by the executive order of April 13, 1942, the opposition between the two was open and direct. One would have to yield or chaos would result.

Wallace was out of the country for most of March and April on a good-will trip through eight Latin-American countries as the President's representative. On the Vice-President's return, Jones sought a *modus vivendi*. An oral agreement was arrived at which when reduced to writing by the BEW included in Jones' view "much more than we had agreed to." Jones would not accept the enlarged version of transfer of activities and in appearances before the Joint Committee on the Reduction of Non-Essential Federal Expenditures (the Byrd Economy Committee) poured out his grievances. Since the continued life of BEW depended on congressional appropriations, Jones's version had to be answered.

Matters came to a head when Senator Kenneth McKellar of Tennessee spoke from the Senate floor on June 4. A member of the Economy Committee, he was also chairman of the Appropriations Committee. He completely endorsed the Jones position and offered an amendment to an appropriation measure to keep final fiscal control in the RFC.

Wallace and his executive director, Milo Perkins, (another Houston, Texas, business man like Jones, with a long record of rivalry with him) worked for two nights to prepare a seventeen-page memorandum of refutation for the Appropriations Committee. Strongly worded, Wallace hesitated to release it, but as "misrepresentations" of the facts continued, he gave it out on June 29. Item by item, page by page, it listed instances of RFC obstruction to the economic warfare program. For the first time the impersonal Vice-President engaged in personalities. Mr. Jones had created a "false impression," had made "harmful misrepresentations," had "done much to harass the administrative employees of the Board in their single-minded effort to help shorten this war." Wallace hoped that in the future his employees would "be free from this hamstringing bureaucracy and backdoor complaining of Mr. Jones and his employees."

In an equally lengthy reply Jones refuted the Wallace allegations, calling some "false" and others "purposely misleading." The whole "implication" of Wallace's charges he felt was that Jones had been impeding the war effort, a "maliciously false" implication.

President Roosevelt, extremely angry at this new spectacle of disunity, took steps through Budget Director Harold D. Smith, "Assistant President" Byrnes, and Hull to unify international economic operations without the participation of either Wallace or Jones. While the mechanics were being worked up, Jones received a letter from a "confidant and friend," John Garner: "Politically speaking, it is more honorable . . . to stand up and be shot than to surrender . . . stay with the ship. Stand your ground even if your head comes off by force. . . . I surely would like to be there [in Washington] for three or four days to have a little conversation with some of my 'amigos' on the Hill and get them to sustain you in your position. I am . . . praying that you will win out."

If the "old guard" was solidly behind Jones, the liberals were no less behind the Vice-President. William Allen White, among others, wrote Wallace a characteristic letter of support. However, the President moved ostensibly to punish both Wallace and Jones. Removing the Vice-President as Chairman of the BEW, he then abolished the agency. He also removed Jesse Jones from his directorship of the RFC subsidiary corporations engaged in international economic operations and transferred these to a new establishment—the Office of Economic Warfare. The real victory, from Jones' viewpoint, lay in the choice of the chief of the new office: Leo T. Crowley. As Jones said in summary: "Mr. Crowley and I went on working together in harmony. He made no changes in what we were doing abroad. Mr. Wallace . . . was once more just the Vice-President with little to do but wait for the President to die."

Six months before the President would admit it, "Old Dr. New Deal" was dead and "Dr. Win The War" was in control. The Roosevelt who had made no concessions to conservatism in 1940 felt he had to in 1943.

Though he had received a rebuff practically unprecedented in the history of the vice-presidency, Henry Wallace offered no public defense, no criticism, no resignation. When pressed by reporters after being "fired," Wallace said: "In wartime no one should question the over-all wisdom of the Commander in Chief." And, in private, when friends remonstrated with him to alter a speech which opened with a fulsome tribute to Roosevelt, he did tone down the adjectives but reaffirmed his faith in his chief: "In the final showdown he always puts human rights first . . . Powerful groups . . . take advantage of the President's concentration on the war effort, to destroy everything he

has accomplished on the domestic front for the past ten years . . .
Sooner or later . . . [they] will . . . be exposed." So Wallace stayed on
as Vice-President confined by the miniature dimensions of the office,
without portfolio in the Executive Department and reduced to presiding in the Senate where he was as lonely as ever.

Since the foray into active administration by Wallace while Vice-
President ended in debacle, it would be easy to dismiss the entire
venture as a fiasco. But perspective must be maintained. The difficulties Wallace had with Hull, Jones and others were more than
matched by other inter-agency feuds. The war was won, the agencies
somehow did their jobs, so feuding and stand-still operations could
hardly have been the order of the day. Perhaps Rosenman is right
when he says there was no more friction in government than among
business corporations with their clashes of ideas and programs and
ruthless competitive drives. The dismissal of Wallace was not because of incompetency in the work of the BEW, that agency "had
successfully performed an enormous job."

Wallace still retained his symbolic position as spokesman for the
liberal-labor-racial minorities wing of the Democratic party, and as
such was unremitting in his attacks on "privileged" groups on into
the election year of 1944. With the formation of the CIO-PAC, it was
evident that the "left" wing of organized labor was going to make its
weight felt in the forthcoming presidential election. Wallace was
asked to speak at a PAC luncheon in New York City on January 15,
1944. He sent a copy of his proposed remarks to the President.
Though conservative newspapers were trumpeting that "Dr. New
Deal was dead" as Roosevelt had indicated in December, Wallace refused to agree. His speech attacked "isolationist" big businessmen,
charged a segment of them with financing anti-semitism and organizing "hatred of the President and discord in the Democratic Party."
Roosevelt's reaction would serve to indicate where he stood. The
President encouraged Wallace: "I like that speech of yours for the fifteenth—and I hope you will like my blast which will go to Congress
probably on the eleventh. I would like to deliver it myself but . . . I
am just in the 'relapse danger' part of the flu."

While it would bold to say Wallace had forced the President's hand,
still the facts are that the State of the Union message of January 11,
1944 was a document not at all encouraging to conservatives. Roosevelt excoriated "people who burrow through our Nation like unseeing
moles" suspicious "that if other Nations . . . raise their standards of
living, our own . . . must of necessity be depressed." He compared
"a noisy minority" demanding "special favors for special groups" with

"pests" swarming through "the lobbies of the Congress and the cocktail bars of Washington" interested in war "primarily as a chance to make profits." He asked, among other things, for "a realistic tax law— which will tax all unreasonable profits" and "a national service law —which . . . will make available . . . every able-bodied adult in this Nation." The line of thinking and the epithetical vocabulary used here were in the style of Henry Wallace.

Despite the fact that Wallace had retrieved some of his influence with Roosevelt, a White House conference was held in January 1944, at which "the political advisability of dropping Wallace and picking up Truman in his place was discussed." George E. Allen, court-jester to Presidents Roosevelt and Truman, has written convincingly on the Democratic vice-presidential question. He gives great credit to Edwin W. Pauley, a California oilman, treasurer of the Democratic National Committee, calling him "the Sir Galahad of the righteous band that set out to beat Wallace" and "the original anti-Wallace man in the Democratic-party camp."

For more than a year before the 1944 Convention, Pauley had been on a money-raising tour of the country for the party and had "incidentally" mobilized opposition to Wallace's renomination. Thus about the time Roosevelt fired Wallace from the BEW, an anti-Wallace movement was started by organization Democrats. Pauley "primed local leaders to mention to Roosevelt, when the opportunities presented themselves, that the Democratic ticket would suffer seriously . . . They were to tell Roosevelt that they were all for him but just couldn't stomach Wallace." Pauley's next step was to make "a deal with General Watson . . . to clear the way for anti-Wallace Democrats to see Roosevelt . . . and to block the way for pro-Wallace Democrats." Allen admits that he was himself too "afraid to preach the anti-Wallace gospel" to Roosevelt, but Pauley was not and "made the most of every opportunity to report on the extent and virulence of the anti-Wallace sentiment at the grass roots." Such was the background of the mounting pressures on the President that had crystallized in the January meeting at the Executive Mansion. If Wallace thought the leftish tone of the annual message of January 11, 1944, was due to his influence with Roosevelt, it could just as well have reflected Roosevelt's decision to embrace Wallace's program and electoral support while dropping Wallace.

An additional factor in the anti-Wallace movement was that the coterie of "practical politicians," as Allen calls them, "realized that the man nominated to run with Roosevelt would in all probability be the next President of the United States, because all of them saw enough of Roosevelt to recognize that his health had deteriorated rapidly in the war years." (The question of whether the 1944 Democrats felt they were picking a future President when they selected Truman remains a mooted point. Again ideological lines hold fast in the matter; Rosenman in his *Working With Roosevelt* scoffs at reports of chronic failing health in 1944, but the testimony of a close observer like Allen —whom even Rosenman admits is "one of the shrewdest and keenest political thinkers I have met"—lends credibility to the idea that the group anticipated FDR's death during his fourth term.)

Among those attending the informal White House caucus in January 1944, were Pauley, Robert Hannegan of St. Louis, (Chairman of the Democratic National Committee), Frank Walker of Butte, Montana (Postmaster General and a loyal Rooseveltian since 1932), and Edward J. Flynn (Democratic Boss of the Bronx, who had been pro-Wallace for Vice-President in 1940). It is Allen's testimony that the aforementioned "agree in a general way about what happened" that night in January. The vice-presidency was brought up, and Roosevelt "indicated that he agreed with the leaders that Wallace should be dropped in the interests of Democratic-party harmony." Substitutes were discussed including Senators Sherman Minton of Indiana (later Supreme Court Justice), Barkley, Truman, Byrnes, Justice William O. Douglas and Speaker Sam Rayburn of Texas. Out of it all came this consensus: "Truman would be the best bet . . . He was making a respected name for himself as chairman of a committee policing war contracts; he was a loyal New Dealer but not a radical; he was from a mid-continental state. The President himself was favorably impressed with Truman's qualifications and said so."

Allen reports that "no final decision came out of this meeting." Pauley was heartened. Probably working on the old political theory that you can't beat somebody with nobody, he campaigned openly for Truman from then on and was joined by Hannegan. The Vice-President was unaware of (or perhaps unconcerned at) these inner circle machinations as he went his rounds of Cabinet meetings, presiding in the Senate, demanding "a people's peace," and warning of the dangers of "American Fascism" and "invisible governments."

It is against the background of the anti-Wallace cabal within the Democratic party and the January 1944 White House caucus, that Wallace's mission to the Far East in the spring of 1944 takes on added significance—wholly apart from any war purposes it served. It seemed that Wallace was being sent to Siberia in more ways than one during the delegate-choosing period of 1944. Ostensibly, of course, the mission was an outward sign of continued presidential confidence in Wallace's ability to perform an arduous, delicate foreign mission. At any rate, the President asked him to fly to eastern Asia, visit Soviet Siberia and then proceed to China where the common war effort was in need of stimulation. Wallace had no alternative but to obey a war-time assignment of the Commander-in-chief. Roosevelt publicly announced the trip on the day it began, May 20: "I have asked the Vice-President . . . to serve as a messenger for me in China . . . Forces are being unleashed there [Eastern Asia] which are of the utmost importance to our future peace and prosperity. The Vice-President, because of his present position as well as his training in economics and agriculture, is unusually well fitted to bring both to me and to the people . . . a most valuable first-hand report . . . He . . . will report to me upon his return . . . about the middle of July."

Meanwhile, Wallace's political mentor, Harold Young of Texas, on the Vice-President's staff as "special assistant," remained at home to work for Wallace during the delegate-hunting season.

For nearly two months the Vice-President was half-way across the world. Always ready favorably to compare the Soviet Union with the United States, Wallace extolled Siberia as the "Wild East of Russia" comparable to our historic "Wild West." And whereas "under the Tsars" Siberia "miserably supported" a small population who were "mostly convicts," under Communism there were "over 40,000,000 busy people." Critics generally agree that Wallace was given the "special" treatment by his hosts, followed a rigidly prescribed route and saw only what the Politburo deemed it advisable for him to see. Since Wallace went to be impressed and the Reds determined to impress him, the result was not surprising. The trip deepened the impact on him of the "fact of Soviet Asia today" and strengthened his persistent myopia in matters Russian.

Wallace's China experiences were more significant, despite Hull's estimate that "So far as I could see, Wallace's trip was without beneficial effect." Strong in his convictions and prejudices, Hull viewed every invasion of his Department's functions in the worst light. It was not simply Wallace he objected to, it was anyone.

Wallace had asked Hull to designate someone to accompany him; the State Department named John Carter Vincent, then Chief of the Division of Chinese Affairs. A third member, Owen Lattimore, was assigned by the Office of War Information to "handle publicity matters." Briefed beforehand by a State Department Far Eastern expert, Joseph W. Ballantine, "on the pitfalls to be avoided," the Vice-President arrived in China during the latter part of June. Wallace's primary purpose was "to see what he could do toward consolidating the

Chinese war effort against Japan." The Kuomintang (Nationalist) - Communist split was seriously hampering the allied war effort, and previous American efforts to find a way of subordinating domestic differences in face of the common Japanese aggression had failed. The Vice-President had five talks in four days (June 21 to 24) with Generalissimo Chiang-Kai-shek, head of the National government. A wide range of topics was covered including Wallace's proffer through Roosevelt of American good offices in mediating the internal split "in as much as the Communists and . . . Kuomintang were all Chinese." On Soviet-Chinese relations, the Vice-President thought all questions "which might result in conflict between China and the U.S.S.R." should be settled, though he rejected (at Vincent's urging) Chiang's suggestion that the United States be a mediator. He expanded his favorite theme, the deep interest "the people of the United States" had "in seeing an increase in Chinese agricultural efficiency which will permit a sound industrialization." The nature of the talks was essentially exploratory, though one immediate and tangible result was Chiang's agreement to permit an American Army unit to enter the Communist stronghold in the North to establish liaison with them and to act as observers.

When Wallace was leaving the Chungking airport, President Chiang requested him to give Roosevelt a twelve point message. Chiang said that the Vice-President's visit "to bring about accord with Russia shows great friendship for China" and his presence "at this dark hour will help the morale of the troops and give hope that America will continue to aid China." Wallace then went to Kunming to confer with General Claire L. Chennault, leader of the "Flying Tigers," on the military picture. Chennault was so pessimistic and so heavily underlined the political crisis of China as he had seen it that the Vice-President decided then and there to cable a preliminary report to the President. The Vice-President was assisted in the preparation of this first report by Vincent, the State Department's representative. Wallace considered the most important part of his message to be his military recommendations, three in number, which were "that China be separated from the command of General Stilwell, that General Wedemeyer should be considered in the choice of a new military commander in China, and that the new commander should be given the additional assignment of 'personal representative' of the President at Chungking."

On the political situation, Wallace's central conclusion was that Chiang had put himself and China into a "hole" by an "unenlightened" administration supported by "landlords, warlords and bankers."

Chiang was "so prejudiced against the Communists" as to leave little prospect of a settlement with them for the purpose of concerted action toward winning the war as quickly as possible. "At this time there seems to be no alternative to support of Chiang, but the leaders of postwar China will be brought forward by evolution or revolution, and it now seems more likely the latter." Chiang was considered a "short term investment," neither intelligent enough nor politically strong enough to rule post-war China. Disintegration of the Chungking regime might occur. This would result in "a political vacuum which will be filled in ways which you will understand."

Arriving back in the United States on July 10, Wallace was immediately presented with the news from Roosevelt's emissaries, Rosenman and Ickes, that he was to step aside and not seek renomination at the approaching Convention. Preoccupied and tired, Wallace was in no mood to talk politics.

Rosenman's reminiscences of the breakfast conference he and Ickes had with Wallace are striking: Wallace's face was "as immobile as stone," "He seemed not even to be listening" while they tried their "best to explain the reasons in back of the President's determination." When he had heard enough, the Vice-President said: "Sam, I've just come back from a country where people are dying by the hundreds of thousands because of lack of food . . . I have no interest now in discussing political matters. I shall do so eventually with the President."

Wallace saw Roosevelt both that day at lunch and the day after, presenting his final formal report and discussing with him the vice-presidential situation. Concerning the Far East mission, one cannot agree with the later charge by Republican Senator Homer S. Ferguson of Michigan that the "secret report" made by Wallace in 1944 was "the basis of United States policy" toward China until 1950. One can agree, however, that the Vice-President's recommendations were not fruitless. In August 1944, Major-General Patrick J. Hurley was sent as special representative of the President to be the military-political liaison officer Chiang had called for and Wallace had seconded and in November 1944 Wedemeyer was sent to replace Stilwell as commander in the area. Hurley made renewed efforts to get the Communists and Nationalists together and, in one way or another, Chinese forces were kept in the field until V-J day.

On the matter of dropping the Vice-President, Roosevelt seems to have strengthened his intent while Wallace was abroad. As long as the opposition to Wallace was confined to organization men, the question was open. But when New Dealers like Ickes and Rosenman also approved the idea, Roosevelt became convinced that the Vice-Presi-

dent was a disruptive force. The urgings of these two had led him to
designate them as bearers of the tidings. They were to intercept
Wallace as soon as he entered the United States and cushion the shock
as much as possible. Wallace, however, managed to avoid the emissaries until he arrived in Washington.

Unlike 1940, the Vice-President had pre-convention delegate
strength (290 pledges). Even George E. Allen admitted Young was
doing "fairly well" at lining up votes. The Vice-President pleaded his
case to Roosevelt, showed him the list of delegates, and said that he
did not expect another 1940 effort on his behalf—nor was it needed.
Wallace's position was that unless F.D.R. repudiated him, he would
stand as a candidate for renomination. Roosevelt, possibly abashed
and probably amazed at the delegate strength Wallace had, said he
would not repudiate him and agreed to write a letter indicating his
faith in him. At the conclusion of the meeting, Roosevelt—with a
half pat, half hug around the shoulder—said: "I hope it's the same
team again Henry." Yet that very night the organization men had
another White House conference at which, after canvassing the field,
Truman was designated to replace Wallace as the vice-presidential
nominee in 1944.

Allen, a member of the group, recorded the scene and the President's
conclusion: "Bob, I think you and everyone else here want Truman."
This was good enough for Hannegan who rose and ushered everyone
out of the room "before Roosevelt had a chance to change his mind."
Frank Walker, also aware of this Rooseveltian propensity, urged Hannegan to get the decision on paper. So Hannegan went back upstairs
and got a "Dear Bob" letter for public use if need be. Hannegan's
letter, written in long-hand on a memo pad, was post-dated July 19
and read: "You have written me about Harry Truman and Bill
Douglas. I should, of course, be very glad to run with either of them
and believe that either one of them would bring real strength to the
ticket."

Allen summed up his own thoughts as he left the White House that
July night, eight days before the fateful 1944 Convention opened:
"Roosevelt was now on record with the party leaders for Truman but
he still . . . was free to change his mind, and all those present at the
White House meeting knew it. They also sensed that Roosevelt
would not live much longer. At this meeting he had seemed tired and
listless. Riding home that night . . . I think all of us felt more strongly
than ever that the man nominated . . . would soon succeed . . . we
knew in our hearts that Roosevelt would not live through another
term."

The suspense concerning the President's decision was to last right down to balloting time. Allen went to the Chicago convention not knowing "whom the President finally would pick for the . . . nomination." Though the politicians thought it was still Truman, they could not be sure. At one point even Hannegan despaired, rushing up to Flynn in Chicago, crying: "It's all over. It's Byrnes." Allen states a profound truth when he writes: "Roosevelt could, of course, have named anybody. All he had to do was say whom he wanted definitely and firmly."

Meanwhile the President had left by special train for the West Coast on his way to an Hawaiian conference with the Pacific commanders. On July 15 the train stopped in the Chicago stock-yards for servicing, and Hannegan and Pauley came aboard for a secret conclave. Hannegan received "Roosevelt's encouragement and support" in pushing Truman's nomination. Leahy, who was on the Presidential train, noted that after the train left Chicago, Roosevelt "gave us the surprising information that he had recommended . . . Truman." So apparently the decision of July 11 was confirmed in the Chicago railroad car conference of July 15.

Of all the party conventions held up to that time, none concentrated as much interest in the vice-presidency as the Democratic Chicago Convention of 1944. It was a foregone conclusion that Roosevelt would be nominated and in fact, outside the so-called "Texas Regulars" (of whom Garner was the spiritual godfather), no organized anti-fourth-term sentiment had formed. Wallace held a press conference after the letter the President had promised him was released. Wallace told the reporters: "I am in this fight to the finish . . . I told the President in justice to himself and myself that there should not be anything in the nature of dictation to the convention. The letter did what I suggested."

Roosevelt's Wallace letter, later termed the "kiss of death," read:

"I . . . give you my own personal thought in regard to the selection of a candidate for Vice President.

". . . The easiest way of putting it is this: I have been associated with Henry Wallace during his past four years as Vice President, for eight years earlier while he was Secretary of Agriculture, and well before that. I like him and I respect him and he is my personal friend. For these reasons I personally would vote for his renomination if I were a delegate to the convention.

"At the same time I do not wish to appear in any way as dictating . . . Obviously the convention must do the deciding. And it should—

and I am sure it will—give great consideration to the pros and cons of its choice."

It was the final paragraph that held the sting; it undid the praise and direction of the preceding one. Yet Wallace fought on, even turning the other cheek by seconding Roosevelt's nomination on July 20th in a warm, glowing tribute.

Until the release of the "Truman-Douglas" letter on July 20th, Wallace was in a strong position. The final pre-balloting Gallup public opinion poll had been released that day and showed the Democratic voters in favor of the Vice-President's renomination: Wallace 65%; Barkley, 17%; Byrnes, 3%; Truman, 2%; and the rest scattered. It was confusing to the delegates that the Administration leaders wanted a man who insisted he was not running and who was working for someone else who had received no presidential benediction at all. This is why Allen admitted "it could have been Wallace if the vote had been taken the night before it was. It could have been a stampede. And it almost was." The schedule called for vice-presidential nominations that night of July 20 and Wallaceites were in control of the galleries. Clearly something had to be done. Allen was in charge of convention arrangements and "tried to find some way out of a night meeting and of silencing the organ"—which was playing over and over *Iowa—That's Where the Tall Corn Grows.* Mayor Ed Kelly (one of the night conferees of July 11) "got me off the hook by proclaiming a fire hazard and thus forcing an adjournment until the following day." The recess was all that was needed. Byrnes withdrew, Truman was persuaded to run and the word began to be passed to switch to Truman. At last the battle lines were clearly drawn— Wallace versus Truman. On the first ballot of July 21, with 639 votes necessary for choice, the tally showed Wallace 429½, Truman 319½, scattered 427. But, on the second ballot, Truman rode to victory 1031 votes to Wallace's 105, with many delegations switching to Truman in the midst of the voting.

For the first time in the twentieth century, a political party had refused a second-term nomination to a Vice-President while renominating the President. Strikingly enough, the first time a national convention had ever done this was in 1864, also in the midst of war— and both times the device of a Presidential letter had been used to signify the President's desires.

Of all President Roosevelt's numerous mooted acts, none is more indefensible than that toward Wallace on this occasion. Even adulators and friendly critics of Roosevelt are hard put to explain his tactics. Though John Gunther agrees it was "a blessing to the country, as subsequent events manifestly proved," the manner of dropping was "brutal" and "can hardly be considered other than as the worst double-cross in Roosevelt's history." One can hardly dispute his further thought: "If one can solve the riddle of this performance over Wallace at the convention, one can solve the riddle of Roosevelt as a whole. It is not enough to say merely that the President equivocated; played two ends, and gave conflicting promises."

Gunther's own solution for the "riddle of Roosevelt" on this occasion is that the President was "bored" by such concerns in 1944. What F.D.R. told Rosenman late in June seems nearer the mark: "I am just not going to go through a convention like 1940 again. It will split the party wide open, and it is already split enough between the North and South; it may kill our chances for election this fall, and if it does, it will prolong the war and knock into a cocked hat all the plans we've been making for the future." The larger political aspect of Truman's nomination was attested to by Harry Hopkins who said to Sherwood: "People seemed to think that Truman was just suddenly pulled out of a hat—but that wasn't true. The President had had his eye on him for a long time . . . he'd got himself known and liked around the country—and above all he was very popular in the Senate. That was the biggest consideration. The President wanted somebody that would help when he went up there and asked them to ratify the peace."

At a luncheon with the President on August 29th Roosevelt told Henry Wallace that he could have any Cabinet post he wished except the State Department. Wallace chose Commerce, Jesse Jones's department. If the third term cost Wallace his BEW chairmanship and the vice-presidency, it cost Jones his career in government.

Wallace campaigned for Roosevelt, avoided references to Truman, congratulated the President on his 60,000,000 jobs post-war goal and predicted that the party would carry 36 states with a Roosevelt majority of three million. The President replied: "I promise to make good on the sixty million jobs if you will do the same on your [election] predictions . . . That was a grand job you did last night in Madison Square [Garden]. Hope to see you soon." Wallace proved to be a good seer. The Roosevelt-Truman ticket carried 36 states with a popular majority of 3,600,000.

Wallace's impact on the vice-presidential office was tremendous. Or perhaps it is better stated that the attitude of President Roosevelt to the office while Wallace was in it caused his profound impact. The precedent of giving the Vice-President regular, continuing and significant administrative work and making him available for missions abroad was established. In 1949, Congress in reorganizing the newly-created National Security Council, included in its membership the Vice-President of the United States. Thus not by Executive Order or whim, but by statutory authority the Vice-President became a member of the highest policy agency of government. After Wallace left the office of Vice-President it was clearly something different than it had been before he entered it. Whether it would remain different only the future would disclose.

CHAPTER 12

Return to the Senate

While the "Missouri Compromise of 1944" was being talked up among Democrats, the Republican party met at Chicago to name its slate. As Wilfred Binkley points out, though governor of Ohio John W. Bricker, an "honest Harding . . . was the personal choice of the Republican delegates for the presidential nomination . . . he had to be content with second place after the convention had reluctantly bowed to the sentiments of the party's rank and file." Before the balloting began Bricker sensed the futility of his presidential aspirations as he walked to the microphone to second Dewey's nomination. Though Ohio delegates shouted "No," Bricker announced that it was evident that sentiment for Mr. Dewey was "overwhelming" and urged his supporters to vote for the New Yorker. Then Bricker conceded that he had no chance to defeat Dewey. He expressed a willingness to accept the vice-presidential nomination. Since Dewey's own second place preference, Governor Earl Warren of California, refused to allow mention of his name, there was clear sailing for both nominees who were unanimously selected on first ballots.

This 1944 ticket represented a balance of regular Republican forces. If Dewey represented young Republicanism, it was not the New Dealish, "one world" Willkie type. Dewey's nomination marked the Republican "return to conventional practice in recognizing the claims of a candidate . . . based on outstanding public service as a party member." Bricker's nomination merely confirmed that the age of surprise in Republican nominations was over.

By far the most fateful selection of 1944 was that of Harry S. Truman by the Democrats. Coming to the Senate in 1935 after a career in petty Missouri politics and office-holding, Truman was a diligent if uninspiring party wheel-horse. There is no reason to doubt the accuracy of his own recollection of his initiation to Washington: "The first thing I did when I came down here as a Senator was to call on him [Roosevelt] and pay my respects and to tell him that I had been elected on his platform of 1932 and that I expected to support him." Truman kept his promise. Well-trained in party discipline while the

210

protégé of Boss Thomas A. Pendergast of Kansas City, he could be counted on to vote correctly for administration measures.

Since freshman Senators are usually lost souls and Harry Truman was anything but exceptional, he was all the more grateful for such considerations as he received. No one ever gave friendship to him without being amply repaid. Thus when Senators Burton K. Wheeler and James F. Byrnes befriended him, they became his idols. Later politics might make it necessary for the liaison to break up (as in the case of Wheeler), or ideological and personal differences might change the friendship to enmity (as in the case of Byrnes), but Truman would never be the first to turn his back on anyone who had helped him out during those lonely first years in Washington. As he said about Wheeler: "His viewpoint is almost opposite to mine but you must understand that sixteen years ago Burt Wheeler was one of the few Senators . . . who was in any way decent to the Junior Senator from Missouri and I can't forget that. That doesn't necessarily mean that he has any influence with me as to policy but I shall continue to like him as long as I live."

These two powerful Democrats, Wheeler and Byrnes, unsuccessful aspirants to the vice-presidency themselves at one time or another, taught him the ropes, gave him entrée to party social and political cliques, and generally brought him along in the Senate. (Wheeler had bolted in 1924 and been Vice-Presidential nominee on the La Follette Progressive ticket. Byrnes sought the nomination both in 1940 and 1944. Truman learned from Wheeler many of the techniques he was later to use on the "Truman Committee." The freshman Senator was assigned to the Interstate Commerce Committee which Wheeler headed, and was occasionally given charge of a subcommittee.)

By these means did Senator Truman make the grade with his colleagues and come to be accepted. By the fall of 1937 he was a luncheon companion of Vice-President Garner along with such other Senators as Sherman, Minton, Byrnes, Schwellenbach and Barkley and was a visitor to Garner's office for a sociable drink or two. According to the independent liberal Senator Norris, Truman "came into public life with somewhat of a cloud because he was probably first elected . . . by the influence of the noted Boss Pendergast. I watched him in his public service more than I otherwise would, and I must say that . . . I never knew an instance . . . that the bosses or the machine controlled his official work. I think he has done some very good work."

Truman, reviewing his work during his first term in the Senate, indicated why he got the reputation of a plodder: "I became a member of the Appropriations, Interstate Commerce, Public Building and Grounds, Enrolled Bills and Audit and Control Committees. I attended every meeting of every committee to which I was appointed."

Truman was no meteor either to Washington or to the people back home. He had difficulty being renominated, but squeezed through in a three-way race between Maurice Milligan (federal district attorney for Kansas City who had just put Boss Pendergast in Leavenworth Prison for income tax evasion), and Governor Lloyd C. Stark (whose star also seemed to be rising, so strong was his appeal among the farmers). Truman strength—"the remnants of Pendergast's empire and the aging men of Battery D"—plus the significant last-minute endorsement of the young leader of the St. Louis Democratic forces, Robert E. Hannegan, managed to prevail. The future was writ large for both Hannegan and Truman in that first coalition compelled by the exigencies of Missouri politics. The Administration Truman had supported lent him no aid in his 1940 primary fight. In responding to an appeal for help, Roosevelt (in contradistinction to his 1938 attitude) answered through Steve Early: "The President asks me to explain to you personally that while Senator Truman is an old and trusted friend . . . his invariable practice has been not to take part in primary contests. This . . . because . . . the President must stand aloof regardless of any personal preference he might have. Of course, after the primary . . . contests then are clear-cut." Nevertheless Truman was re-elected in the third term victory year even though he trailed Roosevelt in Missouri by 28,000 votes. That is why William Hillman, his official biographer, writes, "Indeed, he [Truman] was never elected to an office he did not have to fight for, tooth and nail, unless it was the nomination as Vice-President which he struggled to avoid."

Truman returned to the Senate and introduced the resolution that would ultimately lift him to the vice-presidency and the presidency. This resolution of February 10, 1941 called for the establishment of a committee to investigate the national defense program. The plan was viewed by the administration as a possible source of unfavorable headlines that would further divide the country. Truman insisted his idea was different: "I went to see President Roosevelt and explained that I wanted to help him win the war, that I would keep him informed of what I found, and that if he could remedy the situation he'd hear no more from me beyond that." Truman's motivations for asking for the committee's establishment appear to have been a combination of his knowledge of American Civil War history, his recollections of Army waste in World War I and a tour he took in 1940 because of Senate

Appropriations Committee hearings in various Army camps on rising defense requirements. Truman's erstwhile sponsor, Byrnes, pared his modest $25,000 appropriation request to $15,000, and before an indifferent Senate (with only 16 senators on the floor) the resolution was approved without objection, March 1, 1941.

The value of the Truman Committee became recognized even before Pearl Harbor. Interested in seeking facts rather than headlines, it sought to help the defense program. After its first report on Camp Meade, which constructively showed how savings might be effected, it never had appropriations trouble again. The Committee continued throughout American participation in World War II and submitted forty unanimous reports. It was a shining example of bipartisanship. Truman himself felt that one of the early major post-Pearl Harbor accomplishments of his Committee was the 190-page report on the OPM including its affiliation with Vice-President Wallace's SPAB which, the committee felt, had so confused lines of administration that "chaos and indecision" were rife. The subsequent creation of the WPB under one-man administration was, Truman believed, the result of his committee's "unanswerable indictment." Perhaps the major result was that Truman became a power among Senators and was respectfully listened to. His committee's authority was appealed to in and out of the Senate and he became, in the President's eyes, a Senator apart from the run-of-the-mill party incumbents.

Truman headed the War Investigating Committee for forty months (resigning in August 1944 after his vice-presidential nomination), using total appropriations of $360,000 with an estimated saving of $15 billion to the nation. Beyond the usual credit that goes to the titular head of a constructive agency, Truman received a rare compliment by the Washington newspaper correspondents when he was voted in a poll to be "one of the ten most valuable men in Washington in the war." He was the only member of Congress so listed.

The chief mystery about Truman's selection in 1944 is not why he was chosen, but what his own attitude was. By disclaiming any desire for the place down to the eve of the balloting, Truman was following a well-established pattern. Can it be that here was a truly reluctant candidate? Despite the well-nigh universal belief among practical politicians that the Vice-President of Roosevelt's fourth term would succeed to the presidency, did Truman still not want the office? The record, as so far revealed, is incontestable and harmonious that Truman made no overt moves to promote his own nomination, participated in none of the numerous conferences among party leaders to stop Wallace, and revealed no secret wishes to intimates to capitalize on his political assets of a good press and an honored name through-out the country.

It could be said that Truman had no need to make any overt moves to organize his candidacy, that the facts of the situation were doing that for him anyway. A good case could be made from such premises, for the Truman Committee made him available without any need for action on his own part, while Hannegan and Pauley were beating the bushes for him (either with or without his approval, but probably not without his knowledge and certainly not *against* his wishes). In such circumstances Truman could take the old Theodore Roosevelt stand and be really consistent (where the latter was not) until in essence a wartime order from his commander in chief, Franklin D. Roosevelt, on Thursday afternoon, July 20, 1944 by means of telephone made him agree to accept the place. If the real facts were as the above appar-encies seem to make them, then Truman's candidacy was indeed a true instance of "the office seeking the man," a political rarity in the United States.

Auxiliary questions remain that leave Truman's real purposes in 1944 in doubt. For example, what was the motivation of Hannegan during this period? His political rise was rapid indeed after he gave belated assistance to Truman in the hotly contested renomination battle in Missouri. Truman recommended him as Internal Revenue Collector in St. Louis in 1942 and for Commissioner of Internal Rev-enue in 1943. Finally, when Frank Walker desired to retire as Chair-man of the Democratic National Committee, Truman refused the offer to succeed him, but recommended Hannegan who got the job. So, shortly before the significant January 1944 White House confer-ence, Truman's fellow-Missourian had been placed in the most stra-tegic of all party posts just when the running-mate question was about to come to a head. Leaving aside the interesting implications of why Roosevelt twice tried to shunt Harry Truman from his elective office, it was apparent that something more than reciprocity for a past favor was involved in Truman's sponsoring Hannegan. As Daniels puts it, "Certainly Hannegan owed his entire political status to Truman since he . . . had lost out in . . . the state but [and] in the St. Louis city hall as well."

Pauley and Hannegan frankly campaigned for Truman after Jan-uary 1944 and saw to it that Truman was seen in organization circles that spring. A series of money-raising dinners was held at which the most sought-after speakers were Truman and Speaker of the House Sam Rayburn. Truman crossed the continent to hold committee hearings on various aspects of the war effort and was able to meet

Pauley and Rayburn in San Francisco on March 30, inviting them to his hotel rooms for cocktails before another party banquet. With his fellow-investigators, Harley Kilgore of West Virginia and Mon Wallgren of Washington, the group "got to kidding about the vice-presidency." One of the Senators "mentioned that Harry Truman was a candidate." Pauley said that was fine with him, but that he was already committed to Rayburn. (1950 accounts on the nomination, like Allen and Daniels, emphasize Pauley, while 1952 works, like Hillman and Rosenman, omit even mention of his name. Truman's 1955 *Memoirs* do not speak of Pauley in connection with the 1944 nomination.) Those cocktails started a mutual admiration society. Later that same night at the dinner, Truman toasted Rayburn "as the next Vice-President of the United States" and "just a week later" Rayburn reciprocated at a dinner in St. Louis.

At an undisclosed later time Roosevelt "went over the potential candidates" with Ed Flynn—who tells us that Truman "just dropped into the slot. It was agreed that Truman was the man who would hurt him least." Roosevelt then told Flynn to get the political leaders together for another session at the White House to "inject Truman into the picture." The result was the July 11 meeting, already discussed, out of which came the Truman selection.

Just one week before that second White House political conference, the man from Independence had lunch with Secretary of the Navy James Forrestal. It was Independence Day, and Forrestal noted in his diary that Truman: "said to me that he was being urged to accept the nomination for vice president but that he proposed to resist. I told him that it was his duty to take it in view of the fact that the alternative would be Henry Wallace. This alternative he regarded with the same misgivings as myself but still felt he did not want to take the nomination, saying that he was happy in the Senate and felt that he was able to exercise as much influence in government as he wished." This disclosure at least indicates that *before* the crucial July 11 conference Truman was aware of the movement to have him nominated. (Two things ought to be noted about Forrestal's diaries, as published —they are incomplete, the above quotation being lifted from the context of additional Forrestal remarks as antecedent elision marks indicate, also the White House was the repository for the diaries until they were published, being first "examined by representatives of the White House." Thus from the point of view of Truman's reluctance to run the one item that substantiates all official versions is printed. No other Forrestal information or attitude on the nomination is printed. Whether any exists, the author does not pretend to know.)

Pauley's version of how the field was narrowed on the night of July 11 is terse if incomplete: "Rayburn [was eliminated] because of the split in the Texas delegation; Byrnes because of coming from the Deep South; Barkley because of his apparent lack of loyalty to President Roosevelt, and coming from the South, too."

The man "committed" in March to Rayburn does not seem to have argued for him at all that night. Moreover, when the meeting was over and the leaders were riding home, Allen said to him, "Ed, this is the greatest personal victory you will ever obtain." Whether this ambiguous remark meant getting Wallace dropped or Truman accepted it is impossible to say, but the context in Daniels implies the latter. Thus, even without reference to any other sources, Pauley's pro-Rayburn commitment did not mean much if it had ever meant anything. Rayburn, evidently apprised of his rejection by the leaders at the White House, phoned Senator Truman that "he was not a candidate." Truman now swung to Byrnes, passing the word to his office "boys" and telling them that "he was not personally interested in seeking the nomination and that, if the nomiation was offered to him, he would be forced to decline."

On July 14 (the same day the Roosevelt train left Hyde Park for the West), Truman got ready to leave for Chicago. What follows is Truman's own version of the vice-presidential proceedings from that point: "As I was about to leave . . . the Honorable James F. Byrnes called and asked me if I would nominate him for vice-president, as the President wanted him to have that position on the ticket. I said surely, I'll do it if the President wants it done. Before I could get to the automobile . . . Senator Alben Barkley called and asked me to nominate him for Vice-President. I reported my conversation with Senator Byrnes and told Barkley I was committed."

The peculiarities of this nomination were now fixed: the anointed one was to put in nomination someone else, and work in convention for him while disavowing his own pretensions. There is no parallel for this in vice-presidential history, but it reminds one of the Republican 1880 convention when Garfield, working for Sherman for the presidential nomination, emerged as the dark horse compromise choice himself. At Chicago, Truman relates, "I went to see all the leaders I knew, to try to get them for Byrnes for Vice-President. Each time I saw a leader he would tell me he was for Henry Wallace first and for me second. I told all of them that I was not a candidate. I reported all these interviews to Mr. Byrnes. He would tell me each time that President Roosevelt would publicly say he was for him for Vice-President."

What Truman means is that he went to see all the labor leaders. On July sixteenth he breakfasted with Sidney Hillman, who, in answer to his plea for Byrnes, said "No. We're for Wallace, but we might accept two other men. Our second choice after Wallace would be Douglas. I'm looking at our first choice now." Philip Murray of the CIO, A. F. Whitney and George Harrison of the railroad unions told him the same thing on the following day. William Green of the AFL "fed him another breakfast and the same words" on the eighteenth. Truman was either a master politician or an indispensable man. He was getting clearance from sources while apparently not working for them. When to the labor leaders were added border state delegates and "anti-labor Southerners," all interested in Truman as the means to stop Wallace, Byrnes felt it time to hear from Roosevelt directly. On the day the convention opened, Wednesday the nineteenth, Byrnes phoned San Diego, but could not reach him. He then withdrew "in deference to the wishes of" Roosevelt, which wishes Rosenman states he knew as early as the morning after the night conference of July 11 when Frank Walker was assigned the job of telling Byrnes he would not be the nominee. (Truman in his *Memoirs* also feels now that Byrnes used him wrongly in 1944).

Roosevelt was renominated on July 19, after which, Truman relates: "Bob Hannegan . . . came to see me at the Stevens Hotel and told me that the President wanted me to be the nominee for Vice President . . . I was flabbergasted. I told Hannegan that I wanted to stay in the Senate, and . . . would not take the nomination."

Remembering that two weeks before, Truman had told Forrestal of the pressures that were on him to be a candidate and remembering the prior close relations between Hannegan and Truman, it is impossible to accept Truman's version. How could he have been "flabbergasted", even if he did not know the results of the conference of the 11th, when every significant labor leader had spoken to and for him?

On the next day, July 20th, the vice-presidential nomination was scheduled to take place. This is Truman's statement on how he stubbornly fought to stay in the Senate and out of the White House:

"I [Truman] was asked to come over to the Blackstone Hotel for a conference . . . all the Democratic leaders of the nation . . . began to put pressure on me, the country boy, to stand for . . . Vice-President.

"Finally, Hannegan called President Roosevelt in San Diego, California . . . the President said, and I could hear him, 'Well, if he wants to let the Democratic Party and the country down in the midst of a war that is his responsibility.'

"I was, to put it mildly, stunned.

"I stood around for at least five minutes and then I said, I'll do what the President wants.

". . . After the nomination . . . none of us [Truman, his wife, and daughter] was happy."

While the reminiscences of Allen, Flynn, Pauley, Rosenman and Walker differ in minor details, they all hold fast to the Truman story of intransigeance on the nomination and avow his innocence of any participation in the intricate maneuvers that led to Roosevelt's decision to take him.

The factors determining Roosevelt's selection of the 1944 running-mate were, according to Rosenman, "that the candidate nominated" be "a liberal in complete sympathy with the New Deal and with the Administration's foreign policy and postwar program." In addition, Roosevelt "weighed carefully . . . the potential political strength" of the field. The one who best met these qualifications was Senator Harry S. Truman, on whom the President definitely decided in the night conference of July 11, 1944.

Specifically, Truman met the above factors, in Rosenman's view, because he "had been an undeviating supporter of the President's domestic and foreign policies . . . with only one or two exceptions . . . His service as chairman of . . . the Truman Committee had been thorough, dignified, and painstaking. It had not been used . . . for political propaganda . . . Its work had built up vast public support and good will for Truman. Coming from the central part of the country, he was geographically very acceptable . . . He was from a border state . . . politically doubtful in 1944, and he could be expected to win its . . . votes. He was a combat veteran of World War I, active in veteran's affairs, and would appeal strongly to the soldier vote."

Truman, as we have seen, won the vice-presidential nomination on the second ballot after trailing Wallace on the first. Roosevelt sent him the usual felicitations. The President was busy with war and post-war plans and, while the two did meet for the usual conference on campaigning procedures, that was to be their only meeting "in the entire time between the convention and inauguration."

Truman was a vigorous campaigner. Allen, who was in his entourage, described the campaign vividly. Truman "spoke wherever the train stopped and many times at some stops. No two speeches were identical. He was at his best before a small, intimate audience . . . Nobody paid much attention to the Truman effort unless he got into trouble or got out of potential trouble, as he frequently did."

Truman's troubles during the campaign were concerned largely with Senator Wheeler, Hearst and Vice-President Wallace. Wheeler, isolationist and anti-Roosevelt, was Truman's friend. Allen, as representative of the Democratic National Committee, dreaded the coming Montana tour because that was the home state of Wheeler, and a picture or news story of the two together "wouldn't go down very well in Washington." However Truman had already arranged that no awkwardness should occur; Wheeler was not in sight during the Truman visit.

While the tour of Illinois was in progress, Daniels (a White House secretary at the time) phoned Allen that "the Hearst press was publishing a copyrighted article" exposing Truman "as a member of the Ku Klux Klan." Truman publicly denied it and instituted a libel suit which he called off after his election. Truman, of course, was the very opposite of a Klansman.

The traditional end-of-the-campaign rally in Madison Square Garden was complicated because of the expected presence of the Communists and Wallace. Since the Vice-President was their idol, it was expected that at the very least they would give him a reception that would dwarf Truman's. It was decided that the only thing to do would be to have both enter the Garden together. Truman thus arrived an hour early, kept out of sight and awaited the Vice-President's arrival. Though there were certain anxious moments, the unknowing Wallace "finally arrived one minute before the time set for the meeting to open and was marched into the huge auditorium at Truman's side. It was a great demonstration—probably for Wallace—but Truman took his bows and the publicity was all right."

The election was another clear-cut Roosevelt triumph. In the few remaining months of Roosevelt's life, he was to have only perfunctory relations with Truman. However important the latter was to have been when the anticipated post-war treaty settlement would come before the Senate, he actually never became the confidant Garner or Wallace had been at the outset of their incumbencies. Truman later was to say: "I don't think I saw Roosevelt but twice as Vice-President except at Cabinet meetings." Allen is correct in asserting, "Truman settled inconspicuously into the Vice-Presidency . . Like other Vice-Presidents before him, he was forgotten by most Americans until the day death made him President of the United States."

Truman was to be Vice-President for only 82 days, during which time he conscientiously carried out his senatorial, Cabinet and legislative liaison duties. With reference to the last-named, his only really important task was to help steer Henry Wallace's nomination through the Senate. Roosevelt informed him of the contemplated Cabinet change and asked for his assistance. Though Truman's immediate reaction was an incredulous oath, he recovered to promise that he would "see every Senator" he could in order to put it over. He and Barkley managed ultimately to do it, but it took two months of prolonged public hearings, protracted postponements in the Senate, and special legislation separating all lending-spending activities from the Commerce Department. The new Vice-President felt he played a strategic role in accomplishing the confirmation of the ex-Vice-President. As he reminisced: "Wallace was almost beaten at one point when Barkley was not paying attention and Taft asked to be recognized. He was going to bring up the question of . . . confirmation and Wallace would have been beaten right then. Finally Barkley woke up and I recognized him." Truman thus showed that he would use his powers of presiding as a servant of the Administration, rather than as the unconcerned national officer. So divided was the Senate that only by using the casting vote twice did Vice-President Truman keep Wallace's name from being obliterated as an item of business.

Since President Roosevelt spent not much more than a month of his short fourth term in Washington, there were only a few Cabinet meetings. A session held on the eve of the inaugural, just three days before he left for Yalta, included an item that had overtones of Vice-President Marshall's time and possible application to the incoming Truman. The President informed his Cabinet that "he was quite willing to *have the Cabinet meet under the leadership of whoever was the ranking member at the time* . . . He recalled that . . . Wilson . . . in 1919 . . . became exceedingly angry when Robert Lansing . . . called a meeting because of his expressed doubt as to Mr. Wilson's competence to tend to business. The President said that he did not share that point of view and would be quite willing to have the Cabinet convene whenever anyone thought there was business to be dealt with."

The portion italicized above is interesting if ambiguous. Roosevelt, who had reinstituted the practice of having Vice-Presidents sit in at Cabinet sessions, did not indicate what he meant by "ranking member." Technically and officially, the Vice-President is outranked only by the President himself in the American scheme of things, but as a member of the Cabinet he was (as of 1945) the last officer to be admitted to its ranks and was thus the junior member from that viewpoint). It may also be true that he is not a member at all, since he heads no department and is merely included *ex officio* and by presidential courtesy. Whatever Roosevelt meant by his permission to allow Cabinet meetings in his absence from the country, he made no effort to fix the position of the incoming Vice-President in the hierarchy for chairmanship purposes.

Roosevelt's quoted remarks are also interesting because he confused two things. Wilson distinguished Cabinet meetings during his absence because of his attendance at an international conference and those held during his absence because of illness. He not only permitted the former, but had asked Marshall to preside over them. He forbade the latter type of Cabinet meetings, and dismissed Lansing because he dared to call them. Roosevelt is not clear as to whether he was granting permission under the latter circumstances, though it is clear that Forrestal felt it was a blanket permission and that "anyone" could call the Cabinet together.

As for the Cabinet meetings held in Roosevelt's presence, Truman, like Marshall and Garner, doubted their usefulness for him: "Roosevelt never discussed anything important at his Cabinet meetings. Cabinet members, if they had anything to discuss, tried to see him privately after the meetings." While private meetings occurred, the Forrestal diaries are direct testimony that important subjects were discussed at Cabinet sessions both by the President and other members. Thus on March 9, at least seven different topics were discussed (only three of which are listed in the truncated published diaries) and in addition "the President made some observations about his conception of the trusteeship idea . . . with particular reference to the Pacific Ocean Areas." Roosevelt's remarks were an outline of the method and theory that was to become the ultimate fact of United Nations trusteeships and the strategic areas we would acquire under his formula. As President, Truman would administer the Trust Agreement under the format first divulged at a Cabinet meeting. Again, at a session on March 16, the first item of business was a report by the President on the "considerable difficulty with British relations . . . He stated that the British were perfectly willing for the United States to have a war with Russia any time and that . . . to follow the British program would be to proceed toward that end." This, too, was hardly an unimportant question—either then or at any time after Truman succeeded on April 12, 1945.

Perhaps on balance and in view of the full force of the variety and number of problems he was to face, Truman was warranted in feeling that the Cabinet meetings were disappointing, but his blanket criticism seems scarcely warranted. Within the limitations imposed by the nature of the Cabinet process, Roosevelt gave information and invited discussion on at least some of the problems facing this country. Not that such meetings alone were an adequate preparation for succession, they certainly were not; Roosevelt died so soon after commencing his fourth term that even under the best of circumstances Truman's lot would have been difficult. One can appreciate the remark in the *Memoirs of Harry Truman:* "It is a mighty leap from the vice-presidency to the presidency when one is forced to make it without warning."

During his short tenure as Vice-President, Truman added two points of innovation. He acquired a military aide, an old National Guard crony, Harry S. Vaughn (who went with him to the White House), and he commandeered an Army bomber to take him to the funeral of his old patron, Tom Pendergast of Kansas City. Criticism was intense over both aspects of this January trip, but Truman felt he was merely expressing a final token of loyalty by a rapid means of locomotion that would keep him away from his job at Washington for the shortest possible time.

For the third time in the twentieth century, the Senate had provided a Vice-President. Thus, like Fairbanks and Curtis, Truman remained in the Senate until his inauguration. The last legislative day of the old session, January 18, 1945, took only 36 minutes and though the presidency of Henry Agard Wallace was over at its conclusion, Barkley did not even remark on its termination. He had at least noted its commencement. Truman's resignation as Senator was effective with that adjournment also. When the Senate convened on Monday, the 22nd, he had already been sworn in as Vice-President and knew of Roosevelt's intention to name Wallace Secretary of Commerce. The commencement of Truman's term as President of the Senate was unmarked by speeches, but the ex-Senator knew that he was among friends and his entrance into the Senate chamber was greeted with applause. The Senate was welcoming one of its own, and if the wartime austerity of the fourth term inaugural had to be copied by the Senate, that body could just as effectively underscore the contrast between Wallace and Truman by handclapping.

Practically the first order of business in Harry S. Truman's initial day of presiding was the bombshell of the Roosevelt-Jones exchange of letters, duly incorporated into the *Record* by Taft, and the receipt of the Wallace nomination. Off and on for the next two months, Vice-President Truman was to preside over debate on the issue of Wallace's confirmation, until it should be finally approved on March 1, by 56 to 42.

Truman, according to Daniels, "organized his office, with some contempt for the way Wallace had run his, to be effective for the Administration." The specific steps taken are not mentioned, nor do the

Truman *Memoirs* shed any light on details. As Vice-President, Truman's "feeling" was the office "has great inherent and potential dignity that has been sadly neglected . . . I never . . . had the time even to speculate on what I might have been able to do with the office of Vice-President."

How his succession to the presidency looked to Truman is recorded by him in his diary for April 12, 1945:

"At 3:35 p.m. I was presiding over Senate. After adjournment about 5, went over to Sam Rayburn's office. At 5:05 p.m. there was a call from Steve Early, asking me to come to the White House as quickly as possible. Arrived there about 5:25 p.m. and was ushered into Mrs. Roosevelt's study . . . [she] said, 'The President is dead.' I asked what I could do, and she said, 'What can we do for you?'

"I decided to call a meeting of the Cabinet. While . . . assembling, I telephoned Chief Justice Harlan F. Stone to come as quickly as possible and I sent a car for my wife and daughter. As soon as they arrived, an effort was made to find a Bible . . . Stone administered [the] oath. I immediately asked all of the Cabinet members to remain in office . . . I am not easily shocked, but was certainly . . . that the weight of the Government had fallen on my shoulders. I did not know what reaction the country would have . . . I did not know what effect the situation would have on the war effort, price control, war production and everything. I knew the President had had a great many meetings with Churchill and Stalin. I was not familiar with any of these things, and it was really something to think about, but I decided . . . to go home and get as much rest as possible and face the music."

Thus in circumstances as sudden and portentous as those surrounding the Johnson succession in April 1865 did the seventh change of President through death occur. The significance of the mechanism of this selection by the national convention and the electorate was lost sight of in the great upsurge of emotion at the death of Roosevelt. But the fact remained that the choice of Truman, which seemed to many in April 1945 to have been haphazard, arbitrary and merely political, had been carefully weighed by Democratic leaders who were keenly aware of the danger that F.D.R. would die in office. From this point of view the Democrats—and the people—got what they wanted on April 12, 1945 even if, as Daniels says, they did not know what they were getting.

What did the American people get when Vice-President Harry S. Truman became President on April 12, 1945? They got a man who, if uninformed about details of war and diplomacy, let existing policies work themselves out. No alterations of plans occurred. Truman's displacement of Roosevelt had apparently no effect on lengthening or shortening by a day the duration of World War II or the institution of the United Nations. The new President found out what existing policies were and then made decisions in keeping with them. Thus when some governmental opinion felt that the projected San Francisco Conference which was to write a charter for a new world peace organization ought to be postponed, it was Truman who decided that the projected date of April 25 should be adhered to and that the speech-making tasks originally planned for Roosevelt would be performed by himself. Thus had the successor early indicated that he was not afraid to grasp the nettle, retain a hold, and do his best. (Truman displayed the endearing quality of modesty and humility in these early months of his succession. When Secretary of the Navy Forrestal had congratulated him on the Japanese surrender which ended hostilities, Truman replied: "I deserve no credit for the victory except the little I contributed as United States Senator. It was already won when I became President and all I had to do was carry out the program laid out.")   When new situations arose, not covered by existing plans or policies, Truman would make his own determinations (as, for instance, the decision to use the atom bomb in the war against Japan).

Domestically speaking, the American people were at first unsure of what they were getting. Having been selected as one who seemed to be "all things to all men," Harry Truman enjoyed a honeymoon with all segments of Congress and public opinion until the end of the Japanese war in September 1945. Here again was a striking parallel to the first days of the Johnson succession.

A big difference between Johnson's and Truman's honeymoon periods was in duration. The former lasted about three months, the latter about twice as long. The practically universal attitude of sympathy and support toward the unassuming, industrious Truman came to an abrupt end when on September 6, 1945 he submitted a twenty-one point program for legislative enactment that was even more extreme than the Roosevelt-Wallace New Deal program. The "Fair Deal" was born and from then on the Truman administration was in the maelstrom of storms and struggles.

The mid-term elections in 1946 returned a Republican-dominated Congress which seemed to Republicans and most Democrats the harbinger of a Democratic presidential defeat in 1948. To some, 1946 meant that the people should have an immediate change of executive. Senator J. William Fulbright of Arkansas, a Democrat, had the strange idea that the President had a duty to dismiss his Secretary of State, appoint a Republican and then resign his office. (Since there was no Vice-President, the Secretary of State would of course, have succeeded to the presidency.) This answer to one of the contradictions of the American system of government was crustily (and correctly) rejected by the accidental President (who was less accidental than any preceding successor-by-death). Remarking that what this country needed was more education in land-grant colleges, he subtly indicated that Oxford trained Senator Fulbright did not understand the American constitutional system.

The Senator's movement to install the British parliamentary system of transfer of executive power by means of a vote of "no confidence" died aborning, but periodically, critics of the minority Democratic President raised the old question of whether Truman was really President or only acting President. The public remained indifferent to this abstruse issue and Truman carried on as best he could. The opinion grew that he would not even be nominated for a term in his own right in 1948.

Democratic politicians, except for a corporal's guard of cronies, were convinced Harry Truman was now a liability. He was to experience the same degree of organized opposition to himself as a presidential candidate that Wallace had known as a vice-presidential aspirant both in 1940 and 1944. Since Truman quite definitely was in the running for the nomination, and "you can't beat somebody with nobody," a boom commenced within the Democratic Party for General Dwight David Eisenhower, wartime commander of the African and European Allied invasion forces. The selection seemed a natural one; even Truman himself was on record as deeming the General deserving of the presidency. At the Potsdam Conference in the summer of 1945, during his humble, unassuming period, Truman had told Eisenhower: "General, there is nothing that you may want that I won't try to help you get. That definitely and specifically includes the Presidency in 1948." With the publication of Eisenhower's memoirs in 1948 this offer became common knowledge.

The General himself, with some difficulty, managed to avoid presidential overtures from both parties that year. The Republican boom had more easily been disposed of in January when he said: "I am not available . . . The necessary and wise subordination of the military to civil power will be best sustained . . . when lifelong professional soldiers . . . abstain from seeking high political office." Though the principle behind his refusal applied with equal force to the Democrats, they nevertheless chose to interpret it otherwise. Pressures mounted

on him to accept the Democratic candidacy. In July the important
city bosses of New York and Chicago (William F. O'Dwyer and
Jacob M. Arvey) in coalition with James Roosevelt issued a call for
a party caucus of the leaders to endorse Eisenhower. New Jersey's
boss, Mayor Frank Hague of Jersey City, dramatically switched his
support from Truman to the General. Paradoxically enough, the second choice of this cabal of professionals was Supreme Court Justice
William O. Douglas, on the far left wing of the Democratic party. The
Americans for Democratic Action, a New Deal "holding company"
organization, set up to keep non-communist Democratic left-wing elements from wandering off with Wallace, endorsed the scheme. Most
surprising of all, Senator Pepper of Florida, viewed by many as a most
extreme New Dealer to the left of Wallace, urged the Democratic
party to transform itself temporarily into a national movement, draft
Eisenhower as its candidate and "promise him control of the convention, platform and the Vice-Presidential choice."

In the face of these defections, Truman seemed indeed to be in a
position of greater difficulty than any other vice-presidential successor of the twentieth century. But as is revealed in the *Memoirs,*
Truman already knew from the General himself, that Eisenhower
would not be a candidate. Accordingly, it was no surprise to the
President when Eisenhower sent a public telegram to Pepper on July
10 rejecting a nomination offer. This cut the ground from under the
dissident Democrats. They began frantically to look elsewhere for a
nominee, but on the same day, Douglas rejected the movements
springing up for him.

There was nobody left but Truman. When the convention opened
on the 12th, the delegates were apathetic, more than half-convinced
that the long Democratic reign had run its course. Even a sparkling
keynote address by Barkley whipped up their flagging spirits only
temporarily. Resigned to defeat in November, the convention selected
Truman on the first ballot. (Truman received 942½ votes to 263 for
Senator Richard B. Russell of Georgia. Russell's votes came from
anti-Truman Southern delegates who had not already walked out of
the Convention over the civil rights plank.)

The twentieth century pattern had managed to hold fast. The Democratic party was accepting the facts of life that a candidate selected for the vice-presidency and thus potentially for accidental succession could scarcely be repudiated at the next convention after having succeeded and ostensibly organized his administration on the
principles of his predecessor. It seems likely that, in the future, Vice-
Presidential-successors will have a large claim on subsequent presi-

dential nomination because of the trend established by Theodore Roosevelt in 1904, Coolidge in 1924, and Truman in 1948.

The Truman experience also indicated that party machinery had become more closely knit around the patronage power of the Chief Executive. Thus the independence even of the professionals was curtailed. Long aware of Eisenhower's unavailability Truman alone was unconcerned through all the alarums of the 1948 pre-convention months. He publicly exuded a confidence of his renomination that would be exceeded only by his views of his chances of election.

Truman tried to dominate the vice-presidential picture, but, like many Presidents before him, was rebuffed. In the pre-convention discussions, many names were mentioned. In May, the *New York Times* felt that the situation would require "a Southerner as running mate" if Truman was nominated and that either Senator Barkley or Speaker Rayburn was "indicated."

Reporters, trying to draw out the silent Truman, mentioned Mrs. Roosevelt and Eisenhower as possibilities. The President responded that the former was "acceptable" and "if Eisenhower wants the post that is up to him." The Georgia state convention endorsed a ticket of Senator Richard B. Russell for Vice-President and Eisenhower for President. Senator Joseph C. O'Mahoney of Wyoming became the first publicly to announce his candidacy for the vice-presidency and early in July set up headquarters in the convention city to promote it. Truman's old committee colleague, Mon Wallgren, now Governor of Washington, stated after seeing the President that he would take the nomination if offered it. So the list of names began to grow until it included: Averell W. Harriman of New York, Senator Brien McMahon of Connecticut, Senator Millard F. Tydings of Maryland, General George C. Marshall, William O. Douglas, and Governor Ben Laney of Arkansas.

Out of this welter of names two stood out: the reluctant vice-presidential possibility of both 1940 and 1944, William O. Douglas, and the avid seeker of the office in 1944, Alben W. Barkley. It was at this juncture that Truman moved. The word was passed, as soon as Douglas' rejection of the first place was public, that he was the preferred one for the second. Perhaps Truman wanted to prove his liberalism by naming the liberals' pet. At any rate, he was rejecting the claims of the tested, powerful, organization-minded Senate Majority Leader for the place, just as he had found reasons to refuse to support him for majority leader in 1937 and for the vice-presidential nomination in 1944.

With Douglas re-enacting Truman's 1944 attitude on the vice-presidency, the latter was forced to make the same sort of direct personal appeal he had required Roosevelt to make to him. But in 1948 there was this difference, that Douglas refused to be convinced, even by the telephone call of the President himself, and thus as the Philadelphia convention opened, Truman was without a candidate. He was still in the process of attempting to arrive at a suitable choice when the Convention strongly indicated that it desired Barkley, who had made such a fine impression on the night of July 12 with his fighting keynote speech. After a 24-hour delay, Truman capitulated because he had no alternative. Barkley was nominated if not against his positive wishes, at least with his blessing withheld as long as possible. Truman, in his *Memoirs,* puts the issue in the most favorable light possible when he states Barkley phoned him "at about the time I received Douglas' refusal" to ask if he would "object" to Barkley's running. "Why didn't you tell me you wanted to be Vice-President? . . . It's all right with me," was President Truman's answer.

Until the White House sanction was reluctantly given at the last moment, Barkley "felt he was being left out on a limb." He could not say whether he was a candidate or not and the situation made him "mad." As he told a friend: "I don't want any biscuit that's been passed around the Convention and comes to me cold." Senatorial friends urged him to fight for the nomination anyway, but this proved unnecessary since Truman capitulated. Barkley was nominated by acclamation when the "irreconcilable" South's candidate, Russell, refused to have his name put before the Convention. Why was Truman opposed to Barkley? Probably the reported reason, his age, was the chief factor. Barkley was 70, Truman 64, in 1948. Just as Roosevelt had rejected the Senator in 1944 partly on the ground that he was older than himself, so Truman understandably desired a younger man as running-mate in an office whose main significance was its succession potential. By contrast, the Dewey-Warren ticket was a comparatively young one (47 and 57). Truman also probably wanted a running-mate stronger with the liberal intellectuals than the organizationally liberal Barkley and hence better able to overcome the unknown quantity of Wallace's voting strength. Since the civil rights question was the big issue in the convention Barkley, as a Kentuckian, might lose the support of northern minority groups.

But indeed the very reasons that Truman did not want Barkley made him the choice of both liberal northern Democrats and much of the South. His age was not held against him. Being both a border state organization Democrat and a man with a liberal voting record, he was acceptable to these diverse elements. Wilson Wyatt, spokesman for the Americans for Democratic Action, put him in nomination; Senator Tydings of Maryland, a reputedly anti-Truman Southerner made a seconding speech. Organization Democrats, North and South (like Farley and Rayburn) also spoke for him. The withdrawal of Russell only confirmed that the anti-civil rights South (except its fire-eating segment) found him an acceptable compromise.

Among those who seconded Barkley's nomination was a hitherto minor Democrat, grandson of Cleveland's second-term Vice-President and bearer of his name. As a delegate from the 13th Congressional District of Illinois, Adlai E. Stevenson, Democratic designate for Governor, was making his debut as a convention speaker to signify Boss Jake Arvey's acquiescence in the North-South compromise. In the diffident tones that would become better-known four years later Stevenson said "I will not detain you but for a moment" and spoke of the "brave and beloved" Barkley who "long before the great era of the Roosevelt revolution . . . stood and battled with the southern courage we all know so well, for the new freedom of another great Democrat, Woodrow Wilson."

Barkley was facetiously humble in his acceptance speech, given to the closing Convention session: "If anybody had told me when I left my home for Philadelphia . . . that I would leave here tomorrow as the nominee . . . I would have pronounced such person as a prophet without honor . . . I did not come here as a candidate; I did not become one after I got here, and I was not one." Pledging "my unremitting toil and my loyal support not only to the head of our ticket but to the platform," Barkley "with great pride and with deep humility" accepted the nomination he had really so long sought.

One final anomaly of his nomination was that he had been not only keynoter of the Convention, but Chairman of the "Committee to Notify Vice Presidential Nominee," which led to "Barkley's informing Barkley that he was his party's choice for second place."

The Republicans, who meanwhile had already met in a jaunty mood of confidence, created a precedent for their party by accepting the defeated 1944 presidential candidate, Governor Thomas E. Dewey of New York, on the third ballot. The vice-presidential choice was probably part of the bargain that led to this result. Going into the Philadelphia June Convention, there were two main presidential contenders, Dewey (who led in delegate strength) and Senator Robert A. Taft of Ohio. The liberal Governor of Minnesota, Harold E. Stassen, was a strong minority candidate. The favorite son of California, Governor Earl Warren, controlled his state's bloc and held them firmly to himself through two ballots. These two ballots saw the Dewey strength approach but not reach the necessary majority. The balance of power lay with Warren, and after a recess had been taken, he probably authorized the switch on a "give and take" basis. At any rate, Taft and Stassen announced before the third ballot was taken that they were withdrawing. Dewey's nomination was then unanimously made, Warren's selection following by acclamation. In 1948 as contrasted with 1944, Warren sensed victory in November and wanted part of it. His acceptance talk in which he stated he was so surprised at his selection that he felt as if a ton of bricks had fallen on him can be dismissed, like Barkley's, as just so much convention oratory.

The Dewey-Warren ticket of 1948 represented an advance in liberalism for the Republicans. Warren stood somewhere between Dewey and Stassen in the political spectrum and the two candidates were politically more-or-less compatible.

The Democratic victory in 1948 was an extraordinary achievement in view of the massive Democratic defections on the right and the left in that year. Such strong figures as James F. Byrnes, Henry A. Wallace, and the veteran Senate Democratic leader, Alben Barkley, may well all have felt that they had more right to be seated in the President's chair after Roosevelt's death than Truman. It was not surprising that there should be conflict between them and the President. By 1948 only Barkley was still in the administration. Wallace was leading Democratic left-wing extremists in a third party bid for the presidency on the Progressive Party ticket. Ex-Secretary of State James Byrnes of South Carolina while formally not participating in the campaign, was quietly nurturing the right-wing Dixiecrat secession that was to put its own national ticket into the field with Governor J. Strom Thurmond of South Carolina at its head.

In 1948, disappointed aspirants to political power had seemingly disintegrated the Democratic party into warring components. However with the faithful Barkley preaching party unity, the Southern revolt was contained (though four states were lost) and the Wallace threat proved insufficient to give the election to the Republicans or throw the issue into the House. The Truman-Barkley ticket won tidily. Truman obtained 304 electoral votes; Dewey, 115; Thurmond, 38. In the popular vote, Truman had over 24,000,000; Dewey, just below 22,000,000; Thurmond, 1,168,000 and Wallace, 1,138,000.

Once more the Senate of the United States had provided a Vice-President, thus giving rise to the query whether a new trend had commenced. Was the Senate to be the proving ground for vice-presidential timber? Was the office becoming appreciated as a promotion for a Senator? Or was it that the Wallace experience had been so disastrous that the dominant party felt it had to have a veteran Senator in the chair to guide legislation through the parliamentary intricacies of a perenially closely divided chamber? By 1952 both major parties would, for the first time since 1928, select Senators as their vice-presidential nominees, thus confirming the trend established by the Democratic nominations of Truman in 1944 and Barkley in 1948. For at least twelve years (1945 to 1957) the Vice-President would be an ex-Senator—a record in the history of the office.

WILLIAM ALBEN BARKLEY

The 35th Vice-President of the United States was born in the proverbial log cabin in Kentucky on November 24, 1877. The son of a relatively poor tobacco tenant farmer, Barkley put himself through college and law school. Admitted to the bar in 1901, he commenced his practice in Paducah, Kentucky.

Politically, his career commenced in 1905 as local prosecuting attorney and McCracken County court judge. He began his uninterrupted national service by election to the House in the Wilson victory of 1912. Then followed 14 years in the House and 22 in the Senate. Elected Senate Majority Leader in 1937, he held that post until the Republican 1946 congressional sweep reduced him to minority leadership status.

As a party member, Barkley rose successively to more and more important national convention posts. From a mere delegate-at-large (1920 through 1928) he became keynoter of the 1932 Convention and was selected by President Roosevelt to be keynote speaker again in 1936. Entrusted with the job of seeing that the third term draft was properly put over, Barkley was made permanent chairman of the 1940 conclave. As such Roosevelt had him deliver the message to the convention that neither announced a Roosevelt candidacy nor shut the door to one. In reality it was a nominating speech, as Barkley had intended it to be. One senses that 1940 was the real beginning of Barkley's aspirations for the vice-presidency. He had been signally honored by Roosevelt throughout his second term; the office was open; he was in constant full view of the Convention as its chairman, and had adroitly presented it with Roosevelt's name. But it was not to be even though others felt the Senate leader preferable to Wallace. Farley remembered that he suggested both Bankhead and Barkley to Roosevelt after he had been told the President's choice, but Roosevelt "did not take kindly to them." However disappointed he may have been, Barkley did not lose his equanimity and accepted the result.

Perhaps the most dramatic point in Barkley's long party and legislative career came on February 23, 1944. FDR had taken the unusual step of vetoing a tax bill that Barkley had broken his back to get through the Senate. The veto message had characterized the tax measure as "not a tax bill but a tax-relief bill providing relief not for the needy but for the greedy." Barkley took the floor the next day to tell a hushed and crowded Senate: "That statement, Mr. President, is a calculated and deliberate assault upon the legislative integrity of every Member of Congress . . . I do not propose to take this unjustifiable assault lying down."

Then in a burst of oratory, Barkley outlined his part in the development of the New Deal and the difficulties of a party wheel horse in keeping the team headed on the same course: "For twelve years I have carried to the best of my ability the flag of Franklin D. Roosevelt. For the past seven years I have carried the flag . . . as majority leader . . . frequently with little help from the other end of Pennsylvania Avenue . . ."

Declaring he intended to resign his leadership at a caucus he announced for the following day, he concluded: "Mr. President, let me say . . . that if the Congress of the United States has any self-respect yet left it will override the veto . . ." The Senate broke into prolonged applause; the Senators gave him a rising ovation; the galleries cheered.

Roosevelt that same day wrote another "Dear Alben" letter:

"I regret . . . that you thought I had . . . attacked the integrity of yourself and . . . Congress. Such . . . was not my intention. You and I may differ, and have differed on important measures, but that does not mean we question one another's good faith . . .

"I sincerely hope that you will not . . . resign . . . If you do, however, I hope your colleagues will not accept your resignation; but if they do, I sincerely hope that they will immediately and unanimously reelect you . . . Certainly, your difference with me does not affect my confidence in your leadership nor in any degree lessen my respect and affection for you personally."

The caucus of the 24th re-selected Barkley and on the 25th, Wallace laid before the Senate the veto message which the House had already overridden by a vote of 299 to 95. Only Senator Pepper defended the veto while many senators cried "Vote! Vote!" The Senate killed the veto, 72 to 14.

Seldom has a President been so completely overwhelmed by his own hand-picked majority leader. It was a most bitter pill for Roosevelt to swallow and not a matter he could soon forget. One cannot dispute Allen's conclusion that Barkley's action was one of the reasons Roosevelt turned "thumbs down" on Barkley in 1944, although age was the reason he gave.

Barkley, more politically thick-skinned than Roosevelt, had evidently taken Roosevelt's February apology at its face value and considered that their former close relations were unimpaired. He had reason to think so for the President selected him to put his name in nomination for the fourth term and he was chosen again as permanent chairman of the Convention. Since Barkley knew Wallace was going to be bypassed, it was little wonder that he felt he had a clear road ahead for the vice-presidency. Farley expressed the 1944 organization viewpoint when he said: "By all the rules of the game, and by virtue of his service as Senate Majority Leader, Barkley was entitled to consideration. I cast my ballot for him because I considered him well qualified . . . and, from a party point of view, more entitled to consideration." In vain did the Kentuckian try to organize his candidacy. The Truman-Douglas letter destroyed his chances and now, unlike 1940, Barkley was furious. Farley recalled: "In righteous anger, he was about to tear up the nominating speech he had prepared for Roosevelt . . . A few . . . of us . . . persuaded him . . , to go through with the nomination like a good soldier. This he did and no one guessed the reluctance that lay behind the address, so well did he deliver it."

The 67-year-old Kentuckian had to defer his hopes once more and wistfully watch the transfer of power in 1945 to Truman, relatively an upstart. By 1948, Barkley, now nearing 71, could no longer be denied. As the only disappointed vice-presidential hopeful of 1944 who had loyally stuck by Truman, he felt that his claims were unassailable. Moreover, his hold on the Democratic party organization was possibly even greater than President Truman's. With the assistance of Secretary of the Senate Leslie M. Biffle and a coterie of senators led by Walter F. George of Georgia, he was nominated by acclamation.

Barkley popularized the vice-presidential office. He was known affectionately as the "Veep"; he garnered his share of headlines by a romantic second marriage and an airplane trip to the front lines of Korea. On all occasions he assiduously defended the Fair Deal program. But the most significant event of his tenure was his becoming the first Vice-President to sit on the National Security Council (Act of August 10, 1949).

Of all the legal powers and duties conferred on Vice-Presidents since the establishment of the office, none was remotely so significant as this statutory membership. As the highest councilling body to the Chief

Executive, the NSC comprises the top echelon of presidential policy assistants. And the Vice-President was not merely a courtesy member, but a full legal participant. Since the NSC is charged by law with "the integration of domestic, foreign, and military policies relating to national security" no important aspect of national administration was outside the purview of the Vice-President. Barkley, accordingly, was a participant in such decisions through NSC membership as intervention to stop North Korean aggression in June 1950 and the recall of General Douglas MacArthur in 1951 from his Far Eastern commands.

The circumstances of Barkley's 1948 nomination apparently made no difference to Truman. In late 1951, Barkley attested that: "No President and Vice-President have ever worked more closely together than Harry S. Truman and I." In 1956, ex-President Truman revealed how closely the vice-presidency had been to being a stepping-stone to the presidential nomination in 1952. Two weeks before the Democratic convention met, Governor Stevenson was still refusing to run. "Barkley let it be known that he would like to be a candidate for the presidency." Truman goes on to say that he called in the Vice-President and told him he "would support him." Barkley went to the Convention with that commitment but, rebuffed by the labor leaders there, withdrew. Truman then arranged for him to make the farewell speech to the party at the convention which put him in the presidential race again. The day after Barkley had first "withdrawn," Stevenson announced his candidacy with Truman's approval. The ex-President's summation of the whole confused 1952 picture was: "Actually, if Barkley had not withdrawn when he did, and if he had not made it irrevocable in his call to me, I would not at this late date have been able to tell Stevenson that I would support him, and Barkey would have been the Democratic nominee."

Had Barkley been younger, the vice-presidency might have been the source for the presidential nomination at mid-century, as Senator Lodge had dreamed it might be for Theodore Roosevelt at the century's start.

CHAPTER 13

Crisis at Mid-Century

All the dynamic forces which had been transforming the vice-presidential office from one of insignificance toward one of responsibility and power came into sharp focus during the tenure of Richard Milhous Nixon. For better or for worse, he held that office during four years of trial and anxiety in which the public would, to a greater extent than ever before, scrutinize both the institution and its incumbent. The cardiac crisis of President Eisenhower in the fall of 1955, at a time of continuing international peril, necessarily made the American people fearfully aware of the dangers inherent in the constitutional succession of executive power. As a new presidential election loomed, the issue of the choice of Vice-President assumed an importance to the electorate which it had never before had in the history of the republic.

Richard Nixon exercised greater power and responsibility in the 1953-57 term than had any of his predecessors. He conducted important diplomatic missions; he served as the chief liaison officer between the White House and the legislature; he was the chief campaigner of the Republican Party; he was largely responsible for keeping its conservative and liberal factions at least nominally united behind President Eisenhower. Even more important was the precedent-breaking fact that Nixon ran the meetings of the Cabinet, which theoretically shaped basic government policy, and the meetings of the National Security Council, which in fact did so, during the President's absence.

It is probable that President Eisenhower chose his running-mate with essentially these possibilities in mind. He was realistic about his age and what it implied in terms of death or disability while in office. The corollary was the need for a Vice-President who could assume the terrible duties and responsibilities of the highest office if a medical crisis should occur. With this in mind, Eisenhower emphasized that he wanted a young man for the second place on the ticket. If the Vice-President was to be ready at all times to take over executive leadership, it obviously followed that he must be given responsibilities which would in effect make him the second highest officer in the nation. This approach was entirely in accordance with the military pattern of executive organization which President Eisenhower had known all his life. In terms of the chain of command of the executive power, Richard Nixon was destined not to be a Throttlebottom, but a Chief of Staff.

Nixon was born of Quaker parents on January 9, 1913, in Yorba Linda, California. His roots were average and his upbringing unusual only to the extent that he was obliged, because of illness in the family, to assume heavy responsibilities at an early age. His father was a rolling stone who settled down to run a grocery store in Whittier, California many years after Richard's birth. Young Nixon supplemented his local public schooling by running the produce counter. By his teens, he was permitted to keep whatever profits he made to finance his college education.

His high school principal remembered him as "a very alert, serious-minded student who . . . knew what he wanted and went out and got it." Although he had to drive to the Los Angeles market before dawn to buy produce, help keep books and tend to the store after school hours, he maintained an A average, was elected general manager of student affairs and won the Constitutional Oratorical Contest and the Harvard Award as "best all-around student." He was extremely systematic in his work, a believer in thorough preparation, a boy who would attempt to get to the essence of a problem and to express his views as simply and concisely as possible.

Entering Whittier College, a small coeducational home-town institution founded by the Quakers in 1901, Nixon enrolled as a liberal arts student. At Whittier, he was remembered as "one of the sharpest and most sincere students of constitutional history" with "a passionate interest in the field." As the President of the College remembered him, "he had terrific powers of concentration. He was exceptionally clear in his thinking and brief in his writing." He became president of the student body and a member of the debating team. He wanted to play varsity football, but was too light and had to sit on the bench for four years. The water boy remembered him as "an inspiration . . . always talking it up . . . one of those inspirational guys every team needs."

Upon graduating in 1934, Nixon was granted a partial scholarship at Duke University Law School. The $200-a-year stipend he received was renewable if he maintained a B average. With money always a problem to him, he shared a room in an old farmhouse with three other impecunious students about a mile from the campus. He took advantage of the National Youth Administration Act, was certified as worthy of assistance by a faculty member and was given 35 cents an hour to work in the library. In 1937, Nixon got his law degree, ranking third in a class of twenty-six.

At first Nixon wanted to become an FBI agent and he took and passed the FBI examination. On the advice of Dean Horack of Duke, however, he decided to join a local law firm as a stepping stone to politics. Late in 1937, he was hired by the firm of Wingert and Bewley in his home town of Whittier and a year later was made a partner.

In January 1942, Nixon came to Washington, D. C., in search of government work. On his twenty-ninth birthday, he applied for a job with the Office of Price Administration and was hired immediately. His interviewer recalled him as "a good-looking boy, [who] seemed intelligent and had an excellent record." Assigned to the tire-rationing phase of the OPA, Nixon was one of a battery of young lawyers behind desks in a large open office on the first floor of "Tempo D," one of the temporary sprawling beaverboard structures thrown up to house burgeoning wartime agencies. His salary of $61.50 a week earned four blocks away from the Capitol was in sharp contrast to the annual income of $40,000 he would begin to earn just eleven years later in the Vice-President's office.

As an OPA lawyer, Nixon "was very quiet, self-effacing, conservative and competent. You'd never have thought of him as likely to be successful in politics." But the young man was not impervious to the political atmosphere of the third Roosevelt Administration. According to a close friend: "We were the only Republicans in the OPA . . . I think he got his idea to run for Congress when he was working in the OPA. People in there were more liberal and left-wing than his thinking . . . He just felt we needed sounder thinking . . . We used to talk about that." Soon dissatisfied, Nixon applied for a commission in the Navy. In August 1942, he received the rank of Lieutenant (junior grade) in the Reserve and was sent to the Naval Training School, Quonset, Rhode Island. He served until January 1946, principally as an operations officer in the South Pacific Combat Air Transport Command. Naval officers of Nixon's classification helped to establish and maintain small air bases on the lesser islands to feed into the main transport routes. His early training in bargaining with produce wholesalers seemed to help him in his tasks. "He was a trader by nature and a salesman par excellence. A simple sheet of plywood would set in motion for him a chain reaction of swaps that in a couple of days would have his unit housed and operating."

Nixon could parlay a little into a lot. Political enemies later on would say that that observation was the story of Nixon's life. But his Navy associates gave him a high rating: "He was a good, solid admin-

istrative officer. He ran that air station like it was a law office or a
grocery store—smooth and businesslike." Nor did he ever lose his
temper: "I never saw an enlisted man who didn't like Dick." He was
generous in sharing "everything he had—food, liquor and money."
Nixon in a milieu where there was "quite a bit of drinking among
officers . . . merely sipped beer." The Quaker-bred Nixon was an above
average poker player: "There are one hundred Navy officers who will
tell you that Nix never lost a cent at poker." Nixon would play for
hours "his face like a rock . . . hands glued to the cards."

It was upon his relief from active duty that Richard Nixon entered
politics for the first time in his life. The Twelfth Congressional District of California, comprising three assembly districts in widespread
Los Angeles County, had been represented since 1936 by a Democrat,
Jerry Voorhis. The district Republican leadership needed a new face.
Through the press, a Committee of One Hundred announced it wanted
a young man to run for Congress against Voorhis: "preferably a veteran, fair education, no political strings . . ." Herman L. Perry, a
banker and member of the Committee, knew Nixon, believed he qualified and wired him in Baltimore. Nixon phóned back. Assured by
Nixon that he was a Republican and available, Perry had him fly
back to the coast. He appeared before the Committee and was approved 55 to 22.

Though Nixon's victory against Voorhis was basically due to the
nationwide revulsion against the War and its political leadership, there
were special aspects of the campaign that would linger long in the
memory of his enemies. Among these was one contrasting the "clean,
forthright young American who fought in defense of his country" and
the incumbent Voorhis "who stayed safely behind the front in Washington." Nixon's campaign leaflets said that, in opposing Voorhis, he
was fighting "the PAC, its Communist principles and its gigantic
slush fund." According to an article by Theodore H. White, appearing in *Collier's* for February 3, 1956, an anonymous telephone campaign was attributed to Nixon supporters. Voters answering their
phones heard a voice say: "I just wanted you to know that Jerry
Voorhis is a Communist." After that the phone would go dead. However, Ralph de Toledano, in his 1956 campaign biography of Nixon
claims that this story is a "fabrication."

As a freshman member of the Republican-controlled Eightieth Congress, Nixon might have been totally submerged but for his assignment to the House Committee on Un-American Activities. Here he
heard the conflict of testimony between Alger Hiss, President of the
Carnegie Foundation, and Whittaker Chambers, confessed former

member of a Communist spy ring. Chambers charged that Hiss had been a Soviet espionage agent under his direction. Appearing before the Committee, Hiss denied the charge very effectively. Congressman (now Senator) Karl E. Mundt of South Dakota and other Committee members believed that Chambers had lied to them and that Hiss was telling the truth.

Nixon stubbornly insisted that he felt the Hiss testimony was fishy and evasive. He was advised by a reporter who was friendly to the Committee to drop the Hiss case on the grounds that Chambers was lying and any further investigation was certain to boomerang. Nixon did not follow this advice. He convinced the Committee that its plain duty was to probe the conflict of testimony and find out which was a perjurer. Appointed to head a small subcommittee, Nixon travelled to New York and extracted from Chambers such intimate details of the Hiss household and family that he left convinced that his original hunch had been right.

In mid-August, Nixon arranged a confrontation scene between Hiss and his accuser. The young Carnegie Foundation president now retreated, admitted that he might have known Chambers many years ago under a different name, but continued to deny that he had been either a Communist or a spy. Relentlessly Nixon repeated the scene in Washington at a public hearing before the full committee. The probe continued. As fresh conflicts of testimony came to light, Nixon was chiefly responsible for an investigation of these discrepancies that in each case corroborated Chambers and forced Hiss to take refuge in qualifications, changes of testimony and subterfuges. The rumored Justice Department plan to indict Chambers rather than Hiss was frustrated. The judicial consequence of the Un-American Activities Committee probe was that Alger Hiss stood trial twice for perjury. The first trial resulted in a divided jury, the second in a verdict of guilty. From 1948 to 1950, when Hiss was convicted and sentenced, the case was a *cause célèbre* perhaps without parallel in American criminal annals. As a result, Richard Nixon became nationally known as an enemy of Communism and an investigator of considerable ability and fairness. Writing in 1952, Professor Robert K. Carr of Cornell thought Nixon "the most competent member of the committee," but one who was "guilty of bad errors of judgment, and as time went on . . . [one who] showed increasing signs of partisanship and personal ambition."

Nixon's two terms of service in the House showed him to be internationalistic in foreign affairs and conservative in domestic affairs. He voted for the Greek-Turkish Aid bill and against paring it by $150,-

000,000; he was for extension of the Reciprocal Trade Agreements Act in 1948; and he co-sponsored a resolution committing the United States to promote defensive military alliances and aid to free countries. In internal affairs, Nixon voted for the anti-third term amendment; voluntary price controls; the Taft-Hartley Law; the tax reduction bill of 1948 and overriding President Truman's veto thereof. But his specialty was domestic subversion: he participated in the investigation of the "Hollywood Ten", a group of motion picture writers and directors accused of Communist leanings, and co-sponsored the Mundt-Nixon Bill to control subversives.

In 1950, Congressman Nixon ran for the United States Senate. His opponent was a House colleague, Helen Gahagan Douglas, a prominent actress and liberal. While she campaigned on the manifold issues of the day, Nixon was content to talk about the Hiss Case. But on one occasion when asked to comment on Mrs. Douglas' voting record, Nixon asserted that it was almost identical with Vito Marcantonio's, the fellow-travelling New York Congressman. Many felt this kind of generalization went beyond the bounds of allowable campaign talk, and anti-Nixonites had one more item to add to their bill of particulars against him. Though Governor Earl Warren refused to endorse Nixon's candidacy over his opponent's, it made little difference. Nixon won by 670,000 votes. As Senator, he continued his interest in anti-subversive legislation and also advocated passage of the Immigration and Nationality Act. Sharply critical of the Truman Administration's "softness" toward Communists, he made frequent speeches that irked the President who had once referred to the Communist investigations as "a red herring".

With the 1952 national nominating conventions approaching, both political parties were in a quandary about ticket selections. President Truman had taken himself out of the running and his choice as standard bearer, Adlai Stevenson, was reluctant to run. Republicans were torn between their devotion to Senator Robert A. Taft of Ohio and their feeling that he could not win in the election. Many felt that General Dwight D. Eisenhower was a much more likely victor, but he—like Stevenson—was reluctant to give his consent.

Senator Nixon was one of those who believed that the party's chances would be better with the NATO commander as presidential nominee. As a member of the Senate's delegation to the 1951 World Health Congress at Geneva, Nixon had visited SHAPE in Paris, had met General Eisenhower there for the first time and had been enormously impressed by him. Nixon took a sample poll of his constituents and found overwhelming support for Eisenhower.

The California delegation was pledged to support Governor Earl Warren and, under California law, Warren alone was entitled to release it. Warren's strategy was based on the expectation that the Taft-Eisenhower forces would battle to a deadlock and that he would then either emerge as the compromise choice or be able to throw the state's 70 votes to the candidate he favored. To emphasize a nonexistent unity of sentiment in the California Party, Warren had named Senators Knowland and Nixon co-chairmen of the delegation. "Not once, but several times," Knowland had reportedly been approached by the Taft forces with the offer of the vice-presidency if he "would canvass the California delegation to throw its second-ballot strength" to their candidate. Although he was on the right wing of the Republican Party, Knowland refused.

Nixon was openly for Eisenhower, but pledged to vote for Warren until released by him. Fortunately for the young Californian, the crucial battle came before the actual balloting: the issue being whether Taft or Eisenhower delegations were to be seated from the strife-torn states of Georgia and Texas. Ratification of the pro-Taft recommendations of the Credentials Committee would give the Ohioan an initial lead that might prove decisive. The California delegates met in caucus and the proposal was made to split the vote fifty-fifty. On this issue, Nixon was not bound by state law and he argued vigorously and successfully for support of Eisenhower delegations from the South. This contributed mightily to the ensuing mad scramble to get on Ike's bandwagon while there was still time to be counted and rewarded. As a result, the General was nominated on the first ballot.

Eisenhower men had been working on Nixon. Theodore H. White reports that "the precise moment when the California party began to come apart was nine-thirty on the evening of July 4, 1952." At that moment, Nixon boarded the special train at Denver carrying the California delegation to Chicago. He had already been to Chicago where, the report continues, "the deal was knit" and had doubled back to influence the delegates. As White states: "Within minutes of his arrival, the train sputtered with rumors . . . A new convention strategy rose. Eisenhower could not be stopped, California must not waste its votes, it must go for Eisenhower; in return, Nixon's name would be suggested to Eisenhower as possible Vice-President." Being openly for Eisenhower's nomination did not, however, prevent Nixon from joining in the demonstration that followed when Earl Warren's name was presented for nomination as Republican presidential candidate.

Right after Eisenhower's nomination Nixon strolled over to Senator Leverett Saltonstall of Massachusetts to observe: "Ike's virtu-

ally an Easterner, you know, so I suppose they'll be looking for a running-mate from the Western party of the country—from out my way."
Saltonstall no doubt was amazed to learn that Abilene was the East.
His response is unrecorded. Up to that point, he had had hopes that
he himself might be the other half of the Republican ticket. A group,
including Senator Wayne Morse of Oregon, had been working hard at
the Convention for his candidacy. But it was not to be.

Eisenhower later stated that he was surprised at finding he would
have "great influence" in the choice of his running-mate. Governor
Dewey, Senator Henry Cabot Lodge, Herbert Brownell, Arthur Summerfield of Michigan and Senator Frank Carlson of Kansas asked him
to name his choice. Stating that he had been out of the country too
long and was too much out of touch to insist on a specific candidate,
Eisenhower wrote down seven names acceptable to him. Of these
three were state governors. The others were Lodge, Knowland, Stassen and Nixon. Richard Nixon's name headed the list.

Taft, discharging a pledge, phoned the group at the Blackstone
Hotel to recommend Senator Everett Dirksen of Illinois, but this sug-
gestion aroused no enthusiasm. There was desultory talk of Taft and
Warren. In quick order, the coterie got down to business and chose
Nixon.

Word was passed to the Convention "that Eisenhower didn't want
anybody nominated but Nixon." The reason given was that the
General "wanted the Convention over with . . . quickly . . . because
people were tired and tempers were short." The Saltonstall adherents were indignant to learn that they would not even be given the
chance to put their man in the running. As Senator Morse recalled:
"We [Eisenhower Republicans] beat the Taft forces, in my judgment,
primarily on the ground that there were going to be no deals if Eisenhower was nominated. We've got our man nominated, and the first
thing he does apparently is walk into a hotel room, without consulta-
tion except with a small group, and pick the vice-presidential nominee
for us and then send us instructions. 'That is it—nominate him and
go home.' "

Nixon's version, as told the press a few days after the event, is that
shortly after Eisenhower's nomination, he went over to the Stockyards
Inn across the street from the Convention Building. "I hadn't much
sleep the night before, and I was relaxing with a ham-and-cheese sand-
wich, when I was told Herb Brownell wanted to talk to me. Mr.
Brownell said the steering committee had elected me and that General
Eisenhower wanted to see me in his hotel suite." Upon receipt of this
phoned information (the time was 3:45 p.m. Friday, July 11, 1952),

Nixon went to the Blackstone Hotel for a fifteen minute talk with the presidential choice. The General explained that he wanted to pitch his campaign to a "crusade" with emphasis on the participation of youth. "He asked me if I would join him in such a campaign, and, without too much reluctance, I replied 'I'd be proud and happy to'."

The only conclusion that could be drawn from the reports on the Nixon choice was that there was no inherent inconsistency in any of them. Nixon might well have been promised the vice-presidency in return for his support of the General in California. Eisenhower might well have come to his own independent judgment that Nixon deserved to be on his list of acceptable younger men. (This emphasis on youth, by the way, excluded Saltonstall.) It was not unusual for presidential hopefuls to be committed by their convention managers without their knowledge or consent. Thus it was with Lincoln in 1860 and with Wilson (with respect to Marshall) in 1912. In 1952, there was a fortunate coincidence between the alleged commitment of the campaign managers and the expressed wishes of the presidential candidate. Had Nixon *not* been on Eisenhower's list and unacceptable to him, one wonders whether the presidential candidate would have been persuaded or whether the professional politicians would have had to abandon their plan. President Eisenhower may have had this sort of situation in mind in 1955 when he said: "It seems obvious to me that unless the men (*sic;* i.e. the vice-presidential candidate) . . . chosen were acceptable to the presidential nominee, the presidential nominee should immediately step aside, because we have a government in this day and age when teamwork is so important, where abrupt changes could make so much difference, that if a President, later, is suddenly disabled, or killed, or dies, it would be fatal, in my opinion, if you had a tense period on . . . to introduce now a man of an entirely different philosophy of government . . . I think you'd have chaos . . . if there isn't some kind of general closeness of feeling between these two."

Advocates of a strengthened vice-presidency could take heart from these words. They were a contemporary restatement of the beliefs of such men as Theodore Roosevelt, William Jennings Bryan and Senator Arthur H. Vandenberg. Their applicability to the 1952 selection, however, was a different matter. General Eisenhower had met Nixon only twice and fairly briefly before he placed his name on the list of acceptables and one may therefore question how much "general closeness of feeling" could have existed between the two men.

The strategy behind the Nixon choice was shrewd and self-evident. The post-Civil War Republican Party had won election after election on the issue of "the bloody shirt" of rebellion and treason. Nor was Franklin Delano Roosevelt above "campaigning four times against Herbert Hoover." Thus it was not unnatural that the Republicans should see the advantages of running against Alger Hiss. Nixon was too tough and experienced a politician to let the Hiss case drop simply because that individual was serving his prison sentence. The strategy was to expand the issue from Hiss and the Communists to the fellow-travellers, to the former fellow-travellers, to those who had allegedly protected them and, finally, to those who had not prosecuted them or perhaps had not been sufficiently diligent in prosecuting them. The circle of complicity could be widened almost indefinitely. As for those who opposed Nixon's pretensions, it was always possible to allege that they did so because they sympathized with Communism or were blind to its dangers. In either case, they were obviously unfit for public office.

The Communist issue had been working well for Nixon and others since 1946. Now he could test it on a national scale. According to biographer Ralph de Toledano Eisenhower and Nixon agreed on a basic "one-two campaign technique" two weeks after the Convention closed. Ike was to speak in lofty tones appealing to "militant faith and hope," whereas Nixon "would pound away at the flaws and weaknesses of the Democrats." This division of labor left the enemy confused and defensive. Stung by Nixon's charges and innuendoes, Democrats denounced "the technique of the big smear," while General Eisenhower called for a new birth of political morality and emphasized that he would not descend to personalities.

The greatest threat to Richard Nixon's continuing climb of the political ladder came at the outset of the 1952 campaign. In September, the *New York Post* charged that Nixon had free use of a private fund donated by a group of California business men. Many thought that Nixon was in the pay of the interests and that if he was not immediately dropped from the ticket General Eisenhower's crusade against corruption in government would seem the sheerest hypocrisy. There was a strong demand from liberal Republican quarters that he be ditched. The Old Guard and the professional politicians such as Arthur Summerfield urged Eisenhower to support his young running-mate. The Democratic standard-bearer, Adlai Stevenson, who had himself a fund to supplement the salaries of underpaid Illinois government executives, refused to make political capital of Nixon's alleged turpitude. "I am sure the great Republican Party will ascertain facts," he said, "will make them public, and act in accordance with our best traditions."

Eisenhower was at first staggered and refused to comment on the apparently well-substantiated charges. A decision was made to put Nixon on the air and on TV screens. Suspense was built up by conveying the idea that the General would decide Nixon's future on the basis of the speech and public reaction to it.

A most curious emotional sequence of events then began. With his whole political future at stake and his personal integrity directly challenged, Nixon made a national broadcast and telecast that was designed to tug at the heart strings of the people. By this standard, the talk was an incredible success. It was heard and seen by one of the largest audiences in American history. Some viewers burst into tears and after the speech a deluge of letters and telegrams, supporting Nixon 350 to 1, swamped the Republican National Committee. After this outpouring, candidate Nixon flew to meet General Eisenhower. The latter rushed to the airport to embrace him with the words: "You're my boy." Then, before an audience of 6,000, as hundreds of flashbulbs exploded, the overwrought Nixon found emotional relief on the shoulder of Senator Knowland.

Almost four years later, Vice President Nixon in a talk to fellow Republican politicians on how to utilize television in political campaigns reminisced about this 1952 crisis. CBS correspondent Eric Sevareid described these recollections as follows:

"Now what you do is to ad lib, you speak impromptu, as though straight from the heart. Except that you don't really. Nixon made clear that all good impromptu TV speeches are really very promptu. The road to a real triumph of manner over matter is the road of intense work in advance; naturalness does not come naturally, and great care is required in order to appear careless.

"With charming frankness, Nixon took his audience behind the scenes of his celebrated TV speech of '52, defending his acceptance of that private fund. The reason it was given on Tuesday instead of Sunday was not, as many thought, to clear things with General Eisenhower, but to build up more suspense in the audience and give more time for careful preparation.

"He might have added that he tried out various parts of his speech —the mortgage on the new homestead, the little dog Checkers, the poor working girls in Washington, et cetera—on small West Coast audiences before putting the package together. He did say that his wife was instructed to be always looking at him in case the studio camera beamed on her.

"Anyway it was a great triumph in terms of votes and it seems to have started American politics on the whole present trend toward the promptu impromptu, the calculated spontaneous, the general pre-packaging school of modern statesmanship."

If intellectuals and eggheads thought the 1952 Nixon performance was only pure corn and lacking in dignity, it made very little difference since they were out of step with the majority. The whole affair had the political effect of shifting the spotlight from the inter-party battle to the Republican Party. In it was enacted a great human interest drama, a twentieth century morality play with a heartwarming climax in which the Prodigal Son proved that he had never sinned at all and was then embraced by the good Father.

Nixon's script was unimportant, but it should be noted briefly. He admitted the fund existed but refuted the implication that it was additional personal income. He argued that the fund really saved the taxpayers' money because he refused to pad the government-supplied expense and payroll allottments. Saying "I don't happen to be a rich man," Nixon justified the fund as enabling him to fulfill the political aspects of his Senatorial role. Furthermore, even with the fund: "Pat doesn't have a mink coat. But she does have a respectable Republican cloth coat." Bringing up the fund matter was just a "smear" to have him cease attacking "the Communists and the crooks and those that defend them" in the Democratic Administration.

The budding Eisenhower-Nixon cooperation had survived its greatest test. From then on, Richard Nixon was to be given greater and greater responsibilities by the General.

Meanwhile the Democrats, having finally corralled the elusive Stevenson for the presidential nomination, turned to the question of selecting his running-mte. Ex-President Truman described how this was done: "The convention recessed again after Stevenson had made his speech of acceptance. Meanwhile, Sam Rayburn, Stevenson, [Frank] McKinney [Chairman of the National Committee] and I retired to a small private room behind the stage in the hall and discussed possible candidates . . . I left before a decision was reached, but before leaving I suggested that Senator John Sparkman of Alabama would be the best asset to the ticket. He was nominated by acclamation." The two Democratic candidates held the same basic philosophy.

The election was a great personal triumph for General Eisenhower who received the largest total popular vote (though not the greatest plurality) in the history of the presidency. The Republican Party rightly felt that the Nixon fund had not hurt the ticket at all. Less satisfactory were the congressional returns which gave narrow Republican majorities in both houses.

As Vice-President, Richard Nixon was to have manifold duties thrust upon him. Though only forty, he was probably the most politically knowledgeable member of the Eisenhower team. He was utilized to explain the mysteries of Capitol Hill to the amateurs in the White House. His advice to fledging presidential advisers and executives was: "Get to know personally and promptly the key committeemen for your unit. Don't take with you, or send to represent you at the Capitol, aides prominently associated with the Truman Administration. If you get a formal, tough letter from a member of Congress (and try to prevent such a situation from arising) answer it verbally in a very friendly way." On the other hand, Nixon smoothed ruffled congressional feathers when businessmen officials acted abruptly or disregarded the conventional channels of liaison. The death of "Mr. Republican" in August 1953 increased the administration's dependency on Nixon in all congressional matters.

For his part, President Eisenhower showed deep and serious regard for the second office in the land. He consistently sought to build up its prestige and power. Some of the steps he took in this direction were pathbreaking innovations. He established the rule that Cabinet meetings were to be held on schedule whether he attended them or not. During his absence, the Vice-President (rather than the Secretary of State) was to conduct them. This departure from established presidential tradition was clearly a response to the needs of the office and the exigencies of the modern age. It was in striking contrast to the situation in Harding's regime when Vice-President Coolidge sat at the foot of the table as if to emphasize that he had less rank there than the most junior member of the Cabinet.

Similarly, the President directed that Vice-President Nixon take the chair of the National Security Council whenever he should be absent. This was a move of extraordinary importance, for the NSC had become the most powerful policy-forming and executive board in the nation. It had become what the Cabinet once was and its meetings dealt with the basic problems of American foreign and domestic policy especially in so far as they had security or defense components.

Under President Truman, the Secretary of State had presided over NSC in the Chief Executive's absence. The new rule established by Eisenhower emphasized that the Vice-President had become the second most important person in the Executive Branch, the chief of staff of the President and the heir-apparent. The importance of Vice-President Nixon's role in the NSC was not materially diminished by the fact that the President attended 48 out of the 51 meetings of the Council in the first year of his administration. Whether he presided or not, Nixon had great weight in the NSC. When President Eisenhower suffered his heart attack in the fall of 1955, the new continuity of the executive branch was symbolized by the announcement that the National Security Council was meeting on schedule with the Vice-President in the chair. The contrast that leaps to mind is President Wilson's fury when he learned that Secretary of State Lansing had dared to hold Cabinet meetings while he was ill, on his back, partially paralyzed and incapable of conducting his constitutional duties.

A third, and much less important, step was to appoint Nixon Chairman of the President's Committee on Government Contracts. After the failure of Congress to pass FEPC legislation, this group was set up to enforce anti-discrimination clauses in government contracts. Early in 1955, the Committee reported that it had secured 37 compliances in 79 cases. By 1956, Eisenhower told Congress cautiously that "Progress is . . . being made among contractors." The more ebullient Nixon told a Republican meeting a month later: "We've abolished racial segregation in . . . Federal contracts and civilian employment." The fact that this was an exaggeration did not diminish the importance of assigning regular executive duties to the Vice-President as Roosevelt had done a decade earlier in the case of Henry Wallace.

President Eisenhower also followed an FDR precedent when he decided to send Vice-President Nixon abroad as good-will ambassador and representative of the American people. This gave the Vice-President international, as well as domestic, stature. Perhaps even more important, it helped to familiarize him with the complexities of foreign affairs. The precedent thus established by President Roosevelt and Eisenhower might beneficially become part of the unwritten law of the vice-presidential office.

Nixon's first trip in the fall of 1953 was a ten-week tour of strategically important countries in the Far East and South Asia. Before leaving, he boned up on the ten countries on his itinerary and listened to a two-hour briefing by each State Department national desk concerned. These specialists testified to his energy and ability to absorb a vast mass of information quickly. Abroad, Nixon's easy manners and charm won friends for America. He handled foreign press conferences with skill and made Communist hecklers ridiculous. On his return, he again met the State Department personnel, but this time he met them as a group and it was their turn to listen. They were treated to the unprecedented experience of hearing a Vice-President tell them what he felt the wants and needs of these overseas areas were and how American foreign policy should, in his opinion, be shaped in relation to them. In Cordell Hull's day, the Department would have fought this briefing as if it had been a foreign invasion. The calm acceptance of the changed state of affairs was a measure of what had happened in a brief decade to the vice-presidency.

Nixon likewise went to Latin America twice: on a month's tour in 1955 of all Central American and Caribbean nations; in January 1956, as President Eisenhower's representative at the inauguration of the new President of Brazil. (A trip to troubled spots in the Old World was projected for November 1955, but abandoned because of the crisis arising from President Eisenhower's illness.) So effective were these trips, both as trouble-shooting assignments and as personal triumphs, that the rumor arose that Nixon was being groomed to replace Secretary of State John Foster Dulles.

"Dick is the most valuable member of my team," President Eisenhower once said. An unidentified member of the inner White House group went much further, according to *Life* magazine, and claimed: "For all practical purposes he's running the government here in Washington." This was stated before the President's heart attack.

The Vice-President's influence was considerable, but in some quarters there was some question as to how he used it and for what ends. Columnists like Drew Pearson, the Alsops and Walter Millis dealt critically with Nixon's role in the great crises of war and peace that came before the National Security Council in 1953 and after. Most of these writers were Nixon's political opponents and their testimony was not authoritative, most of it being based on sources which they could not reveal. The gist of Pearson's columns was that Nixon on several occasions voted for policies that risked involving America in an Asiatic war. Toledano confirmed this when he stated in his biography that Nixon gave consistent public support to President Eisenhower's politics, but urged his own course in the privacy of NSC meetings. Here "he sided" with Admiral Arthur Radford, the Chairman of the Joint Chiefs of Staff, on Far East policy. In 1954-55, Admiral Radford favored helping China defend the offshore islands by atom-bombing Chinese cities if necessary and at the risk of starting World War III. He argued for preparing the Formosa armies for eventual invasion of the Chinese mainland to be supported by American air and sea power. During the Indochinese crisis, Radford held the view that America should intervene militarily rather than accept a negotiated peace.

After the Vice-President had come back from his trip to Asia, he joined Admiral Radford in urging that a military alliance be set up to extend from Turkey to Japan. As a step to this end, Nixon recommended that Pakistan be given American arms as an offset to India's neutralism. Nixon's opponents felt that this policy was short-sighted and would only further promote Asian ill-will and suspicion toward the United States. According to Toledano, Nixon's basic foreign policy premise is that the conflict between the Soviet Union and the United States cannot be compromised, but must continue until one or the other system goes under. As Toledano puts it: "He [Nixon] was no advocate of 'coexistence' which he realized from the start to be a maneuver aimed at lulling the nation into a series of diplomatic defeats." Since coexistence means living together, its only alternative in the framework of the contemporary world is struggle until one of the two rival coalitions is destroyed.

The Vice-President first publicly indicated where he stood in these matters in April 1954. During the height of the Indochinese crisis, he gave an "off the record" speech to 700 editors. Considering the nature and size of the audience, this was a contradiction in terms. Being asked whether, in case French forces withdrew, the United States should send troops into Indochina in order to prevent Communist occupation, Nixon denied that French withdrawal was probable. He then added that: "if in order to avoid further Communist expansion in Asia and particularly in Indochina, if in order to avoid it we must take the risk now by putting American boys in . . . I personally would support such a decision." This roused a storm of criticism. Some journalists believed that Nixon had planted the question, that he was fully aware his remarks would leak out, and that the whole maneuver was a trial balloon of the Administration to see if the people were ready for a second Korea. Whether this was so or not, Nixon's remarks raised such furore that both he and Secretary Dulles were subsequently obliged to reduce them to nothing by qualification. Despite Nixon's hopes, the French discontinued the fight in the tropical jungles and American public opinion rejected Nixon's idea that our troops should replace them. Viet Nam was partitioned later in the same year in the Korean fashion.

Nevertheless Nixon's basic thinking remained unchanged. In June 1954, when President Eisenhower and Secretary Dulles were negotiating with their British counterparts for a united policy in Asia, Nixon gave a speech in Milwaukee which roused every lurking foreign fear of American "recklessness" and "irresponsibility". The speech defined American foreign policy as based largely on massive retaliation. Nixon said: "A policy of weakness leads only to war. The only language the Communists understand is a policy of strength and firmness. To carry out this policy, we adopted a new military program which provides that when overt aggression occurs we will place our primary reliance on our massive mobile retaliatory power to be used at our discretion wherever or whenever it occurs."

The Democrats were annoyed. They felt this was not the way to maintain that bipartisan approach that the President had consistently stated he desired. Stevenson decried "that threatening talk by the . . . Vice-President about massive atomic retaliation, which scared our allies half to death, if not our enemies." Minority Leader Rayburn told the House: "We have witnessed a startling exhibition of . . . statements from immature voices high in Republican circles . . . The Vice-President . . . announced one day that American ground troops were going to be sent to Indochina. Another day, the White House denied it. 'Massive retaliation' was threatened against Red aggressors . . . Yet the Reds march on and prove his words empty."

But these Democratic reactions were mild in comparison to what they said about another section of the Milwaukee speech. Nixon had analyzed the Truman Administration's foreign policy as: "A policy characterized by weakness and surrender of principle at the conference table . . . the Acheson policy was directly responsible for the loss of China. And if China had not been lost, there would have been no war in Korea and there would be no war in Indochina today." Democratic Representative Emanuel Celler of New York became almost incoherent with rage when he spoke to the House. The Vice-President was "a broken down, maladjusted purblind Throttlebottom" and a "hoax of a statesman." Accusing him of attacking Democrats on the one hand while striving to win their support for administration bills on the other, Celler concluded by calling Nixon "Little Boy Blue" and "an inept, naive Piltdown statesman." Though the atomic age has not been noted for restraint in political language, it would still be hard to find the equal of Celler's castigation. In the other chamber, Senator J. William Fulbright made the same point in much milder fashion. He accused Nixon and his party of "working both sides of the street . . . a completely immoral way to conduct politics." Earlier in the same year, James Reston of the *New York Times* had complained that Nixon had "boasted . . . that the Eisenhower Administration, unlike its predecessors . . . had seized the 'initiative' from the Communists—a remark that was promptly followed by a progression of Communist victories in Indochina and Geneva."

Meanwhile, Nixon was preparing for the midterm campaign. In purely intra-party matters, his goal was to preserve unity. He tried consistently to keep the dissident Republican elements tied to Eisenhower so that the party could show a united front to the American people in 1954 and 1956. Thus in 1953 he worked hard but unsuccessfully to persuade the White House to agree to some kind of compromise language acceptable to Bricker Amendment advocates.

More serious was the problem of McCarthy. Nixon was the only official close to the President who could approach Senator Joseph R. McCarthy of Wisconsin with any expectation of making him "play ball" with the Administration. Their association extended back to the Senator's notorious 1950 Wheeling, West Virginia speech which touched off charges about Communists in the State Department. Congressman Nixon was reported to have extended the Senator the use of his files. It was Nixon who pulled McCarthy away and led him off when the Senator had physically attacked columnist Drew Pearson. Nixon unsuccessfully tried to tone down McCarthy's methods, advising him not to make charges unless he was sure of his facts, to avoid exaggeration, and to conduct his hearings more on the basis of fair play than on headline hunting.

As Vice-President, Nixon pursued these same goals but McCarthy could not be contained for long. Soon he was attacking Republicans as well as Democrats. When McCarthy began to speak of "twenty-one years of treason," it was clear that he felt the Eisenhower Administration was cut from the same cloth as the Roosevelt-Truman Administrations with regard to the Communist issue. After many attempts to curb McCarthy and confine him to attacking only Democrats, Vice-President Nixon could no longer avoid decision as a showdown loomed between the Administration and the Wisconsin Senator. In a national radio and television speech, Nixon took his stand: "Communism threatens freedom and when we use unfair methods for fighting Communists we help to destroy freedom itself . . . When you do it unfairly and with irresponsibility all that you do is to give ammunition to those who oppose any action against the Communists . . . Men who have in the past done effective work . . . have, by reckless talk and questionable method, made themselves the issue rather than the cause they believe in."

At all events, in high Republican circles it was recognized that the Vice-President was the man to see about party problems. Nixon called this type of work "liaison" and admitted that it took "'a great proportion" of the time whereas "anyone" could preside over the Senate. He was the first Vice-President from the legislative branch to express a preference for his new job: "I like it much better than service in the House or Senate. In the vice-presidency you have an opportunity to see the whole operation of the government and participate in its decisions."

The Vice-President set Republican strategy in the 1954 midterm elections. The watchword was down-the-line support for all Republican candidates of whatever shade, and unremitting attack on the Democratic opposition. Nixon bore the brunt of the actual campaigning. From September on he travelled 30,000 miles, covering thirty states. As in all his previous campaigns since 1946, Nixon's vigorous attacks raised angry outcries. But there was this difference: Heretofore, Nixon's imprecations had concerned only Californians or had been muted by Eisenhower's loftier approach to the issues. In 1954, Nixon was the leading spokesman of the Republican Party until the President finally joined the battle in late October in a desperate effort to hold control of the Congress.

Nixon concentrated on the "four K's": Korea, Communism, Controls, and Corruption. He argued that the Democrats had failed and the Republicans succeeded in each area. Among his more controversial statements were these: "The issue is the inexcusable activity of a few leaders of the previous administration who, by underestimating the danger of Communist infiltration, ignoring the warning of J. Edgar Hoover and the F.B.I., and by covering up rather than cleaning up when disloyalty was brought to their attention, rendered a terrible disservice to their country and discredit to their party . . . The Democrats either did not understand the magnitude of the Communist threat or ignored it." By contrast, the Eisenhower administration had "kicked the Communists, the fellow travellers and security risks out of government not by the hundreds but by the thousands." If a Congress of Adlai Stevenson Democrats should be elected "the security risks which have been fired . . . will all be hired back." Finally, Nixon told Californians at the close of the heated campaign: "In 1952 the issue was 'kick the rascals out.' In 1954 it is 'keep the rascals out.' "

Nixon's campaign efforts did not prevent the usual pattern of a midterm decline in the popularity of the party in power from holding true. With about 20 per cent fewer voters at the polls, the Democrats won control over Congress, and made a net gain of eight gubernatorial contests to control executive mansions in 29 states. In pivotal New York, Averell W. Harriman became the first Democratic governor in twelve years. These results seemed to demonstrate that the Republican Party needed Eisenhower more than he needed it. His absence from the ballot confirmed that the Republican Party was still in the minority. Elated Democrats read the midterm results as harbingers of victory in 1956, for only once—in 1948—had a President been re-elected after losing both houses at midterm.

When the Eighty-Fourth Congress met, the Democratic majority showed it was fighting mad at Nixon for what he had said during the campaign. The persistency of the Democratic attacks indicated that if Nixon were on the Republican ticket again in 1956 they would make his character one of the major campaign issues. The Democrats interpreted his 1954 remarks as a charge of treason levelled against all Democratic office-holders during the Truman Administration. The attitude was that if Nixon had not actually called the Democratic Party the party of treason, he had tried craftily to create that impression.

The Republicans retorted that Nixon's remarks had been fair comments on the record and that the real Democratic strategy was to strike at Eisenhower through Nixon. Leonard Hall, Chairman of the Republican National Committee, said heatedly: "The technique is to smear him [Nixon] by falsely accusing him of smearing others. This is one of the lowest tricks in politics." When queried on the matter, President Eisenhower was quick to throw his support to Nixon: "Any sweeping condemnation of any party . . . he had never heard of Mr. Nixon making . . . On the contrary, Nixon had assured him time and again he had never by any implication tried to condemn the whole party . . . He certainly believed in the loyalty and patriotism of Dick Nixon. So he would be loath to believe that Nixon had been guilty of indiscretion."

The storm around Nixon was directly related to President Eisenhower's divided mind on the issue of a second term for himself. There was widespread fear among Republicans that he would decide to retire and that Nixon would be the standard-bearer. During 1955, the President avoided any direct answer to this question, stating merely that he felt no political party should gamble too much on the future actions of any individual. He added that the Republican Party had many first-class young men and mentioned several, with Nixon heading the list.

These perspectives were suddenly changed by the news that Eisenhower had suffered a heart attack. For the third time in American history, the nation was presented with the question of whether or not its Chief Executive was incapacitated and, if so, what it should do about it. The seizure occurred at 2 a.m., Saturday, September 24, 1955. It was first passed off as "a digestive upset"; seven hours later, the announcement was changed to "a mild coronary thrombosis." A night bulletin made the further alteration of eliminating the adjective "mild." Only when the eminent heart specialist, Dr. Paul Dudley White of Boston, had flown to Denver and examined the President was an authoritative diagnosis announced. On Sunday, September

25, the people were told: "The President has had a moderate attack of coronary thrombosis without complications. His present condition is satisfactory."

From the time of Eisenhower's arrival at Fitzsimmons Army Hospital on Saturday afternoon to Thursday, September 29, he was in an oxygen tent all or part of the time. The following day, he performed his first presidential business since the seizure, signing a few papers. Thus passed the first of two weeks his physicians described as critical—critical because of the possibility of complications. The second week opened with a pessimistic bulletin on October 2 which failed to note continued satisfactory improvement and emphasized his complaint of fatigue. This deterioration proved only temporary and the nation rejoiced when complications failed to develop. During his initial period of recovery, Eisenhower saw only three officials: Press Secretary James C. Hagerty, Presidential Assistant Sherman Adams and, on October 8, Vice-President Nixon. This was the first medical crisis of the American presidency in which the Vice-President had been permitted to see the Chief Executive.

Three weeks after his hospitalization, the President was lifted out of bed for the first time; a month after the seizure he was able to stand unassisted; three weeks later, he left the hospital and flew to Washington. The second phase of his recuperation took place at the White House and for a month at Eisenhower's Gettysburg farm. By December, Dr. White was able to pronounce him "out of danger." The doctor recommended a trip to the South and the President flew to Key West. He returned to Washington in mid-January and told his first press conference that he was still undecided on the second-term issue because of his illness. Twenty weeks after the heart attack, Dr. White announced that there was no medical barrier to a second term. Prophesying that the President's chances for carrying on active life for another five to ten years were good, White added that work did not hurt cardiac cases, but that worry did. (Later, the comment about worry was made "off the record," but some of the newspapers reported it.) After another vacation in Georgia, the President returned to Washington. In accordance with his statement that he would endeavor to give his decision by March 1st, he announced his intention to run at a February 29th press conference and detailed his reasons in a broadcast and telecast that evening.

During this partial interregnum, Vice-President Nixon had assumed his new responsibilities with unostentatious efficiency and firmness. He presided at Cabinet and NSC meetings and remained at all times within overnight distance of Washington.

Although he tried to stay out of the limelight, Nixon made one major blunder that earned him criticism from Democrats, independents and a good many newspaper editors. Before a Lincoln Day meeting in New York, he boasted: "And speaking for a unanimous Supreme Court, a great Republican Chief Justice has ordered an end to racial segregation in the nation's schools." There was an immediate, angry and general reaction to the effect that it was outrageous to bring a Supreme Court decision into partisan politics and to designate a Chief Justice by his former party affiliation. Even President Eisenhower, who had hitherto defended Nixon on every occasion, observed: "Once a man has passed in to the Supreme Court, he is an American citizen and nothing else in my book until he comes out of that court." The feeling grew that the reappearance of Nixon on the ticket in 1956 might alienate those Eisenhower Democrats and Independents necessary for Republican victory. The most charitable explanation of Nixon's blunder was advanced by James Reston of the *New York Times:*

"The popular image of Nixon as a well-heeled young leader of the conservative Republican right putting over carefully calculated arguments is a joke. He has less staff help in his office today than he had when he was a Senator from California. He spent five nights with a big yellow pad writing his speech in Boston the other day, and the social and professional demands of his job are constantly in danger of outrunning his budget . . .

"Unlike his predecessor, Alben Barkley of Kentucky, he does not accept fees for public speaking. He uses a Government plane on his outside speaking engagements only when he is representing the President, and most of the time his hosts at public speaking occasions do not even pay his hotel and traveling costs.

"Accordingly, he devotes to these speeches whatever time he has personally to do the job, and this means that he often goes off with a few typewritten notes which he expands extemporaneously when he gets on his feet."

The President had not mentioned his views on his 1956 runningmate when he announced his personal decision. At a news conference, he replied to a question concerning Nixon's future as follows:

A—"As a matter of fact, I wouldn't mention the vice-presidency in spite of my tremendous admiration for Mr. Nixon for this reason: I believe it is tradition that the Vice-President is not nominated until after a President is—a presidential candidate is—nominated; so I think that we will have to wait to see who the Republican convention nominates, and then it will be proper to give you an expression on that point."

Q—"Mr. President, I just wonder if you could clarify that further; should you be nominated by the convention would you like to have the Vice-President?"

A—"I will say nothing more about it. I have said that my admiration and my respect for Vice-President Nixon is unbounded. He has been for me a loyal and dedicated associate, and a successful one. I am very fond of him, but I am going to say no more about it."

The "stop Nixon movement" was encouraged by the President's failure to make a firm statement. Speculation advanced such names as Governor Christian Herter of Massachusetts, Thomas E. Dewey of New York and Chief Justice Earl Warren as liberals who could provide the assurance that independents wanted in view of Eisenhower's uncertain health. The movement proved too fragile and premature. There was as yet no anti-Nixon candidate on whom the liberals were agreed and who commanded impressive support.

Meanwhile, GOP Chairman Leonard Hall said flatly that he "assumed" Nixon would be the vice-presidential candidate. An Associated Press poll of Republican leaders across the nation showed them supporting Nixon thirteen to one.

President Eisenhower explained that he had told Nixon to weigh alternatives carefully and decide what he wanted to do. This was probably in reference to a proposal—advanced originally by some anti-Nixon groups, but taken seriously by the President—to give Nixon a major Cabinet position as a means of grooming him for the presidency in 1961.

Eisenhower waited, allowing tempers to subside and forces to resolve themselves.

The liberals had shown their hand early and produced vigorous pro-Nixon support. The Vice-President's strength was seemingly overwhelming within the Republican Party. In the New Hampshire Republican primaries, 22,000 voters wrote in Nixon's name for the second place on the ticket. Eisenhower followed up this unusual performance by a statement to his press conference that seemed to end doubts and uncertainties: "Anyone who attempts to drive a wedge of any kind between Dick Nixon and me is—has just as much chance as if he tried to drive it between my brother and me. We are very close, as I have told you before . . . I am very happy that Dick Nixon is my friend. I am very happy to have him as an associate in government. I would be happy to be on any political ticket in which I was a candidate with him. Now, if those words aren't plain, then it is merely because people can't understand the plain, unvarnished truth."

If these Mid-March events left any doubt as to Nixon's future they were completely shattered on April 26, when the Vice-President emerged from the White House to announce that he "would be honored to accept . . . nomination again." Significantly, Presidential Press Secretary James C. Hagerty interjected this announcement with the observation that Eisenhower was "delighted" with Nixon's decision.

It was apparent that, barring unforseeable developments, the Eisenhower-Nixon team would again be the standard bearers of the Republican Party. For the first time in twenty years an incumbent Vice-President was virtually certain of a second nomination. It was apparent, too, that Nixon would be the outstanding political target—a rare distinction for a Vice-President of the United States—in the campaign of 1956.

Select Bibliography

MAJOR BOOKS

A History of the Vice-Presidency of the United States, Louis C. Hatch and Earl R. Shoup, New York, 1934.
Seven by Chance: The Accidental Presidents, Peter R. Levin, New York, 1948.
Presidential Succession, Ruth C. Silva, Ann Arbor, 1951.
The American Vice-Presidency: New Look, Irving G. Williams, New York, 1954.

MAJOR ARTICLES

"The Vice-Presidency", G. Homer Durham, *Western Political Quarterly,* I (1948), 311-15.
"The Vice-Presidency of the United States", Oliver P. Field, *American Law Review,* LVI (1922), 365-400.
"The Vice-Presidency of the United States", Louis C. Hatch, *Americana,* XXVII (1934).
"Casting Votes of the Vice-Presidents, 1789-1915", Henry B. Learned, *American Historical Review,* XX (1915), 571-76.
"Some Aspects of the Vice-Presidency", Henry B. Learned, *American Political Science,* Supplement, VII (1913), 162-71 passim.
"The Vice-President and the Cabinet", Charles O. Paullin, *American Historical Review,* XXIX (1924), 496-500.
"Reform of the Vice-Presidency", Clinton L. Rossiter, *Political Science Quarterly,* LXIII (1948).
"Renaissance of the American Vice-Presidency", Irving G. Williams, *Redman,* V, no. 2 (1954).
"The Vice-Presidency", Lucius Wilmerding, Jr., *Political Science Quarterly,* LXVIII (1953).

CHAPTER 1

"The Changing Role of the Vice-President", Robert Bendiner, *Collier's,* Feb. 17, 1956.
"A New Look at the Vice Presidency", James M. Burns, *New York Times,* Oct. 9, 1955.
Forty-Two Years in the White House, Irwin H. Hoover, Boston, 1934.
"The Issue of Presidential Disability", Sidney Hyman, *New York Times,* Feb. 26, 1956.
"Does the Presidency Shorten Life?", *Statistical Bulletin,* Metropolitan Life Insurance Co., 1946.
"Presidential Inability", Lyman Trumbull, Thomas M. Cooley, Benjamin F. Butler, and Timothy W. Dwight, *North American Review,* vol. 133 (1881), 417-46.
Constitutional Law of the United States, W. W. Willoughby, New York, 1929, vol. 3.

CHAPTER 2

Documentary History of the Constitution of the United States of America, 1786-1870, vols. I, II, III, Department of State, Washington, 1894-1900.
The Debates in the Several State Conventions on Adoption of the Federal Constitution, as Recommended by the General Convention at Philadelphia, in 1787 Jonathan Elliott, editor, 5 vols., Philadelphia, 1866.
The Records of the Federal Convention of 1787, Max Farrand, editor, New Haven, 1937.

CHAPTER 3

The Works of John Adams, Charles Francis Adams, editor, 10 vols., Boston, 1856.
The Writings of George Washington From the Original Manuscript Sources, 1745-1799, 39 vols., John C. Fitzpatrick, editor, Washington, 1931-44.
The Writings of Thomas Jefferson, 10 vols., Paul L. Ford, editor, New York, 1892-99.
The Writings of Thomas Jefferson, 20 vols., Andrew A. Lipscomb and Albert E. Bergh, editors, Washington, 1903.
The Journal of William Maclay . . . 1789-91, Edgar S. Maclay, editor, New York, 1890.
Jefferson, Saul K. Padover, New York, 1942.
Aaron Burr, Samuel H. Wandell and Meade Minnigerode, 2 vols., New York, 1927.

CHAPTER 4

Memoirs of John Quincy Adams, Charles F. Adams, editor, 12 vols., Philadelphia, 1874-77.
Correspondence of Andrew Jackson, John S. Basset, editor, 6 vols., New York, 1926-35.
John Quincy Adams and the Union, Samuel Flagg Bemis, New York, 1956.
John C. Calhoun: American Portrait, Margaret L. Coit, Boston, 1950.
Democracy in the Making: The Jackson-Tyler Era, Hugh R. Fraser, New York, 1938.
Reminiscences of Sixty Years in the National Capital, Benjamin Perley Poore, 2 vols., Tecumseh, Michigan, 1886.

The Age of Jackson, Arthur M. Schlesinger, Jr., Boston, 1945.
The Diary of Philip Hone, 1828-1851, Bayard Tuckerman, editor, 2 vols., New York, 1889.
John C. Calhoun, Charles M. Wiltse, 3 vols., Indianapolis, 1944-51.

CHAPTER 5

The Critical Years A Study of Andrew Johnson and Reconstruction, Howard K. Beale, New York, 1930.
Twenty Years in Congress, 1861-1881, James G. Blaine, 2 vols., Norwich, Conn., 1884-86.
The American Commonwealth, James Bryce, 2 vols., London, 1891.
Abraham Lincoln and Men of War Times, Alexander McClure, Philadelphia, 1892.
James K. Polk: A Political Biography, Eugene I. McCormac, Beverley, California, 1922.
Ordeal of the Union, Allan Nevins, 2 vols., New York, 1947.
Complete Works of Abraham Lincoln, John G. Nicolay and John Hay, editors, 12 vols., London, 1894.
Andrew Johnson: A Study in Courage, Lloyd P. Stryker, New York, 1930.
Congressional Government: A Study in American Politics, Woodrow Wilson, Boston, 1885.

CHAPTER 6

Theodore Roosevelt and His Time, Joseph B. Bishop, 2 vols., New York, 1920.
Across the Busy Years, Nicholas Murray Butler, vol. 1, New York, 1939.
A Journal of the McKinley Years, Charles G. Dawes, Chicago, 1950.
Notes as Vice President, Charles G. Dawes, Boston, 1935.
From Harrison to Harding, Arthur W. Dunn, 2 vols., New York, 1922.
Notes of a Busy Life, Joseph B. Foraker, 2 vols., Cincinnati, 1917.
Selections From the Correspondence of . . . Roosevelt and Lodge, Henry Cabot Lodge, editor, New York, 1925.
The Senate of the United States, Henry Cabot Lodge, New York, 1921.
The Letters of Theodore Roosevelt, Elting E. Morison, editor, 8 vols., Cambridge, 1951-2.
Theodore Roosevelt: A Biography, Henry F. Pringle, New York, 1931.
An Autobiography, Theodore Roosevelt, New York, 1920.
The Gentleman From Massachusetts: Henry Cabot Lodge, Karl Schriftgiesser, Boston, 1944.

CHAPTER 7

The Letters of Archie Brett, Lawrence F. Abbott, editor, Garden City, 1924.
Woodrow Wilson and the Great Betrayal, Thomas A. Bailey, New York, 1945.
Woodrow Wilson: Life and Letters, Ray Stannard Baker, 8 vols., Garden City, 1927-39.
Forty Years in Washington, David S. Barry, Boston, 1924.
The Story of Congress, 1789-1935, Ernest Sutherland Bates, New York, 1936.
The Memoirs of William Jennings Bryan, William Jennings and Mary B. Bryan, Chicago, 1925.
Taft and Roosevelt, Archibald W. Butt, 2 vols., Garden City, 1930.
My Memories of Eighty Years, Chauncey M. Depew, New York, 1922.
Eight Years With Wilson's Cabinet, 1913-1920, David F. Houston, 2 vols., Garden City, 1926.
From McKinley to Harding, Herman H. Kohlsaat, New York, 1923.
Wilson: The Road to the White House, Arthur S. Link, Princeton, 1947.
Crowded Years, William Gibbs McAdoo, New York, 1931.
Making Woodrow Wilson President, William F. McCombs, New York, 1921.
Recollections of Thomas R. Marshall, Thomas R. Marshall, Indianapolis, 1925.
Breaking New Ground, Gifford Pinchot, New York, 1947.
The Life and Times of William Howard Taft, Henry F. Pringle, 2 vols., New York, 1939.
The Works of Theodore Roosevelt, Theodore Roosevelt, vol. 13, New York, 1926.
As I Knew Them: Presidents and Politics from Grant to Coolidge, Henry L. Stoddard, 1927.
Thomas Riley Marshall: Hoosier Statesman, Charles M. Thomas, Oxford, Ohio, 1939
Woodrow Wilson as I Knew Him, Joseph P. Tumulty, Garden City, 1921.
My Memoir, Edith B. Wilson, New York, 1938.

CHAPTER 8

Incredible Era: The Life and Times of Warren Gamaliel Harding, Samuel Hopkins Adams, Boston, 1939.
The Autobiography of Calvin Coolidge, Calvin Coolidge, New York, 1929.
Journey Through My Years, James M. Cox, New York, 1946.
The Wilson Era: Years of War and After, Josephus Daniels, Chapel Hill, Raleigh, N.C., 1946.
Calvin Coolidge, Claude M. Fuess, Boston, 1940.
Memoirs: The Cabinet and the Presidency, Herbert Hoover, vol. 2, New York, 1952.

Crowded Hours, Alice Roosevelt Longworth, New York, 1932.
Fighting Liberal, George W. Norris, New York, 1946.
F.D.R.: His Personal Letters, Elliott Roosevelt, editor, 3 vols., New York, 1948-1950.
A Puritan in Babylon: The Story of Calvin Coolidge, William Allen White, New York, 1938.

CHAPTER 9

That Man Dawes, Paul R. Leach, Chicago, 1930.
The Wallaces of Iowa, Russell Lord, Boston, 1947.
The Ghost Talks, Charles Michelson, New York, 1944.
The 1928 Campaign, Roy V. Peel and Thomas C. Donnelly, New York, 1931.
Agricultural Discontent in the Middle West, 1900-1939, Theodore Saloutos and John D. Hicks.
This Was Normalcy, Karl Schriftgiesser, Boston, 1948.
From Kaw Tepee to Capitol, Don C. Seitz, New York, 1928.
They Also Ran, Irving Stone, New York, 1943.
Portrait of an American: Charles G. Dawes, Bascom N. Timmons, New York, 1953.

CHAPTER 10

The Era of Franklin D. Roosevelt, Denis W. Brogan, New Haven, 1950.
The Man of Independence, Jonathan Daniels, Philadelphia, 1950.
Behind the Ballots, James A. Farley, New York, 1938.
Jim Farley's Story: The Roosevelt Years, New York, 1948.
"This Job of Mine", John N. Garner, *American Magazine*, vol. 118 (July, 1934), 23 ff.
Roosevelt in Retrospect, John Gunther, New York, 1950.
Mr. President, William Hillman, New York, 1952.
The Memoirs of Cordell Hull, Cordell Hull, 2 vols., New York, 1948.
The Autobiography of a Curmudgeon, Harold L. Ickes, New York, 1948.
Secret Diary of Harold L. Ickes, 3 vols., New York, 1953-54.
Fifty Billion Dollars: My Thirteen Years With the RFC, Jesse H. Jones, New York, 1951.
"This Vice-President of Ours", Anthony Lee, *American Magazine*, vol. 118, (July, 1934), 22ff.
After Seven Years, Raymond Moley, New York, 1939.
The Roosevelt I Knew, Frances Perkins, New York, 1946.
"Can The Vice-President Be Useful?", F. D. Roosevelt, *Saturday Evening Post*, Oct. 16, 1920.
Roosevelt and Hopkins, Robert E. Sherwood, New York, 1950.
Garner of Texas, Bascom N. Timmons, New York, 1948.

CHAPTER 11

Presidents Who Have Known Me, George E. Allen, New York, 1950.
Shirt-Sleeve Diplomat, Josephus Daniels, Chapel Hill, N.C., 1947.
You're The Boss, Edward J. Flynn, New York, 1947.
Our Vichy Gamble, William L. Langer, New York, 1947.
White House Physician, Ross T. McIntire and George Creel, New York, 1946.
Henry Wallace: The Man and the Myth, Dwight MacDonald, New York, 1947.
This I Remember, Eleanor Roosevelt, New York, 1949.
The Public Papers and Addresses of Franklin D. Roosevelt, 1928-45, Samuel I. Rosenman.
Working With Roosevelt, Samuel I. Rosenman, New York, 1952.
Seven Decisions That Shaped History, Sumner Welles, New York, 1951.

CHAPTER 12

That Reminds Me, Alben W. Barkley, New York, 1954.
Crusade In Europe, Dwight D. Eisenhower, Garden City, 1948.
Mr. President, William Hillman, New York, 1952.
The Forrestal Diaries, Walter Millis, editor, New York, 1951.
"Is Truman Really President?", Raymond Moley, *Newsweek*, July 14, 1947.
Memoirs By Harry S. Truman, Harry S. Truman, 2 vols., Garden City, 1955-56.

CHAPTER 13

Presidential Nominating Politics in 1952, Paul David, Malcom Moos, 5 vols., Baltimore, 1954.
How We Drafted Adlai Stevenson, Walter Johnson, New York, 1955.
This Is Nixon, James C. Keough, New York, 1956.
Eisenhower the President, Merlo J. Pusey, New York, 1956.
"The President — After a Year", James Reston, *New York Times*, Magazine, Jan. 17, 1954.
Affairs of State: The Eisenhower Years, Richard H. Rovere, New York, 1956.
"Most Likely to Succeed", Richard H. Rovere, *Harper's*, Sept. 1955.
Nixon, Ralph de Toledano, New York, 1956.
"The Gentlemen From California", Theodore H. White, *Collier's*, Feb. 3, 1956.
"The Case For Nixon", Richard Wilson, *Look*, Nov. 29, 1955.

Index

262